Development Debacle:
The World Bank in the Philippines

Development Debacle: The World Bank in the Philippines

Walden Bello
David Kinley
Elaine Elinson

Institute for Food
and Development Policy
Philippine Solidarity Network

Copyright © 1982 Institute for Food and Development Policy
All rights reserved.

To order additional copies of this book, please call or write:
Institute for Food and Development Policy
1885 Mission Street
San Francisco CA 94103 USA
(415) 864-8555
Please add 15 percent for postage and handling ($1 minimum).
Bulk discounts available.

Distributed in the United Kingdom by:
Third World Publications
151 Stratford Road
Birmingham B11 1RD
England

Development Debacle, the World Bank in the Philippines.
Includes bibliographical references.
Contents: Introduction: Cracking the World Bank / by David Kinley and Walden Bello—"Colonization without an occupation force"; "The making of McNamara's second Vietnam" / by Walden Bello, David Kinley, and Elaine Elinson—"Containment in the countryside" / by Walden Bello, David Kinley, and Vincent Bielski—[etc.]
1. Economic assistance—Philippines. 2. Investments, Foreign—Philippines. 3. Philippines—Economic conditions—1946-1982. 4. World Bank.
I. Bello, Walden F. II. Institute for Food and Development Policy (San Francisco, Calif.) III. Philippine Solidarity Network. Congress Task Force.
HC455.D487 1982 332.1'532'09599 82-9386
ISBN 0-935028-12-9 (pbk.) AACR2

Cover: A Bogobo woman in Davao del Norte province, the Philippines.
Photo by A. Lin Neumann.

Table of Contents

For Macliing Dulag, the Kalinga and Bontoc people, the urban poor of Tondo, the peasants of Samar and all the other victims of development from above.

Foreword

by Richard Falk
Department of Politics,
Princeton University

The story of Robert McNamara and the World Bank is told these days in dramatically different ways. For most Americans who think about such matters, McNamara was seen during his thirteen years of presidential tenure as leading the World Bank down a path of creative idealism resulting in a major reorientation of development thought and action away from the preoccupation with mindless growth and toward an emphasis on growth-with-equity. For McNamara, this emphasis meant using the Bank's leverage to encourage projects and development strategies that would bring vital services and economic opportunities to the poorest sectors of a society and also a tilting of concerns in the direction of the poorest countries in the Third World, which meant especially sub-Saharan Africa.

This concern with the moral content of the development process made McNamara and the Bank controversial here in the United States. For the right, McNamara became a symbol of soft-headed liberalism whose help to Third World governments was seen as both a foolish waste of taxpayer dollars and a wrongheaded preoccupation with poverty to the detriment of trade and investment opportunity and, as such, was regarded as virtually a treasonous abandonment of the market in favor of state enterprise and public sector financing. McNamara's World Bank was also hostilely regarded by the political right as a bastion of internationalism. A conservative U.S. Congress in the latter McNamara years tried hard to insist that the Bank's lending programs conform more closely to the dictates of American foreign policy, being particularly incensed about a small proposed loan to Vietnam during the 1970's. In this setting, too, McNamara was generally perceived as trying hard, although bending as necessary, to protect the independence of the Bank from such regressive pressures and to maintain lending policies based on Bank policies rather than succumbing to the ideological likes and dislikes of its principal contributor or, for that matter, of the United Nations, OPEC, or other powerful international actors. In these respects, McNamara's early retirement as Bank President in mid-1981 and replacement by A. W. Clausen, a California banker, was widely regarded as a defeat for enlightened efforts to use international influence and capital to humanize the Third World development process

Of course, more careful students of the development process were never really convinced by this portrayal of virtue. They noticed that McNamara remained a hero for the Council on Foreign Relations and Trilateral Commission, that is, for the main bastions of international capital and imperial geopolitics. For these "enlightened" architects of a new international order, the flavor of their preferred response to challenges confronting wealthy nations in the 1970's was caught by their central formula: "the management of interdependence." The World Bank, along with other international financial institutions (IFI's), had a vital role to play in coordinating economic relations between North and South, that is, in acceptably managing the Third World development process for capitalist interests in a period of postcolonial inhibition on direct involvement, thereby buffeting the profit-making operations of multinational corporations and banks against a rising tide of economic nationalism.

Despite the publicity attached to McNamara's inspirational annual reports with their exhortatory appeals for a common effort to reduce mass misery in the non-Western world, the operational policies of the Bank were quite a different matter. It became clear over the last decade that the Bank, together with IMF, was policing the development process often in a manner that directly opposed the mandates of a supposed ideology of empathy. IFI technocrats were leaning heavily on Third World government officials to impose regimes of fiscal austerity, which tended to raise prices of basic commodities and tighten credit in ways that impinged mainly on the poor. Increasingly, it became clear that the real impact and function of the Bank was to integrate Third World economies into the world capitalist trading and investment systems for the sake of the First World.

Nowhere has this real story of the World Bank's actual role in the life of a Third World country been told in more devastating detail than by the authors of *Development Debacle: The World Bank in the Philippines.* This study demonstrates beyond all reasonable doubt that the World Bank has directly and systematically engineered a disastrous development path for the Philippines that is an antithesis to McNamara's development philosophy. In all aspects of Filipino economic life the role of the Bank has been to foster top-down development oriented away from domestic needs and carried forward by corrupt henchmen in a manner detrimental to both workers and peasants. *Development Debacle* displays the dismal reality that has emerged in the Philippines that until now has been generally obscured behind the high-flown rhetoric of internationalism. As Walden Bello and his colleagues amply document, McNamara has achieved in the Philippines precisely the kind of "victory" he earlier sought as Secretary of Defense for American imperial interests in Vietnam, namely, the subjugation of a people to priorities and interests set by distant economic and political power centers.

How are we to explain this sinister gap between idealistic illusion and exploitative reality? Are we to say that McNamara is a crude mercenary for capitalist forces, or worse, that he is a bumbler who doesn't realize that his homilies on poverty were at odds with the policies of the institution he administered? And must we dismiss the attacks from the right on McNamara and the Bank as a diversionary sideshow or, possibly, as one more confirmation that the addled reactionary mind has not yet been able to figure out how to protect capitalist interests in the complex world of the late twentieth century?

Well, in my judgment, some partial insights are suggested by these rhetorical questions, but the main explanation lies elsewhere. I think McNamara was largely sincere in his professions of well-meaning concerns, yet deeply confused about their implications for development. The main confusion concerns the functioning of the modern state system in the setting of world capitalism. To participate actively in the world economy as a latecomer it is necessary to enter on terms that serve that wider market at the expense of the domestic population. If the world economic situation is buoyant and the domestic political framework reasonably honest, then there may be enough of a capital surplus generated by economic growth to combine satisfying the greed of the rich, while taking some action to alleviate poverty and hardship. But the logic of the global market is such that a Third World country like the Philippines has little to offer other than commodity exports (that generally divert productive resources from the domestic economy) and cheap labor (that attracts foreign investment). This cycle has dreadful political effects, as well; the export compulsion capitalizes agriculture at the expense of marginal peasants and domestic demand, while the investment compulsion both depresses real wages and represses the efforts of workers to resist. In such a development context, a Third World leader is necessarily alienated from his people, serving interests that are primarily external to those of his country, a situation that is psychologically salvaged by personal aggrandizement, including a sharing of payoffs with a tiny indigenous elite that gets rich while the masses are drawn ever more forcefully into a maelstrom of poverty and intimidation.

Another part of the explanation of McNamara's "sincerity" has to do with the abstractions of imperial geoeconomics. There is little effort made by the McNamaras of this world to distinguish state and society, or to consider the relevance of class structure and class conflict; they are both structure-blind, a conceptual defect useful for their careers, but a decisive impairment if the goal is to comprehend reality. The World Bank "helps" a poor country by assisting its government, but its government is a reflection of the play of social forces and is generally faithful to the service of dominant class interests. To help the Philippines has been translated into practice, without pause, into helping the Marcos regime, which, of course, reinforces the dominant position of an exploitative faction of the Filipino ruling class. The Bank ignores such social realities unless a socialist leadership that offends the United States Congress comes to the fore, and then it must either turn its back, allegedly, as with Allende's Chile, to preserve its overall credibility with donors (that is, patrons), or press hard to offer a nominal contribution and maintain the pretense of ideological neutrality. In its essence, however, the World Bank is a creature and instrument of world capitalism. Once this is clearly understood almost everything else falls into place. Perhaps McNamara never could understand this central reality; indeed, his failure of comprehension, if that is what it was, undoubtedly enabled him to play his part convincingly as the leading savant of contemporary internationalism.

The recent history of the Philippines is a tragic embodiment of these various tendencies, and the World Bank has played a ghastly role, facilitating the process in crucial ways and covering it over with a heavy smokescreen of mystification. We can only be grateful to Walden Bello's talented team for telling it like it is in such a careful, responsible, readable fashion, sensitive to broader implications as well as being fully in command of the specific complexities of the Philippine narrative.

There is a policy puzzle left unsolved for the reader with progressive sympathies. Are we to conclude, what even the most progressive Third World governments have yet to contend, that the World Bank, given its role in the capitalist support structure, is an evil force in world affairs whose apparent offers of assistance are always a variety of honied poison? Or is there still room for selective sophistication, conditioning a positive potential for the World Bank upon reasonable domestic political health for the country involved? That is, as long as Marcos rules the Philippines, the contributions of the Bank will necessarily contribute, whatever their avowed intention, to the further deterioration of the quality of Filipino political life, but should a governing process emerge that is dedicated to the well-being of the people as a whole, then, perhaps, it could handle some degree of connection with the IFI's, perhaps not. There is a Catch-22 dimension: if a Third World government is strong, progressive, and intelligent enough to benefit from the IFI connection, then it is the IFI's that will probably break or, at least, weaken it. Obviously, easy answers are not yet forthcoming, but we can be grateful to this volume for posing the right, hard questions.

Acknowledgements

This book has benefited from the assistance of many friends and colleagues around the world. First of all, we wish to thank our friends at the World Bank who courageously provided us with all the key documents in the Bank's Philippine file; without them, this book would not have been possible. We wish to express our gratitude as well to our colleagues at the Institute for Food and Development Policy and the Philippine Solidarity Network for their support of this unique collaborative undertaking.

We also would like to offer special thanks for the contributions of Joel Rocamora of the Southeast Asia Resource Center, Geline Avila of the Coalition Against the Marcos Dictatorship, John Kelly of *CounterSpy* magazine, Arjun and Annie Makhijani, Pacita Bunag, Christine Araneta, Nancy Rocamora, Konrad Ege, Leida Labianca, Guy Gran, John Melegrito, Odette Taverna, Jessica White, Jim Morrell, Martha Wenger, Ricky Polintan, Mary Racelis Hollnsteiner, Lloyd Jansen, Herb White of the United Church of Christ, Nenita Sola, Alan Miller, the Union of Democratic Filipinos, the Third World Studies Center of the University of the Philippines, and the Consumers' Alliance for Citizens' Protection. In addition, we owe special thanks to Nick Allen, Jan Newton, Nancy Guinn, and Gretta Goldenman of the IFDP for their editorial, production, and promotional assistance, to Kerry Tremain for his excellent design work, to Wendy Ward for proofreading, and to Steve Goldfield for his work at the keys of the word processor.

In developing the analysis in this book, we benefited enormously from the pioneering intellectual contributions of Jose Maria Sison, as well as Renato Constantino, Cheryl Payer, and Alejandro Lichauco, both on the nature of Philippine underdevelopment and its structural causes within the international economic system.

We also owe a special debt to colleagues in the media who have assisted us in exposing the real impact of World Bank programs in the Philippines over the past year while this book was in preparation: Amy Wilentz and Barbara

Dudley Davies of *The Nation*; Claude Julien of *Le Monde Diplomatique*; the late Jerry Landauer of the *Wall Street Journal*; Jose Burgos of *We Forum*; Matthew Rothschild, Patricia Perkins, and Jonathan Ratner of *Multinational Monitor*; Jerry Underdall of *The Asia Record*; Jack Clark of *Food Monitor*; Sandy Close and Jon Stewart of Pacific News Service; the editorial staffs of *Southeast Asia Chronicle* and *Solidaridad II*; and Wayne Ellwood of *New Internationalist*.

We wish to express our personal appreciation to a number of close friends who gave us valuable moral support throughout the long and sometimes trying process of developing this manuscript: Rene Cruz, Linda Baker, Matthew Emiliano, John Cavanagh, Annie Newman and the San Francisco JVC Community, and Araceli M. Domingo.

Finally, all of us involved in this collaborative project wish to express our deepest gratitude for the very generous support of the J. Roderick MacArthur Foundation.

W. B.
D. K.
E. E.
R. B.
D. O.
V. B.

San Francisco June 30, 1982

INTRODUCTION

Cracking the World Bank

This book, a collaborative effort of the Philippine Solidarity Network (PSN) and the Institute for Food and Development Policy (IFDP), tells the story of the devastating impact of World Bank development strategy on the Philippines. Through an analysis of the Bank's own internal documents, we illustrate how Bank programs, promoted as meeting the "basic needs" of the impoverished Third World, resulted in increased poverty and repression for the Filipino people. The book was written in the midst of momentous developments in U.S. government policies in 1981, as the triumphant American right proceeded to undo what it considered to be decades of liberal blundering in both domestic and foreign affairs.

Deep cutbacks in social programs and tax reductions for the rich are coupled with a policy of aggressive militarism. The New Cold War ideologues are deadly serious when, like Ronald Reagan, they tell us that a limited nuclear war is possible, or, like Alexander Haig, they threaten military action against Cuba and Nicaragua.

Reagan, Marcos, and the World Bank

Two of the protagonists in this book—President Marcos of the Philippines and the World Bank—have been greatly affected by Reagan's reorientation of U.S. foreign policy. Marcos has received a warm *abrazo* from the new administration after years of arms-length treatment by Jimmy Carter. In what will probably go down as one of the classic statements of the Reagan years, Vice President George Bush toasted Marcos after the dictator's "victory" in rigged presidential elections in June 1981: "We love you, sir . . . .

We love your adherence to democratic principles and democratic processes."

The Marcos-Reagan embrace is part of a bold new policy of increased U.S. support for repressive right-wing regimes throughout the Third World. The rationale for the complete abandonment of human rights considerations in dealing with America's allies has come to be known as the "Kirkpatrick Doctrine," after Reagan's shotgun at the United Nations, Jeane Kirkpatrick. Stripped of its pretentious philosophical trimmings, the doctrine boils down to one fundamental premise: Third World people are incapable of democratic government. Accordingly, the United States is faced with a choice of supporting authoritarian regimes like Marcos' or "revolutionary autocracies" such as the Sandinista government in Nicaragua. Since the latter are anti-American, it concludes, the U.S. has no choice but to shore up its right-wing friends.[1]

Ignoring the fact that Jimmy Carter's human rights policy was more rhetorical than real, Kirkpatrick has asserted that the great sin of Reagan's predecessor was not to perceive this grand truth. It has, therefore, been left to the white knights of conservatism to rectify the mess in foreign affairs created by naive liberalism. In 1981, this "rectification" took the form of a parade of reactionary leaders, like South Korea's Chun Doo-Hwan, Argentina's Roberto Viola, South African Foreign Minister Pik Botha, and El Salvador's José Napoleón Duarte, who visited the White House to receive a benediction from the new U.S. president. Marcos' turn, says the White House, will come sometime in 1982.

The other protagonist affected by Reagan's new foreign policy is the World Bank, the world's largest development aid institution. It has not fared quite so well. The right has not disguised the fact that it views the Bank as the international equivalent of the Welfare Department—that is, as a giant international charity institution. To the applause of the *Wall Street Journal*, the Reagan Administration sternly informed the Bank that the U.S. was no longer interested in sinking capital into the agency's proposed energy affiliate, which was to provide loans on soft terms for the energy needs of Third World countries. Next, Reagan told liberals in Congress that he was scaling down replenishment funds for the Bank's concessional aid window, the International Development Association (IDA).

To no avail did the Bank protest that it holds a triple-A credit rating in the international capital market and that no country has ever defaulted on a World Bank loan. Even the

Bank's sister institution, the International Monetary Fund (IMF), has failed to escape the fusillade from the proponents of "supply-side economics." The IMF was told in no uncerain terms that it was getting too "loose" in the terms it imposed on Third World governments, such as India and Pakistan, borrowing funds to bridge their balance-of-payments difficulties.

The Reagan assault on multilateral lending has been accompanied by a renewed emphasis on bilateral (country-to-country) channels of foreign aid, with Secretary of State Haig declaring that from now on bilateral aid will be tied more closely to the economic and security objectives of the United States. The Administration's aid proposals sent to Congress already reflect the new thrust: military aid and sales to selected regimes have been dramatically stepped up and now comprise the single largest component of the foreign aid package; budgetary support and project aid are ever more concentrated on countries deemed "strategic"; and humanitarian assistance, in the form of food aid, has been significantly cut back.

Reagan's recently unveiled "Caribbean Basin Initiative" illustrates the priority given to short-term military and political goals in the new aid policy. El Salvador's bankrupt junta will get over half of the $60 million in military aid proposed for the region, and over half of the $350 million in supplemental economic aid. This will bring total U.S. bilateral aid to the junta to over $315 million in fiscal 1982—the largest commitment in all of Latin America.

Meanwhile, almost all channels of U.S. bilateral aid to neighboring Nicaragua have been shut. And the U.S. is now using its tremendous veto power in the World Bank to block loans to the popular Sandinista government, which Reagan has denounced as a "Marxist-Leninist dictatorship."

The Reaganites' successful initiative in 1981 to scale down U.S. contributions to multilateral lending institutions has provoked a sharp debate within the U.S. establishment. The *Washington Post*, the *New York Times*, and other liberal opinion-makers took up the cudgels in defense of the World Bank, arguing that the institution actually serves U.S. economic and political interests in vital ways. A *New York Times* op-ed piece by Robert Ayres of the Overseas Development Council (a body headed by former World Bank President Robert McNamara), illustrates the thrust of the liberal counterargument. World Bank aid, says Ayres, "has forestalled and preempted revolutionaries. This is obviously congruent with any realistic conception of American national security interests in the developing world."[2]

But the division within the U.S. establishment could not be strictly characterized as a classic conservative-liberal split. The *Journal of Commerce*, a business daily whose conservative credentials are unquestionable, took issue with the views of the *Wall Street Journal*:

> Over the years, conservative Republicans have systematically accused World Bank supporters of wasting taxpayers' money. . . . What is undeniable is that the World Bank and the IDA have made life a lot easier for U.S. investment in developing countries. . . . It is paradoxical and senseless for conservative Republicans to take action which runs counter to the interests of American business.[3]

Thus the argument that the World Bank has served as an instrument for protecting U.S. interests in the Third World—though long derided by many liberals—is now being used *in extremis* by both liberal and conservative defenders of the Bank. This is an unexpected, but not unwelcome, confirmation of what critical voices like IFDP and PSN have been saying all along. The kernel of our thesis was stated in *Aid as Obstacle* in 1980:

> Foreign aid . . . has not transformed antidemocratic economic control by a few into a participatory, democratic process of change. It cannot. Rather, official foreign aid reinforces the power relations that already exist . . . the influx of such outside resources into those countries where economic control is concentrated in the hands of a few bolsters the local, national, and international elites whose stranglehold over local and other resources generate poverty and hunger in the first place . . . . Ending foreign aid to most Third World countries may be our most important contribution in overcoming hunger and poverty abroad.[4]

Ironically, then, the Reagan assault on multilateral aid could very well be a boon to movements for genuine social change in the Third World. Unfortunately, this offensive by the far right, after scoring several initial victories, is now faltering. The practitioners of *realpolitik* in the Reagan camp, like Haig, will probably prevent the ideologues from cutting the Administration's own throat. Indeed, the more moderate stance toward multilateral aid has been strengthened by the findings of a special 1982 Treasury Department study which concludes that multilateral aid is superior to bilateral assistance in ensuring the strategic economic objectives of the United States. The Reaganites, we predict, will eventually reconcile themselves to the necessary functions that the World Bank and IMF perform in the service of U.S. foreign policy.

Introducing the Cast

Before we unfold the story of how the World Bank attempted to serve American interests in one Asian country, a brief introduction to the main characters is in order.

The World Bank Group. The World Bank, or International Bank for Reconstruction and Development (IBRD), founded in 1945, was one of the key financial institutions set up at the Bretton Woods Conference, which laid the basis for the postwar international economic order dominated by the United States. Originally involved with financing the reconstruction of war-ravaged Europe under the Marshall Plan, in the 1950's the Bank shifted to funding development projects in the Third World. Although the Bank has 134 member countries, most of them from the Third World, it is dominated by the advanced industrial countries, particularly the United States, which, as the holder of the largest capital subscription, controls over 20 percent of total voting power in the institution and appoints the president of the Bank. Backed by the capital subscriptions of member countries, the Bank raises the bulk of its funds by borrowing on world private capital markets. These funds are then parceled out to members as long-term loans for specific projects at below market rates of interest. The volume of lending in FY1981 exceeded $8.8 billion.

Affiliated to the World Bank are two other agencies, the International Development Association (IDA) and the International Finance Corporation (IFC).

Established in 1960, the International Development Association specializes in lending at concessional (interest-free) terms to about 50 Third World countries whose GNP falls below an established "poverty level." Funds for IDA operations come from appropriations of the governments of the industrialized and OPEC countries. Last year it lent almost $3.5 billion worldwide. The largest contributor is the United States, which also holds over 20 percent of voting power.

The International Finance Corporation, founded in 1956, is specifically geared to promoting the private sector in Third World economies by extending credits for private capital ventures, buying shares in such ventures, or identifying and bringing together investment opportunities and qualified investors.[5] Thirty-seven percent of voting power in IFC is wielded by the United States.

In the 50's and early 60's, World Bank group financing went mainly to infrastructure projects. Under Robert McNamara, who became president in 1968, rural development projects became a Bank priority under a strategy of "meeting the basic needs" of the 800 million people in the Third World that the Bank identified as living in "absolute poverty." Recently, the Bank has initiated program—as contrasted to project—lending through "structural adjustment" loans which affect whole economic sectors, such as industry, trade, or energy.

The IMF. While the International Monetary Fund is not the focus of the following account, it nevertheless has played a central role in aiding and complementing the World Bank development effort in the Philippines.

Founded at the same Bretton Woods Conference that set up the World Bank, the IMF is a financial pillar of the capitalist world system. Dedicated to the expansion of international trade and to monetary convertibility and stability, the IMF is composed of 138 member countries. The agency, however, is also dominated by the United States, which has over 20 percent of voting power.

As Cheryl Payer has shown in her pioneering study, *The Debt Trap*, the IMF wields tremendous power over the economies of debt-strapped Third World governments.[6] In order to borrow more than its established quota, a member government has to agree to certain conditions of economic performance required by the IMF. Typically, these "stabilization programs" include currency devaluation, cuts in government spending, wage controls, higher interest rates, and removal of barriers to foreign investment and external trade.

The Bank and the IMF have a close working relationship. While the IMF provides medium-term (one to three-year) credits to bridge temporary shortfalls of foreign exchange created by negative swings in a country's balance of payments, the Bank offers long-term (5 to 20-year) loans for development projects. The two organizations jointly head the "Consultative Groups" of bilateral and multilateral donors that monitor the economic performance of individual Third World countries.

The IMF makes special efforts to preserve its image as a neutral institution. Thus, by tradition, its head has usually been a European, whereas the president of the Bank, also by tradition, has been an American.

The Philippines. Our choice for a case study of World Bank development efforts is a country that attained the dubious distinction of being one of America's most reliable Third World allies long before the Bank entered the scene in the early 1970's.

The United States formally acquired the Philippines at the turn of the century after crushing a national liberation struggle that had freed virtually the whole archipelago from over 300 years of Spanish colonial control. Between 1899 and 1941, the Philippines was transformed into a colonial dependency of the United States. Its foreign trade was monopolized by the U.S., and American investors achieved significant influence in practically all sectors of the economy, from export agriculture to utilities. Through such mechanisms as the Payne-Aldrich Act of 1909, the economic relationship between the United States and the Philippines was structured into a classical colonial tie: the Philippines specialized in the production of agricultural commodities like sugar and copra (dried coconut meat from which coconut oil is extracted) for the United States and became a market for American manufactured goods.

To maintain stability in the colony, the U.S. made an alliance with local landed elites and forged them into a national ruling class. In return for the political loyalty of this class, the U.S. allowed it to maintain the semifeudal system of land tenancy that formed the basis of its wealth. Thus, the American colonial period saw the expansion of the landlord-tenant system at the expense of freeholding sectors of the peasantry. This, in turn, sparked peasant resistance, and even rebellion, especially in Central Luzon, which had some of the highest tenancy rates in the country.

The confrontation between landlord and peasant was interrupted in 1941 by World War II and the Japanese occupation. As in Vietnam, however, the peasant movement, led by the Communist Party, gained legitimacy not only as a vehicle of civil protest, but also as a nationalist, anti-imperialist movement.

The end of the war brought with it formal independence from the United States and a constitutional democratic form of government. But it actually meant a shift to a status of semicolonialism, since the United States secured the right to maintain over 20 bases and military installations in the country and U.S. citizens acquired—through the Parity Amendment to the Philippine Constitution and the Bell Trade Act—equal rights as Filipinos to exploit the country's natural resources.

The end of the war also marked the resumption of civil strife between the landed elite and the peasantry. From 1948 to 1953, the People's Liberation Army (Hukbong Magpapalaya ng Bayan, commonly known as the Huks) led an insurrection against neocolonial control and for land redistribution. The movement was eventually put down by the Philippine government with the assistance of U.S. weaponry and advisors, including the "legendary" CIA officer, Col. Edward Landsdale.

The defeat of the Huks inaugurated a period of stifling McCarthyism during which the slightest expression of nationalism provoked the accusation of being a Communist. However, the 1950's also saw the rise of a fragile national industrial class dependent on a protected domestic market that had been accidentally spawned by foreign exchange controls. Nonetheless, due to liberal investment laws, U.S. business maintained a strong presence throughout the economy.

By the late 60's, the social contradictions suppressed by Philippine-style McCarthyism in the 1950's resurfaced in the form of student demonstrations, peasant marches and workers' strikes, and widespread articulation of nationalist sentiment, even in Congress. Most alarming to the local elite and the United States was the rebirth of the Communist Party in 1968 and the founding of the New People's Army, the Party's military arm, in early 1969. President Ferdinand Marcos tried to halt this society-wide civil and national protest with the imposition of martial law on September 22, 1972.

With a stroke of the pen, Marcos shut down the free press, disbanded Congress, and imprisoned thousands of workers, peasants, students, and other opponents of the regime. Significantly, Marcos also invalidated the Supreme Court's "Quasha" decision which declared that U.S. citizens' and corporations' privileges to own and control resources on an equal basis with Filipinos had expired. But the brutal repression of martial law did not end resistance; it drove the resistance underground. Many political organizers joined the New People's Army fighting in the countryside. In 1973, the National Democratic Front (NDF) was established as a coalition of groups opposed to the Marcos dictatorship and to U.S. economic and political domination of the Philippines.

The NDF has developed into the main force coordinating various sectors of the resistance. In 1981, for example, peasant struggles for land, teachers' and health workers' strikes for higher wages, and student protests against tuition hikes were organized into a successful nationwide boycott of Marcos' fake presidential elections. The groups within the NDF currently have a total of 50,000 full-time organizers operating in two thirds of the country's provinces.

The Philippines, an island nation of 48 million people, has a strategic importance to the United States far beyond its size. It is the home of two of the largest U.S. military bases outside of the United States, Clark Air Base and Subic Naval Base, the only remaining U.S. bases in Southeast Asia since the American defeat in Vietnam. The bases are a springboard for U.S. military intervention in the region and even as far away as the Middle East.

The U.S.-Philippines Bases Agreement was renewed in 1979, with a guarantee of $500 million in U.S. military aid to the Marcos regime. The strategic importance of the Philippines was underscored by U.S. Defense Secretary Caspar Weinberger visiting Manila in April 1982. At a meeting with Marcos about the future of the U.S. bases, Weinberger pledged, "The defense of the Philippines . . . from a very real and very near Communist threat, is a very big job and will require a great deal of effort by everyone concerned with preserving peace."[7]

As a leading member of ASEAN (Association of Southeast Asian Nations, the successor to SEATO), the Philippine government willingly acts as a local mouthpiece for U.S. political goals—particularly anticommunism—in the Southeast Asia region.

Penetrating the World Bank

A number of factors led us to select the Philippines for a case study of the impact of World Bank programs. For the Institute for Food and Development Policy, the decision to carry out an in-depth investigation of the Bank in one country was a logical followup to *Aid as Obstacle*, our comprehensive study of "aid" to Third World countries provided by the World Bank and other U.S.-funded agencies. The Philippines seemed an ideal country to focus on because the Bank and the Marcos dictatorship have enjoyed an extremely close relationship ever since the agency declared the Philippines a "country of concentration" almost a decade ago.

The Philippines was ideal for another reason—the confidential World Bank reports available on it. Over the last three years, the Congress Task Force of the Philippine Solidarity Network has been able to acquire over 6,000 pages of secret World Bank reports, memoranda and assessments of the Bank's program in the Philippines. Covering the whole range of World Bank projects, these very candid documents constitute straight-from-the-horse's-mouth evidence that the Bank's programs have directly served U.S. strategic and corporate interests, supported authoritarian control by a brutal dictator, and worked against the welfare of the majority of the people in the Philippines. The documents provide, moreover, an extraordinarily revealing insight into the mentality of World Bank bureaucrats—their goals, and their reactions to and rationalizations of the contradictions and resistance spawned by their authoritarian policies.

This effort would not have been possible without the cooperation of people within the World Bank, who courageously searched for, photocopied, and leaked thousands of pages of documents. How the thick wall of secrecy surrounding the Bank—long regarded as one of the most tight-lipped international financial institutions—was breached is a story in itself. It is a story, however, that cannot yet be spelled out in detail.

For now, it is sufficient to say that a network of whistle-blowers formed within the Bank in the beginning of 1979. Most of these dissenting technocrats had one thing in common: they had entered the World Bank as young liberals in the early and mid-1970's, attracted by a combination of high pay and the lofty rhetoric of reform of Bank President Robert McNamara. Their work for the Bank in the Third World was a chastening experience which led them to understand the huge gulf between the Bank's claims of assisting the world's 800 million people trapped in absolute poverty and the reality of its service to U.S. economic and political objectives. While this experience did not necessarily turn these people into radicals, it did make "cold-blooded cynics" out of many of them, to use the words of one disillusioned technocrat.

By 1980, the network was spiriting out an average of one document a week. The controversial 400-page "Report on Poverty" was smuggled out in first-draft form while Bank management was still editing it. The even more explosive "Ascher Memorandum" on the political prospects of the

Marcos regime was leaked in November 1980, two weeks before a highly secret staff meeting that acted on its recommendations.

By early 1981, the internal Bank network began to move beyond the Philippines, providing sensitive documents on South Korea and Indonesia and even leaking the World Bank blueprint to integrate China into the international capitalist order. Released to the press by PSN and *CounterSpy* Magazine, the leaked documents created major diplomatic strains between the World Bank and the governments of the Philippines, Indonesia, and China.

The significance of a disenchanted faction within one of the nerve centers of the international financial system was not lost on the Bank's top management. It was especially alarming at a time when the Bank was faced with a heavy assault from the other end of the political spectrum, the right. Before his resignation in June 1981, Bank President McNamara launched a manhunt for the whistle-blowers. Dozens of staff members were grilled, a secretary was forced to hire a lawyer to fend off harassment, and a key officer in the Philippines division was threatened with a lie detector test, then abruptly transferred to another division. The FBI was quietly brought in to investigate links between Bank people and "anti-Marcos elements," according to some staff members. "They've even instituted random waste basket checks," groaned one official. "I guess they think we search trash cans for confidential drafts." Mail was opened and building security was tightened.

While his most publicized moves have been directed at shoring up the Bank's defense against the right, new Bank President Tom Clausen, former head of the Bank of America, has continued McNamara's silent war against the leaks. Duke Merriam, McNamara's public relations chief, was the first high-level victim of the Clausen era. While he was ousted for general ineptitude, some staffers say that his clumsy handling of the Philippine and Indonesian scandals, which served to fan rather than douse them, also played a role in his firing. Merriam's replacement recently instructed all top and middle-level officials to clear interviews with non-Bank people with the public relations office. Clausen is also said to have instituted a system of "anonymous mail drops" designed to encourage Bank staff members to spy on their peers and report suspicious or undesirable behavior to superiors.

The dissident Bank network is being more cautious now, but the dissenters have already contributed much to our understanding of the *real* World Bank. In a true sense, they are among the authors of this book.

A Road Map

This book examines in detail and assesses the impact of all the key components of the World Bank development effort in the Philippines from 1970 to late 1981.

The first chapter, "Colonization Without an Occupation Force," details the growing influence of the World Bank in the early 1970's and shows how and why this influence increased significantly after the imposition of martial law in 1972. It explores the relationship between the authoritarian form of government created by Marcos and the technocratic model of development promoted by the Bank. Finally, it shows why the World Bank became a valuable instrument of U.S. foreign policy in the post-Vietnam period.

The second chapter, "The Making of McNamara's Second Vietnam," attempts a sweeping survey and interpretation of the whole World Bank economic development effort from 1970 to late 1981, focusing on the emergence of the key factors that eventually torpedoed the strategy.

"Containment in the Countryside" and "Counterinsurgency in the City," the third and fourth chapters, provide a detailed examination of the dynamics of the Bank's rural and urban development efforts and the contradictions that brought about their demise. Rural development and urban development were the two "pacification" components of the World Bank strategy.

The fifth chapter, "Export-Oriented Industrialization: The Short-Lived Illusion," examines the Bank's desultory and unsuccessful effort to reconcile the demands of indigenous Philippine industrialization with the needs of the multinational corporations.

In chapters six and seven, "Structural and Other Adjustments" and "Technocrats Versus Cronies," we detail the unfolding of the purely repressive components of the Bank program—the "liberalization" of industrial, financial, and trade structures—and the political conflicts which this effort engendered.

The "Conclusion" assesses the significance of the failure of the Bank's Philippine program, restates our basic argument, and essays an explanation of why Bank technocrats think, act ... and fail the way they do.

While the chapters were authored by different teams, they were written as integral parts, as sequences of one story.

CHAPTER ONE

Colonization Without an Occupation Force

> The International Monetary Fund and the World Bank have been the main stumbling blocks of our economy since 1946. . . . The American (World Bank/IMF) formula of giving us $100 million in exchange for our right arm is no longer in our interest. The armchair economists of the World Bank and their Filipino counterparts will sink us if we don't look out. This colonization without an occupation force is not comfortable.[1]

This statement is notable not only for its substance but also for its source. It was written by Teodoro Valencia, an editor of the Marcos-controlled *Daily Express*, who is widely regarded as the chief propagandist for the Philippine president. Valencia's angry remark, provoked by leaks of highly incriminating secret World Bank reports in late 1980, amounted to a startling official admission of the powerful influence exerted by the World Bank and the IMF—the world's two most important public financial institutions—over economic policy-making in the Philippines. It also reflected the severe strains among three key partners in a decade-long experiment in authoritarian development that is now unraveling in spectacular fashion.

Ascher's Secret Report

The Philippine government was especially enraged by the release of the highly confidential "Ascher Memorandum." Prepared by a World Bank team headed by William Ascher, a "political risk" analyst at John Hopkins University and a member of the influential Council on Foreign Relations, the report called attention to the "increasing precariousness" of the Marcos dictatorship.[2] It underlined a painful dilemma: the legitimacy of the government was eroding, yet all likely alternatives to Marcos were unpalatable since they would probably follow nationalist economic strategies. Such an outcome was alarming since the Bank was all too aware that it was widely regarded as an agent of foreign interests. As the Ascher Memorandum noted: ". . . the World Bank's *imprimatur* on the industrial program runs the risk of drawing criticism of the Bank as the servant of multinational corporations and particularly of U.S. economic imperialism."[3]

The political fallout from the Ascher Memorandum triggered a series of frantic moves on the part of the Marcos government. Warned by Ascher that martial law " increasingly has become a liability,"[4] Marcos lifted martial law on January 17, 1981, but secured his political grip by arrogating dictatorial powers to himself by predated decrees. The following months brought a few more cosmetic changes: the April plebiscite, which approved Marcos' proposal for a six-year presidential term and the presidential elections of June, in which Marcos ran against himself in the face of a successful boycott by the political opposition. But the full meaning of the Ascher memo became evident in July 1981, when leading Filipino technocrats with close ties to the World Bank and the IMF were constituted as a cabinet, headed by Cesar Virata, a longtime favorite of the two agencies.

To most politically aware Filipinos, the last move was significant for several reasons. First, the assets and resources of the Philippines were being placed in receivership by the World Bank, with Prime Minister Virata as the trustee, to guarantee payment of the country's huge $15 billion external debt. Second, it was a last-ditch attempt to salvage the Bank's multibillion-dollar investment in the country. Third, it represented the ultimate effort of the Bank to "liberalize" the Philippine economy, that is, open it up to the unrestricted entry of foreign investment and commodities. Finally, it signaled a strong attempt by the World Bank and the U. S. government to provide the technocrats with a decisive advantage over their competitors in the Marcos ruling coalition in the struggle to determine the regime's economic priorities.

Valencia was not far off the mark when he wrote, "Now, we're completely under the thumbs of the IMF because our principal planners are IMF boys." And he predicted,

"These economists will cause the country to sink faster and with more assuredness than the MNLF [Moro National Liberation Front], the NPA's [New People's Army], or the Communists."[5]

The Philippines' new "World Bank Cabinet" was the culmination of a decade of illusions, false hopes, and unmitigated economic and social disaster. To fully understand how a whole country could be placed in receivership, to understand how the World Bank could attain such overwhelming power in determining the economic destiny of 50 million Filipinos, it is necessary to review the concatenation of political and economic events that precipitated it.

An Overview

Between 1970 and 1982, the World Bank became a massive presence in Philippine affairs. Its dramatic entry was provoked by a deep-seated crisis of the postwar social order characterized by an "elite democratic" state presiding over a stagnant, underdeveloped economy. The World Bank effort had two fundamental objectives: to stabilize the deteriorating political situation and to more thoroughly integrate the Philippine economy into the international capitalist order dominated by the United States.

Rural and urban development projects aimed at defusing discontent among the rural poor and the burgeoning urban underclass formed the core of the Bank's program of political stabilization. Tighter integration into the international capitalist economy was to be accomplished by a strategy of creating a favorable climate for foreign investment, knocking down tariff barriers to U.S. imports ("liberalization"), and fostering a strategy of "export-oriented industrialization" geared toward satisfying the demand of markets in the United States, Japan, and Western Europe rather than the domestic market.

This ambitious plan of stabilization and integration could not be achieved without an appropriate political framework, that is, without a state dedicated to repressing those sectors which stood to lose the most from more intensified subjugation of the economy to U.S. corporations and financial interests. The declaration of martial law on September 22, 1972 was a vital first step in fashioning the necessary political superstructure. Authoritarian rule united the interest of U.S. business in "rationalizing" the Philippine economy to serve U.S. needs more effectively and the drive of Ferdinand Marcos and his faction to monopolize political power within the Filipino elite.

The economic and political crisis of the postwar order in the Philippines was not unique. A similar crisis was wracking elite democratic political regimes in other underdeveloped countries, such as Brazil and Chile. What was new in the Philippines in the 1970's was the leading role that the World Bank played in restructuring the economy. The country was, in fact, deliberately chosen as the site of a World Bank experiment in "authoritarian" or "technocratic" modernization, the lessons of which could later be applied in other countries. Key to this experiment in repressive modernization were the U.S.-educated Filipino technocrats whom the Bank cultivated as a base of support within the ruling Marcos coalition.

The role of the Bank as the lead agency in the economic restructuring of the Philippines stemmed partly from the crisis of U.S. foreign policy after the debacle in Vietnam. Popular disillusionment with U.S. foreign policy translated most concretely into growing unpopularity of bilateral aid to repressive allies like Marcos. Thus, the World Bank, the IMF, and other multilateral lending agencies emerged as alternative conduits of U.S. influence to authoritarian regimes allied to the U.S.

The Crisis of the Post-War Regime: I. The Economy

In the late 1960's and early 1970's, Philippine society underwent a fundamental crisis. In its economic dimension, the crisis was precipitated by the intersection of three developments: the failure of the strategy of import substitution as a path to sustained industrialization, the increasing inability of agriculture to meet the country's basic food needs, and the growing pressure from foreign capital to "open up" the economy more completely.

Like many countries in Latin America, the Philippines had stumbled across import substitution as an industrial strategy when the government, in an attempt to stem a serious foreign exchange drain in the late 1940's, enacted foreign exchange controls and quantitative import restrictions. Complemented by the erection of discriminatory tariffs on imports in the late 1950's, these mechanisms sparked the creation of an industrial sector which filled the domestic demand for light consumer goods such as processed food, shoes, and garments which could not be filled by increasingly expensive imports.

By the late 60's, however, the strategy of import substitution ran up against the limits of a restricted domestic market—a market which could not be expanded without a fundamental redistribution of income. While the strategy created and subsequently benefited a small national entrepreneurial class, it carried out no substantial change in the realities of economic power in the Philippines: in 1970, an estimated five percent of the population controlled 25 percent of the national income.[6] As postwar growth leveled off, stagnant Philippine industry could no longer absorb the half a million youths entering the labor force each year or the waves of urban immigrants expelled from the countryside by a backward, semifeudal land tenure system. The number of workers employed in manufacturing in 1969—1.3 million—was practically the same as in 1963.[7]

The stagnation of Philippine industry was paralleled by the crisis of Philippine agriculture. By the early 60's, agriculture could no longer accommodate a growing labor force. The statistics are eloquent: in 1971, the number of people employed in agriculture—6.4 million—was virtually the same as in 1963.[8] Even more significant was the growing inability of agriculture to meet the country's basic food needs. In 1960, the Philippines imported $2 million worth of rice, the country's basic food staple; by 1972, the import figure had risen to $34 million.[9]

Institutions like the World Bank mainly blamed the increasing scarcity of new land that could be brought under cultivation and low farmer productivity for the crisis. But perhaps more significant causes were the expansion of the cultivated area devoted to cash crops for export at the expense of food crops and the retrograde system of land tenure in which millions of peasants were trapped. The landlord system stifled the full productive power of Philippine agriculture.[10]

The failure of the import substitution model provided a powerful ideological weapon with which representatives of foreign business interests and their local supporters sought to sweep away the barriers to a freer inflow of foreign manufactured imports and ward off the threat of nationalist controls on foreign investment. As a former U.S. colony, the Philippines hosted a powerful U.S. business presence. Estimated at $1.5 billion to $2 billion by the early 1970's, U.S. investment in the country was the largest in Southeast Asia.[11] While protectionist measures spawned a small national industrial elite, the failure to supplement those meassures with strong controls on foreign investment allowed the growth of U.S. businesses, many of which were themselves able to take advantage of the high tariff walls to edge out their European, Japanese, and other American competitors. Indeed, U.S. business in the Philippines was so lucrative that, according to the University of the Philippines Law Center, for every dollar invested by American corporations between 1946 and 1976, the net profit came to $3.58. Of this amount, $2 was repatriated to the U.S.[12]

The drive to "export" capital to the Philippines and the Third World, however, intensified sharply in the 60's in response to what establishment economists euphemistically called the "crisis of maturity" of the advanced metropolitan economies, or what Marxists termed the "crisis of overproduction": a marked slowing down of growth due to, among other factors, limits to domestic consumption, declining rates of profit, and rising labor costs.[13] To offset the profit squeeze in their home economies, corporations and banks controlling large quantities of surplus capital stepped up their drive to more fully penetrate Third World markets and gain access to cheap Third World labor—in addition to intensifying the traditional role of the Third World as a source of vital raw materials. Data on capital flows illustrate this. While the book value of all foreign direct investment by Japanese, British, West German, and American multinationals stood at $45.8 billion in 1960, by 1971 the figure had risen to $121.8 billion.[14] Bank lending showed an even more dramatic rise: the total debt to international banks of the less developed countries rose more than threefold, from $8.9 billion to $30 billion in barely five years, from 1968 to 1973.[15] By 1976, 40 percent of the profits of the five largest U.S. banks originated in foreign lending—with Chase Manhattan drawing as much as three-fourths of its profits from its foreign operations.[16]

In the Philippines, however, as in Latin America, the intensified foreign corporate drive came up against the interests of the national entrepreneurial class entrenched in the existing state apparatus. From this position, the national capitalists were able to wage a desperate rearguard action against the offensive of the pro-foreign capital faction of the elite which was by then ensconced in the presidency of Ferdinand Marcos. This political reality was captured in the World Bank assessment that "heavily protected and inefficient manufacturing industries, controlled by *politically connected* ethnic Filipinos . . . were gradually increasing in importance despite their inefficiency and the existing [*sic*] of some foreign competition. . . ."[17]

The same frustration was reflected by Vicente Paterno, Marcos' technocrat in charge of the Board of Investments: "Although in the past there have been expressions of the desire to attract foreign investments into the Philippine economy, these were negated by other statements in Congress and in the Constitutional Convention, proposing to make changes in the law of the land to impose further restrictions on foreign investment."[18]

In the eyes of U.S. investors and Marcos' technocrats, the deadlock had become intolerable. Something extraordinary was needed to break it. As Paterno candidly admitted later: "The logic of foreign investment to participate in the generation of labor-manufactured exports is clear and incontrovertible, but the country needed martial law to attract such investment."[19]

The Crisis: II. The State

The economic crisis was paralleled and deepened by an equally deep-seated crisis of the institutions of political rule. Since the granting of formal independence in 1946, the Philippines had been governed under a formal, constitutional democracy—the political regime promoted by the U.S. throughout the Third World as an alternative to national liberation movements in the early post-World War II period.

The Philippine political system from 1946 to 1972 gained fame as proof of the success of the American recipe. Within the framework of a written constitution, factions of the landlord elite alternated in power, the masses were mobilized through traditional patron-client relationships, and political organization along horizontal or class lines was embryonic. The play of politics took place above an immobile class structure which occasionally generated rebellions. But while flashpoints did occur, as in 1948 with the Communist-led Huk Rebellion, these were of a scale that could be contained by the Philippine military with a generous helping of arms and advisers from the United States.[20]

The equilibrium of this system, however, began to be seriously upset by the late 60's. One of the main reasons for this destabilization was the intensifying competition within the elite for political power. Although Philippine politics has always been characterized by some degree of violence, elite politics between 1946 and 1969 was marked by a notable degree of adherence to parliamentary competition.

The unwritten rule of elite constitutionalism was that each elite faction would get its chance to control the government machinery and dole out the spoils of victory to its followers. The presidential elections of 1969—the same event that, as we shall see, paved the way for greater World Bank-IMF influence on policy-making—broke with this pattern. By having himself reelected to the presidency in 1969, in the most corrupt and violent elections in post-war history, Marcos broke the unstated law of patronage politics. He triggered the rapid degeneration of elite competition into violent vendettas between the huge private armies of oligarchical "warlords."[21]

An even more important factor destabilizing the regime of elite democracy, however, was the growing success of the Filipino middle and lower classes in utilizing their constitutionally guaranteed freedoms to articulate mass demands. As the upper classes divided in internecine strife over political office and over the response to U.S. economic domination, thousands of youths, workers, and peasants burst out of the straitjacket of patronage politics and rocked the country with massive demonstrations, strikes, and marches for anti-elite and anti-American causes.[22] With class and nationalist consciousness taking hold, the capacity of the elite democratic system to co-opt, fragment, and defuse mass demands through patronage began to break down. Instead, its formal rights and freedoms transformed it into Frankenstein's Monster—a dangerous, uncontrollable creature about to undo its creator.

This movement toward genuine participatory democracy was most alarming to the World Bank and U.S. interests, for *it threatened to break the stalemate in the conflict over the direction of economic policy that had developed between the nationalist, entrepreneurial faction and the pro-U.S. Marcos faction of the elite*. Indeed, in 1972, massive nationalist demonstrations forced the normally conservative Supreme Court to issue decrees unfavorable to U.S. investors for the first time. With the controversial "Quasha Decision," the Court ruled that private lands bought by U.S. citizens since 1945 had essentially been acquired illegally and had to be transferred back to Filipino hands.

This turn of events sent shock waves through international finance circles, and foreign investors responded by disinvesting. Between 1970 and 1973, the foreign investment account showed a net disinvestment of $55 million.[23]

The declaration of martial law on September 22, 1972 represented the Marcos faction's dramatic attempt to break the "democratic stalemate" and resolve these multiple contradictions unraveling the postwar political and economic regime in the Philippines. U.S. business did not hesitate to give its stamp of approval to the move, which came in the form of a congratulatory telegram to Marcos: "The American Chamber of Commerce wishes you every success in your endeavor to restore peace and order, business confidence, economic growth, and well-being of the Filipino people and nation. We assure you of our confidence and cooperation in achieving these objectives. We are communicating the feelings of our associates and affiliates in the United States."[24]

In the view of U.S. business, martial law and a good investment climate have been indissolubly linked since then. As the director of the American Chamber of Commerce in Manila asserted in December 1980: "If not for the drastic changes in the country's social, economic, and political fiber initiated in September 1972, the country's drift to oblivion might have preceded Iran by six years."[25]

Enter the World Bank-IMF Conglomerate

It was in the midst of this all-sided crisis of the postwar Philippine regime that the IMF and the Bank forced Marcos to devalue the peso in 1970 in the name of "liberalization"—a euphemism for opening up the economy to foreign investment and imports.

This action was the second key intervention carried out by the two institutions, the first being their successful effort to force the Macapagal administration in 1962 to lift foreign exchange controls and devalue the peso by almost 100 percent relative to the dollar. The results of the earlier devaluation were, however, unsatisfactory: the heavy import substitution and protectionist "bias" of the economy remained.

The presidential elections of November 1969 created the opportunity for the Bank and the IMF to once more force liberalization. Ferdinand Marcos won a second term, but in the process he used up the government's foreign exchange reserves and left the country with few resources to cover a huge trade deficit and to service or pay interest on the mounting external debt.[26] Desperate, the government turned for assistance to the IMF and the World Bank. A "stand-by agreement" was negotiated, but only after the government agreed to a more than 60 percent devaluation of the peso relative to the value of the dollar.[27] In theory, devaluation would bring the trade account into balance by increasing foreign exchange earnings from "cheaper" Philippine exports while stemming the foreign exchange outflow for now more "expensive" imports. The deficit in the trade account was indeed reduced, from $257 million in 1969 to $7 million in 1970—but at a savage price. The move also triggered a sharp rise in the domestic inflation rate from 1.3 percent in 1969 to 14.8 percent in 1970, depressed the growth rate, provoked the bankruptcy of scores of Filipino entrepreneurs suddenly confronted with more expensive imported inputs for their products, and created windfall profits for the most important faction of the Philippine elite—the barons who controlled sugar export production and trade.[28]

The World Bank congratulated Marcos for the devaluation—a "commendable display of political courage. . . ."[29] It was not until much later that the Bank acknowledged that the very temporary relief in the Philippines' balance-of-payments position provided by the devaluation had been obtained "at the cost of a slower growth of GNP."[30]

Devaluation was followed by the creation of a joint "Central Bank-IMF Commission" to overhaul the debt management policies of the government and the installation of an IMF resident officer right in the Philippine Central Bank. According to one report, this representative "sees reports, official figures and analyses from government agencies. Because of interagency secrecy, he probably has access to more documents than some high Central Bank officials."[31]

Even more significant was the formation of a "Consultative Group" of "interested nations and agencies," under the joint leadership of the IMF and the World Bank, to monitor the external position of the economy and coordinate foreign assistance to the government.[32] This body was modeled after the "Inter-Governmental Group for Indonesia" (IGGI), which was created by the IMF and the Bank to directly manage the external finance policies of the pro-Western Suharto military clique that overthrew the nationalist Sukarno government in the mid-1960's.[33]

In a key confidential memo, the IMF Managing Director delineated the complementary responsibilities of the two institutions in such bodies as the Philippine Consultative Group: ". . . the Bank is recognized as having primary responsibility for the composition and appropriateness of development programs and project evaluation, including development priorities." The IMF, on the other hand, "is recognized as having primary responsibility for exchange rates and restrictive systems, for adjustment of temporary balance-of-payments disequilibria, and for evaluating and assisting members to work out stabilization programs as a sound basis for economic advance."[34]

The scope of active interest of both institutions, however, did not end with their areas of primary concern. "In between these two clear-cut areas of responsibility of the Bank and Fund," the directive continued,

> there is the broad range of matters which are of interest to both institutions. This range includes such matters as the structure and functioning of financial institutions, the adequacy of money and capital markets, the actual and potential capacity of a member country to generate domestic savings, the financial implications of economic development programs both for the internal financial position of a country and for its external situation, foreign debt problems, and so on.[35]

The memo stressed: "In connection with all such matters, efforts should be made to avoid conflicting views and judgments, through continuing close working relations between the respective area departments and other means."[36]

With the scope of World Bank-IMF interest defined so broadly, so was the potential arena for World Bank-IMF intervention. Indeed, both institutions were soon using their power to manage the Philippines' external debt as a beachhead from which to criticize what they saw as negative tendencies in other areas of the Philippine economy. "Investment efficiency," the Bank asserted, was on the decline, resulting in "poor utilization of growing savings and large capital inflows."[37] The root of "inefficiency" was traced to the "highly protected" character of Philippine industry.[38] The Bank was particularly worried about the nationalist wave engulfing the country in the late 60's and early 70's, and it warned Marcos against "legislative or administrative action which would unduly restrict the scope for foreign investment in the country. . . ."[39]

The Strategy Unfolds

According to the Ascher Memorandum, one of the "reforms" made possible by the imposition of martial law on September 22, 1972 was the "renewed opening up of the economy to the inflow of foreign capital."[40] As if on cue, the Bank made a massive financial commitment in the months following the advent of martial rule. "The size of our lending program increased substantially in FY 1974 (July 1, 1973—June 30, 1974)," noted one Bank report.[41] "Our lending in FY 1974 amounted to $165.1 million compared to an average of about $30 million a year in the previous five years."[42] This fivefold increase in aid followed the designation of the Philippines as a "country of concentration," to which the flow of Bank assistance would be "higher than average for countries of similar size and income."[43]

Indeed, the financial build-up was impressive. Between 1950 and 1972, the Philippines received a meager $326 million in Bank assistance. In contrast, between 1973 and 1981, more than $2.6 billion was funnelled into 61 projects.[44] Whereas prior to martial law, the Philippines ranked about thirtieth among recipients of Bank loans in cumulative terms, by 1980 it placed eighth among 113 Third World countries.[45]

The significance of the World Bank's post-1972 relationship to the Philippines, however, did not so much lie in the actual value of its loans as in the central position that it was able to carve out in national policy making. "The Bank's basic economic report," asserted the confidential 1976 Country Program Paper, "proposes a framework for future development, which the government has accepted as a basis for its future economic plans."[46]

The Bank strategy accepted by the government was trumpeted as a broad front development effort with these components:[47]

- massive lending for "rural development," to raise agricultural production by "improving the productivity of smallholders";
- industrialization efforts emphasizing the manufacture of labor-intensive exports with the strong participation of foreign capital;
- a continuing drive to "open up" the economy by abolishing protective tariffs and foreign exchange restrictions;
- massive spending on energy and infrastructure to lay the underpinnings for agricultural and industrial advance.

Rural Development (RD) was the Bank's response to the agricultural crisis. The centerpiece of the strategy was increasing the productivity of small farmers through the delivery of "technological packages" and upgrading agricultural support services like credit systems. Rural Development, however, had implications that went beyond improved efficiency. As one specialist close to the Bank put it:

> . . . the underlying political rationale behind the Bank's poverty focus is the pursuit of political stability through what might be called defensive modernization. This strategy rests on an assumption that reform can forestall or pre-empt the accumulation of social and political pressures if people are given a stake in the system. *Reform thus prevents the occurrence of full-fledged revolution.*[48]

Rural development was counterinsurgency. And its targets were obvious: the independent peasant movements and armed rural-based revolutionary forces like the New People's Army, which the volatile countryside had spawned in the late 60's.

While rural development was the immediate priority, the linchpin of the Bank strategy was "export-led industrialization." The Bank rationale read: "Agriculture has in the past been the main source of export earnings; it will continue to play an important role in the future . . . but it can no longer provide sufficient earnings to cover the economy's import needs. Hence, a fundamental change seen as necessary during the next decade should be the emergence of manufacturing exports as a significant contribution to foreign exchange earnings. . . ." It warned: "The expansion of manufacturing exports may be the most difficult to achieve of the changes outlined in this report."[49]

The Bank had reason to be apprehensive since export-led industrialization would necessarily involve a radical reorientation of Philippine industrial development. It meant virtually abandoning the domestic market as the basis for industrial advance and tying the fate of economic growth almost completely to favorable external factors. It was not surprising that such a prescription would provoke hesitation, even within the Bank. Thus, one key officer at the Philippine desk wrote, ". . . in a fiercely competitive and fickle international market, Philippine handicrafts will be in fashion today, and tomorrow [sic]. The bread and butter and the basis of a modern manufacturing sector will always be at home."[50]

Some Filipino technocrats argued for a compromise: while import substitution in light consumer goods had reached its limits, there was still room for replacing imports of capital and intermediate goods—especially since foreign exchange went, for the most part, to paying for such commodities as machinery, petrochemicals, and motor vehicles.

The Bank, however, vetoed this compromise, forcing government acceptance of what amounted to a drastic, total shift to labor-intensive manufacture of light consumer goods like garments, footwear, and handicrafts. As Shahid Husain, a vice president of the World Bank, stressed at the Consultative Group meeting in December 1978,

> . . . the Philippines' export-oriented growth strategy provides an opportunity for both more rapid and more equitable growth than does import substitution. By the late 1960's, the Philippines had exhausted the potential for economic import substitution in consumer goods. *The possibilities for efficient import substitution in capital and intermediate goods industries are limited by constraints of market size, the need for advancing technology in a large number of areas simultaneously, and the capital intensity of many of the processes involved.* Faced with this reality, the Philippines quite appropriately chose an industrialization strategy based on the growth of labor-intensive export industries.[51]

Behind this rhetoric of neoclassical economics lay the World Bank's fear that import substitution in capital and intermediate goods would threaten the interests of American and other Western corporations that dominated the production of these commodities.

The new strategy required providing attractive incentives for export manufacturing. It also meant dismantling the mechanisms protecting the import substitution industries. "For the future," the Bank directed the government, "it should be the government's policy to remove gradually the quantitative restrictions on imports, to restructure and lower tariff levels, and to delete the protective element from other fiscal and monetary policies."[52]

But perhaps most critical to the Bank's strategy was the need to attract foreign investors to labor-intensive export manufacture. To meet these objectives, the Bank projected the need for a $1.6 billion inflow of foreign investment between 1976 and 1985.[53] As one of the Bank's closest associates in the Marcos regime asserted,

> One of the most important strategic devices that can now be effectively employed is the attraction of foreign investment. . . . Foreign investment in labor-intensive export enterprises will accelerate the development of these exports. They will employ Filipinos and earn foreign exchange for the country to an extent beyond what the Filipino-owned enterprises can achieve because of the lack of experience, know-how, and the contacts in international marketing.[54]

These elements, then, constituted the economic scaffolding for what Marcos technocrats called the coming "Philippine miracle." Such a structure, however, could only be erected and consolidated if there were a system of political rule that would nurture and guard it.

Authoritarian Modernization

During the martial law period, certain social sectors were designated as "losers" in the World Bank strategy of export-led growth. This was a key determinant of the system of political rule that arose during this period. The proposed dismantling of protectionism meant that the Filipino industrial elite would have to be sacrificed, for as one World Bank memo put it, protectionism was "one of the few bulwarks of the precarious private entrepreneurial sector. . . ."[55] Another victim of the Bank's strategy was to be the urban working class, whose cheap labor was seen as the main incentive for foreign multinationals to locate in the country. This necessity was euphemistically explained: "The basic objective of the government's wage-price policy has been to promote the growth of employment and investment through, among other things, wage restraint."[56]

To control these two classes, their strongholds within the political system had to be destroyed. In the case of the national capitalist class, this meant Congress; in the case of the working class, it was the trade union movement. The dismantling of Congress was thus sanctioned by the Bank, which noted approvingly that "the proclamation of martial law in 1972 and the abolition of Congress provided the government with almost absolute power in the field of economic development."[57] The Bank also went out of its way to act as an apologist for acts of repression against the labor movement such as General Order No. 5 and Presidential Decree 823, which outlawed strikes. For example, despite the strike ban, arrests of labor leaders, and raids on union offices, Michael Gould, head of the Philippine program office at the Bank, stated, "While the country is formally under martial law, the basic strategy of government is to resort as little as possible to outright coercion and to broaden popular support through the development of effective economic and social programs."[58]

Repression was seen as an unfortunate necessity to create the social arena for the Bank's "technocratic solution" to the country's development problems.[59] The purveyors of this technocratic solution were the key agents of the Bank within the regime—a relationship admitted in a number of internal memos. As one document asserted, "Bank staff have enjoyed very easy access to ministers and other high-level government staff."[60] Another stated: "An active Bank presence . . . has the effect of strengthening the position of the highly trained technical leadership in the government and helping them to achieve policy objectives, which we endorse."[61]

These Bank-favored technocrats included Wharton-trained Cesar Virata, Minister of Finance; MIT graduate Gerardo Sicat, chief of the National Economic Development Authority; Cornell-educated Arturo Tanco, Jr., Minister of Agriculture; Harvard-trained Vicente Paterno, head of the Board of Investments; Executive Secretary Alejandro Melchor, who had studied at the US Naval Academy at Annapolis; and Harvard Ph.D. Placido Mapa, Jr., Executive Secretary for the Philippines at the World Bank.[62]

Similar educational and generational experiences gave these technocrats a strong sense of fraternity with their World Bank and IMF counterparts. Most of them were strongly influenced by the Keynesian Revolution in economics during the 1950's and the ideology of "technocracy" that spun off from it. The "fine tuning" approach advanced during the Kennedy years by Walter Heller and the Council of Economic Advisors provided their model of smooth, top-down economic management.

But while technocratic ideology could manage an uneasy coexistence with liberal democratic ideology in the advanced capitalist states, these soon came into conflict in the developing world. The technocrats experienced mass participation and the give-and-take of the formal democratic arena as uncontrollable variables that sabotaged neat development plans formulated in economic ministries. Both World Bank and Filipino technocrats were thus susceptible to the conservative reformulation of technocratic ideology in the late 60's by such American academics as the influential Harvard professor Samuel Huntington. Huntington argued that in the Third World, the building of order and authority had to precede the granting of political representation to the masses.[63] It was an argument that had been profoundly influenced by such experiences as the "Brazilian miracle," where an 11 percent annual rate of GNP growth went hand in hand with mass depoliticization and the rise of a military-technocratic alliance.

In the Philippines, the Huntington thesis was popularized by such technocrats as O. D. Corpuz, Minister of Education, as "constitutional authoritarianism"[64]—a construct which legitimized the Marcos-instigated and World Bank-sanctioned destruction of the vehicles of political representation. The basic argument was outlined by the dictator himself: "All that people ask is some kind of authority that can enforce the simple law of civil society. . . . Only an authoritarian system will be able to carry forth the mass consent and to exercise the authority necessary to implement new values, measures, and sacrifices."[65] The less sophisticated Ministry of Public Information did not bother with philosophical sugar coating: Filipinos were not capable of democratic government because "we are a people whose flamboyant self-indulgence is legendary. Most of us live by the day, and *bahala na* [or, 'let fate take its course'] for tomorrow. Among such an aimless people Marcos is remarkable."[66] Diplomatically, the World Bank would have dissociated itself from the form but probably not from the substance of this statement.

Modifying the Power Structure

Authoritarian rhetoric and technocratic justification masked a profound rearrangement of the structure of social and political power to meet the serious challenges to elite control and U.S. influence in the 1970's. A major thrust of the new arrangement was the centralization of political power by Marcos which enabled him to better control the revolutionary movement. By 1975 it was clear that under martial law, the following fundamental changes had taken place in the Philippine power structure:

First, the Philippine elite had been forcibly united under the hegemony of the Marcos faction of the elite. As the Bank noted with approval, martial law had "adversely affected the interests of various groups that had been well represented in the old Congress but that lost much of their power after 1972."[67] The quasifeudal autonomy of the political dynasties of regional and local "warlords" was broken and the political and economic power that had been more dispersed in the pre-martial law Philippines was concentrated in the hands of the Marcos clique.

The political necessity of this concentration of class power can be better understood by comparing it to the rise of the "Absolutist State" in early modern Europe. The absolute monarchy, though resisted by feudal lords defending local privileges, triumphed because it represented the centralized redeployment of the power of the whole feudal ruling class against the spreading challenge of peasant revolts.[68] Bearing in mind the limits of historical analogy, something akin to this occurred in the Philippines in the seventies: the Marcos state represented the centralized redeployment of the power of the Philippine elite in order to better contain the revolutionary upsurge of the lower classes that began in the late 60's. Some elements of the old elite could not adjust to the curtailment of their privileges. Indeed, a few, like the powerful Eugenio Lopez family, which boasted of extensive interests in both agriculture and industry, had to be sacrificed. But the centralization of power by Marcos was essential to the survival of the *whole* elite.

The concentration of power served another purpose equally important to the Bank. The abolition of Congress, with its competing power centers, was seen as a prerequisite for a more efficient and all-sided penetration of the Philippines by significantly reducing the "irrationalities" and "uncertainties" faced by foreign investors and aid agencies.

This technocratic distaste for the legislative process was frankly expressed by Board of Investments chief Vicente Paterno, who remarked that measures favoring foreign investors were "steps that would have been difficult to accomplish prior to the proclamation of martial law and would certainly have consumed many months, and probably years, of debate. . . ." Government agencies, he noted, "might face attack from any of several fronts—denunciation in the press or in the halls of Congress, injunction from taking action that may be issued by some courts, investigation of one sort or another, or, in some cases, reduction of the agencies' operating budget appropriations." Paterno concluded that "many of these risks are now eliminated" and technocrats could now "count on a stability of national policies clearly articulated, since there is no longer a multiplicity of the sources which formulate such a policy."[69]

Second, the nationalistic business sector was expelled from the ruling bloc and the center of gravity of elite power shifted from the traditional landed oligarchs like the sugar barons to a new coalition whose power derived from monopolistic control of key industrial and financial institutions, support of foreign capital, and direct control of the state machine. As the Ascher Memorandum saw it, "the political decline of regional, rural-based leaders" was paralleled by the emergence of a "new ruling coalition consisting of the

Marcos family and personal associates, high-level technocrats, key bureaucrats and military officers, and some wealthy businessmen. This alliance is cemented by personal loyalty to the President and by the fact that many of these figures, even in the military, are from Marcos' home region of Ilocos."[70]

Third, the three key pillars of the martial law state were the civilian technocrats, the military, and the president's cronies. As the technocrats took the lead in refashioning the economy, the military became the linchpin of the power structure, "replacing," the Bank pointed out, "the earlier network of political mechanisms."[71] The Bank assessment continued: "Military commanders have, for the first time in modern Philippine history, become an integral part of the power structure, particularly in provincial administration, and through their influence (both personal and official) in judicial and administrative matters."[72] While repression was the primary role of the military, it had also gained an "unprecedented role" in the economy, "moving the policy making and business environment in the Philippines closer to that prevailing in Indonesia and Thailand."[73] Marcos' civilian administrators were, indeed, united to many among their military brethren by the ideology of authoritarian technocracy. Reflecting this philosophy of "technocratic militarism," the Armed Forces Civic Action Manual asserted that military structures "are imbued with a spirit that is tied to rapid technological progress. In a sense, they often represent islands of modernity in the troubled seas of preindustrial societies striving for modernity."[74] With military technocrats placed at the helm of many key state agencies, the Bank concluded, "The power, prerogatives, emoluments, and prestige of the military establishment have never been greater."[75]

The cronies were dubbed bureaucrat capitalists because of the way they manipulated their ties to Marcos and state agencies to build economic empires. They were, in the Bank's view, the irrational element in the ruling coalition, for their moves made a mockery of the technocrats' attempts to project economic policy as neutral and scientific. Unlike the military, which was tied to U.S. military assistance, and the technocrats, who were close to the Bank, the cronies were dependent only on Marcos and utterly loyal to him.

Finally, under the rationale of technocratic centralization, martial law brought major areas of economic life, such as energy and communications, and key industries, such as sugar and coconut, under the direct control and surveillance of the Marcos coalition of technocrats, officers, and bureaucrat capitalists. This coalition rejected nationalistic economic goals. Instead, it forged a state devoted to implementing what the Bank described as a "strategy of liberalization, export-oriented industrialization, and a positive climate for foreign investment."[76] The martial law state, therefore, served as a powerful and unprecedented mechanism for the domination of the economy by external, particularly U.S., interests—as the main instrument of what Valencia described as "colonization without an occupation force."

The U.S. Connection

As the World Bank attained a greater voice in determining the Philippines' path to economic development, so the United States acquired even greater influence over Philippine affairs. For, contrary to its propaganda, the Bank does not stand as an autonomous institution far above the material interests of specific nation-states. It has been responsive above all to the needs of its dominant members, the advanced capitalist countries of the West, and in particular to those of the United States, which controls more than 20 percent of total voting power in the institution.

U.S. officials have made no attempt to hide the dominant influence of the United States at the Bank, the goals for which this influence has been employed, and the means for attaining these goals.

As a U.S. Treasury Department report, commissioned by the Reagan administration, asserts, "The magnitude of U.S. financial participation in the MDB's [multilateral development banks] and the central U.S. role as a founding member has assured us a major role in the MDB decision-making process by tradition, law, and practice."[77] The report elaborates:

> The United States was instrumental in shaping the structure and mission of the World Bank along Western, market-oriented lines. . . . We were also responsible . . . for the emergence of a corporate entity with a weighted voting run by a board of directors, headed by high-caliber, American-dominated management, and well-qualified professional staff. As a charter member and major shareholder in the World Bank, the United States secured the sole right to a permanent seat on the Bank's Board of Directors.[78]

Then comes a passage laden with a sense of might:

> Other significant actors—management, major donors, and major recipients—have recognized the United States as a major voice in the banks. They know from past experience that we are capable and willing to pursue important policy objectives in the banks by exercising the financial and political leverage at our disposal.[79]

To what key ends has the U.S. employed its power? Again, the Treasury report is candid:

> The basic long-term, systemic goal has been to build and to maintain an international economic framework that is open, predictable, growing and characterized by increased efficiency and development. Such an international economic system was expected to encourage development of democratic, pluralistic and capitalistic societies similar to ours.[80]

And how well have the World Bank and other multilateral banks performed in the achievement of this objective? The report replies:

> The MDB's, by and large, have been most effective in furthering our *global economic and financial objectives*, and thereby also serving our long-term political/strategic objectives. . . . Neither bilateral assistance nor private sector flows, if available, are as effective in influencing LDC [less developed countries] economic performance as the MDB's.[81]

The multilateral banks are seen by U.S. officials as complementing the U.S. Agency for International Development (USAID) and other American bilateral assistance agencies:

> U.S. bilateral and multilateral aid have different comparative advantages depending upon the U.S. objective in question and complement, rather than substitute for, each other. The U.S. bilateral aid program holds some advantages in serving U.S. short-term political interests; multilateral assistance primarily serves long-term U.S. interests and promotes a stable international economic environment.[82]

The seeming "impartiality" of the World Bank is its major advantage over bilateral aid. As a Congressional Research Service (CRS) analysis puts it, the World Bank and other multilateral agencies "perform the difficult task of requiring performance standards of their borrowers, a task which the United States and other lenders may be reluctant to impose on a bilateral basis."[83]

Strong U.S. influence at the World Bank has not been limited to setting broad policy orientations for Third World countries. The Bank often serves as a tool for attaining short and medium-term U.S. political-strategic objectives. For instance, "the MDB's can . . . be helpful as relatively apolitical institutions in allowing the U.S. to show some indirect support for countries with whom U.S. bilateral relations are still sensitive but which are susceptible to improvement, such as Yugoslavia and Rumania."[84] But there have been more controversial objectives: the Treasury report reveals that out of fourteen of the "most significant issues" which sparked debate at the Bank—ranging from blocking observer status for the Palestine Liberation Organization to halting Bank aid to Vietnam and Afghanistan—the United States was able to impose its view as Bank policy in twelve cases.[85]

The extent to which the United States can manipulate Bank policy was dramatically illustrated by the cutoff of World Bank funds to the prosocialist Allende government in Chile in 1971—an experience repeated in 1980, when the Bank ceased aid to the Socialist Republic of Vietnam to appease the U.S. Congress. "Overall, the United States has been successful," concludes the CRS report, "in effectively influencing the operations and policies of the institutions. . . . For the most part the banks . . . have refrained from lending to countries with which the United States has had investment disputes."[86]

The World Bank, U.S. Policy, and Repressive Regimes

Preventing assistance from reaching governments perceived as hostile to U.S. interests was one prong of American policy within the Bank. Another was harnessing the Bank's resources for those regimes that were regarded as particularly vital to U.S. security and economic interests. With the onset of the general crisis of U.S. foreign policy triggered by the disastrous U.S. intervention in Vietnam, the World Bank became even more important as a conduit of U.S. aid and influence to favored client-states. To understand this development and its significance for U.S.-Philippine relations, it is worth exploring briefly the roots and dynamics of this crisis.

A key dimension of the crisis was the contradiction between the new political requirements to maintain U.S. presence in the Third World and the traditional ideological justification for that presence articulated by the foreign policy establishment.

In the early post-World War II period, U.S. "overseas commitments" had been legitimized by the ideology of spreading western-style formal democracy as an answer to the challenge posed by national liberation movements. "The idea that the mission of the United States was to build democracy around the world had become a convention of American politics in the 1950's," wrote Frances Fitzgerald. "Among certain circles it was more or less assumed that democracy, that is electoral democracy combined with private ownership and civil liberties, was what the United States had to offer the Third World. Democracy provided not only the basis for American opposition to Communism but the practical method to make sure that opposition worked."[87]

The creation of and support for narrow formal democracies dominated by landed elites was the expression of this compromise between ideology and practical politics. This was the general thrust of U.S. foreign policy, though there were, of course, exceptions to the rule, like the case of Guatemala, where the CIA installed a dictatorship in 1954. However, by the mid-sixties, this political formula was in jeopardy—a situation evidenced not only by events in the Philippines, but also by the parallel crisis of traditional oligarchical democracies in countries like Brazil, Chile in 1970-1973, and Uruguay in 1971-1973, and by the failure to implant the elite democratic model in Vietnam.[88]

In all these countries, the system of formal, elite democracy was driven to the breaking point by the same constellation of forces that destroyed it in the Philippines: factional or policy disarray within the local elite, agricultural and industrial stagnation coinciding with a strong drive by U.S. capital to restructure the economy, and increasingly effective manipulation of the constitutional machinery by the lower classes. In the Philippines, Chile, and Uruguay—all countries renowned for long-standing democratic traditions—there emerged from the wreckage the same formula pioneered by the Brazilian junta in the late 60's: a military or presidential-military dictatorship "sanitizing" the social situation with massive repression, justifying its existence with the ideology of controlled modernization with the indispensable participation of foreign capital, and resting on a social coalition of technocrats, officers, local bureaucrat-capitalists, and foreign investors.

The crisis of the traditional political formula precipitated a conflict within the U.S. foreign policy establishment that dovetailed into the debilitating debate over Vietnam. Partisans of *realpolitik* like Richard Nixon and Henry Kissinger were ranged against traditional "liberal internationalists" like George McGovern, Edward Kennedy, and Rep. Donald Fraser of the House Foreign Affairs Committee. The policy debate within the political elite was articulated in the language of human rights, but its substance lay in the question: *should U.S. influence in the Third World be mediated by authoritarian regimes or formal democratic systems?*

The struggle over the orientation of U.S. policy manifested itself most acutely as a battle over bilateral foreign aid. Supported by mass pressure—polls at the time showed that 87 percent of the American public favored cutting aid to repressive regimes[89]—proponents of the traditional democratic formula were able to score key congressional victories. For example, in 1974 police aid to Third World countries was banned by an amendment sponsored by Sen. James Abourezk; in 1975 the Kennedy-sponsored termination of aid to Pinochet's Chile was approved; and in 1976 the "Human Rights Amendment" to the Foreign Assistance Act was passed, which stipulated that "no security assistance may be provided to any country the government of which engages in a consistent pattern of gross violations of internationally recognized human rights."[90]

With bilateral aid increasingly hemmed in by human rights restrictions, State Department bureaucrats were forced to rely more and more on the World Bank and other multilateral agencies as an instrument of diplomacy. By the mid-70's, right-wing repressive regimes—in particular, Indonesia, Brazil, the Philippines, and South Korea—were at the top of the list of recipients of Bank assistance. In all these countries, multilateral aid flows outstripped U.S. bilateral assistance.

The case of the Philippines is illustrative. Pressure from congressional liberals forced a reduction of U.S. military aid from a peak of $45.3 million in 1973 to $31.8 million in 1979 and of bilateral economic aid from $125 million to $72 million. In such a political atmosphere, assistance from the World Bank became especially critical, as the 1976 Country Program Paper states:

> We do not expect commitments from the major bilateral donors, the United States and Japan, to increase in real terms due to the presently unfavorable climate for foreign aid and other competing claims on their aid resources . . . . Overall, the [bilateral] grant element of official assistance is relatively low . . . and is likely to decrease even further . . . [C]ontinued IBRD [World Bank] and ADB [Asian Development Bank] assistance on a large scale would not only help to ensure that the overall maturity structure of external debt would remain within manageable limits, but also would help the Government to increase its borrowings from Ex-IM [Export-Import] Banks and other commercial sources.[91]

Just how decisively the Bank stepped into the breach is revealed by the statistics: As U.S. bilateral economic aid dropped from $125 million in 1973 to $72 million in 1979, Bank assistance climbed steeply from $39.5 million in 1972 to $561 million in 1979.

The World Bank not only made up for the drop in bilateral economic aid but for the decline in military assistance as well. The massive financial commitment it provided enabled Marcos to shift domestic resources: funds which would otherwise have gone for other purposes were directed to the military. Thus, with the economic gap filled by the Bank, Marcos was able to hike the defense budget by about 350 percent, from $77 million in 1972 to $367 million in 1976. To finance the expansion of the Philippine military from 60,000 to 250,000 troops, Marcos hiked the defense budget from $77 million in 1972 to $367 million in 1976. The latter figure was roughly equivalent to the $384 million the Bank committed to Marcos that year.

Jimmy Carter's ascent to the presidency in 1977 did not alter the World Bank-Marcos relationship. Despite his human rights rhetoric, which contributed to his winning the election, Carter had barely been in office for two months when he found himself aping his Republican predecessors—that is, opposing congressional cuts in bilateral aid for Marcos because of "overriding security considerations."[92] These considerations were the two military bases, Subic Naval Base and Clark Air Force Base—the only major U.S. installations remaining in Southeast Asia following the American debacle in Vietnam.

When Congress nevertheless reduced aid to Marcos in 1978, Carter increasingly depended on the World Bank to quietly channel American assistance to Marcos. The hypocrisy of the administration's human rights policy toward the Philippines is shown in the fact that during the Carter presidency the U.S. never voted against any project for Marcos at the Executive Board—despite the fact that a "no" vote was required under the Human Rights Amendment on any multilateral aid project that could not be shown to "directly benefit needy people." In all such cases, the administration abstained.[93]

Even more glaring was Carter's active effort to make the Philippines eligible for concessional or interest-free lending from the Bank's "soft loan" window, the International Development Association (IDA), in 1978, after Congress reduced bilateral aid. The Philippines had "graduated" from IDA in 1974 but was readmitted, according to the Treasury report, "in large part at the urging of the U.S., despite the fact that the economic case for . . . readmission at that time was weak."[94]

The significance of the World Bank-Marcos relationship for the U.S. was not, however, exhausted by its usefulness as a conduit of U.S. assistance at a time of crisis for bilateral aid programs.[95] The theory of "technocratic modernization" which was being put into practice by the World Bank in the Philippines and elsewhere in the Third World, represented a marked departure from the obsolete postwar ideology of missionary democracy. The model of a strong, centralized regime capable of "imposing development from above" provided many U.S. policy makers with the beginnings of a new ideological rationale for defending U.S. interests in a world beset by national liberation movements. Technocratic modernization, therefore, provided a crucial bridge between the old democratic formula and the full-blown justification for authoritarian rule that was to be advanced in the form of the "Kirkpatrick Doctrine" by the Reagan presidency.

Conclusion

The dramatic emergence of the World Bank as a major force in Philippine affairs in the early 1970's was a response to a fundamental crisis of the postwar neocolonial regime. The massive World Bank effort had two objectives: to stabilize the deteriorating political situation, especially in the countryside; and to completely open up the economy to the free flow of foreign capital and commodities.

Centralization of political power in one section of the elite—the Marcos faction—was essential to the achievement of these goals. This concentration of power made administration of the repression and co-optive functions of the state more efficient and effective. It was also seen as necessary to "rationalize" the economy to integrate it more decisively into the U.S.-dominated international capitalist order. Within the reigning Marcos coalition, the U.S.-educated technocrats became the most trusted and reliable executors of the World Bank strategy of rural development and export-led industrialization.

The role of the World Bank and its sister agency, the IMF, in the Philippines was magnified by the crisis which gripped U.S. foreign policy toward the Third World after the disastrous American intervention in Vietnam. The U.S. establishment became sharply divided between liberals, mainly in Congress, who hewed to the traditional line of promoting elite-dominated democracies as the means of U.S. control, and the practitioners of *realpolitik* in the executive branch, who realized that the maintenance of U.S. domination in the Third World required the presence of repressive allied regimes.

As the Congressional liberals struggled, with some success, to attach human rights restrictions to U.S. bilateral aid, the executive was increasingly driven to rely on the IMF, the World Bank, and other multilateral aid agencies to serve as channels of U.S. influence to the growing number of authoritarian regimes that took the place of constitutional, elite democracies in places like South Korea, Brazil, Chile, and the Philippines.

CHAPTER TWO

The Making of McNamara's Second Vietnam

The World Bank experience in the Philippines has been compared to the U.S. military odyssey in Vietnam. The image is apt, for the economic buildup in the Philippines and the military buildup in Vietnam were both massive, capital-intensive "technical fixes" to societies rent by deep-seated social conflicts. Like McNamara's military adventure in Vietnam, his development experiment in the Philippines exhibited the same pattern of early superficial successes, followed by a protracted stalemate, then spectacular collapse.

The following pages paint, in broad strokes, the origins and dynamics of this crisis, as well as the Bank's frantic attempts to salvage the sputtering strategy.

In this chapter we shall examine the entrance of the World Bank into the Philippine economic scene with its various sectoral projects. Its rural development plan included irrigation, credit, and advice to the government's land reform. In the cities, the Bank focused on slum upgrading. Throughout the country, it financed road building, hydroelectric dams, and other projects to create the infrastructure for the Bank's vision of development of the Philippine economy.

The main elements of this development were to be the pacification of the countryside through Rural Development and the transformation of the industrial sector from import-substitution manufacturing to export-oriented industrialization. This strategy was to plug the Philippines more firmly into the international capitalist economic order.

The strategy, of course, had its own natural enemies: the Filipino working class, who were to become the "cheap labor" of the international pool; the Filipino businessmen, whose interests were to be sacrificed in favor of foreign multinational corporations; and poor peasants and tribal people, who stood to lose, not gain, from Rural Development. The Bank worked hand in hand with the repressive martial law regime to quell this resistance in its various forms.

But the Bank strategy faced other limitations as well. An increasingly hostile international market began closing its doors to Philippine exports and foreign capital became wary of investing in the debt-ridden regime.

In the beginning of the 80's, the Bank and its sister agency, the International Monetary Fund, stepped up their efforts to restructure the Philippine economy, despite the failure they had encountered. The principal mechanism was a "structural adjustment" loan, the granting of which was tied to political changes and economic reforms orchestrated by the Bank. This chapter provides an overview of these developments. The sectoral projects and the major structural transformation will receive more extended analysis and more thorough documentation in the succeeding five chapters.

Beginner's Luck

The early moves and "accomplishments" of the martial law regime impressed Bank bureaucrats. GNP rose by 10 per cent in 1973. That same year major efforts by the government to attract foreign investment resulted in a net inflow of $55 million—a sum that equalled the net outflow of the previous three years. Even the international market seemed to favor Marcos, as high prices for Philippine agricultural exports turned the trade deficit of $120 million in 1972 to a surplus of $270 million in 1973.

On the agricultural front, the Bank observed through rose-tinted glasses: "The Government has vigorously implemented a program of agrarian reform among rice and corn tenants, concentrating mainly on the larger holdings in the first phase."[1] Rice production rose by 30 percent over 1972 "due to increased use of fertilizer, more supervised credit, and increased investments in supporting rural services as part of a general drive for rice self-sufficiency."[2]

But 1973 was the high point and the one bright spot of the martial law economy. The next three years, 1974-77, saw the development offensive grind to a halt on almost all fronts. In the period 1977-81, the program began to unravel in spectacular fashion as several factors converged: authoritarian inefficiency, political paralysis, basic flaws in the "productivity" approach, adverse external conditions, contradictions within the ruling coalition, and, most important, growing resistance from the victims of the experiment in authoritarian development.

The Myth of Authoritarian Efficiency

In 1972, the Bank welcomed Marcos' centralization of power in the belief that it was necessary for a strong, unobstructed effort in national development. A few years later, however, the Bank confessed that, "One of the major constraints affecting the development of the Philippines has been the tendency of the administration to centralize authority and to exercise excessive control."[3] There was, it continued, a "persistent resistance of many agencies to regionalization and decentralization." Then, in a noteworthy passage, it admitted, "Historically, Bank staff have enjoyed easy access to ministries and other high-level government staff. This has certainly facilitated the Bank's work, but we have a lingering concern that we may be taking up too much of top officials' time and contributing to continuing centralization."[4]

What the Bank seemed to forget was that this elitist mode of relating to the Philippines was built right into its own structure. The Bank was the mirror image of the dictatorship. It was itself an authoritarian institution with decision making and control highly concentrated at the top. Like Marcos, McNamara had "the reputation for being an authoritarian boss and for running the Bank in an authoritarian fashion."[5]

Overcentralization in the Philippines was compounded by bureaucratic ineffectiveness. One of the justifications advanced for the sharp increase in lending to the Philippines under martial law was the allegedly "high absorptive capacity" for Bank funds by its economic agencies.[6] But by the end of the decade, the Bank had been disabused of this illusion.

The Philippines, supervision mission reports warned, showed a "deteriorating trend in project implementation."[7] Whereas the Bank regarded 30 percent of all projects as "problem projects" in 1977, the proportion rose to 63 percent in 1979[8]—a figure substantially above the figure for the whole East Asian and Pacific region.[9] "Our basic assessment," noted the 1980 Country Program Paper, "is that the Philippine performance is far below what could be reasonably expected for a country with its income and manpower standards."[10]

One consequence of worsening implementation was a serious backlog in disbursements of already approved loans—a trend criticized by the Consultative Group.[11] The Bank did not relish having to explain the obvious contradiction between the inability of the government to absorb funds and the public posture of the Group that the Philippines urgently needed large inflows of development capital.

The frustrations of Bank bureaucrats were vented in scathing internal attacks on agencies they were praising in public. A typical in-house attack was that directed at the National Power Corporation (NPC), the recipient of more than $200 million worth of Bank loans: ". . . since 1968 NPC has never met the target rates of return agreed with the Bank; today it is unable to meet even its debt service requirements from internally generated cash, let alone make any contribution to new investments. . . . Such a situation will become increasingly difficult to justify in the context of the limited resources available."[12]

It became obvious to the Bank that it was tied to an administration that combined the paralyzing effect of authoritarianism on the initiative of lower or local bodies with the notorious inefficiency of the premartial law government machinery—in short, to the worst of all possible bureaucracies. In the words of the Ascher Memorandum:

> . . . the Philippine public administration remains basically unchanged beneath the thin layer of technically competent technocrats. Except in those agencies devoted to showcase programs enjoying high priority from the President, the traditional tendencies of administrative inertia and corruption are still manifest. To complicate matters, bureaucrats who cannot claim the status of "technocrats" face the insecurity caused by the purges, by periodic attacks on bureaucratic waste, and by the elimination of civil service tenure under the post-1972 rules. The danger of defensive reactions, even paralysis, is significant, and the implementation of economic reforms is still vulnerable to the collapse of morale and effectiveness in various agencies.[13]

The Panacea of Productivity

Authoritarian inefficiency, however, was only one problem inherent in the Bank's approach to development. A more serious flaw was the *overwhelming focus on raising productivity combined with the absence of measures to alter wealth and power inequalities.*[14] Indeed, so as not to antagonize privileged groups, Bank projects were consciously designed to make sure that the benefit of its projects also went to these sectors.[15] Thus, despite the claim that the Bank had abandoned the discredited "trickle down" strategy of development, it was actually that strategy, in a modified form, which was the basis of Bank programs like Rural Development (RD), which was officially billed as targeting smallholders.

It is hardly surprising, then, that the same social consequences associated with the supposedly discarded approach were produced by the Bank's Rural Development projects.[16] By the late 1970's, bank bureaucrats began to doubt whether any benefits from the massive irrigation projects—the biggest component of the RD and agriculture program—were going to smallholders. Indeed, supervision reports and postproject evaluations revealed that a number of projects, like the Smallholders Tree Farming Project and rural credit projects, were actually benefitting mainly big landlords, medium and big commercial farmers, and foreign agrocorporations.[17] The costs of the Bank's basic prescription for upgrading small farmers' productivity—the adoption of a mechanized chemical-intensive and fertilizer-dependent rice technology—drove many small farmers to bankruptcy, while bringing windfall profits to farm machinery manufacturers, the fertilizer cartel, and the U.S. pesticide monopoly.[18] Fixated on the panacea of productivity and sidestepping the redistribution problem, the Bank helped unleash a typhoon of "modernization" in the Philippine countryside that submerged the very people it was supposed to benefit: the peasantry.

Political Paralysis

With the Bank's projects being undermined by the inherent contradictions of the trickle-down "productivity" approach, the antipoverty strategy in the Philippines countryside came to rest principally on the regime's promise to carry out land reform. While Marcos' land reform program was mainly oriented toward increasing productivity and excluded the large foreign-exchange earning cash-crop plantations, still its stated objective of expropriating the property of landlords in rice and corn areas promised a significant alteration of economic power in the rural Philippines.

With this stated objective, Marcos seemed to be promising the expropriation of the wealth of a key sector of his base of support—i.e., to cut his own throat. For Filipinos, the prospect was too good to be true. So, most were not surprised when, in practice, the landlords won the day. Over 600,000 tenant farmers, out of the million target beneficiaries promised ownership of the land they tilled by the Land Reform Decree of 1972, were eliminated from "Operation Land Transfer." This was accomplished by a 1975 government decree allowing landlords owning seven to 24 hectares to retain seven hectares of their holdings. And what legal exemptions failed to accomplish, intimidation by landlords and bureaucratic timidity did.[19] By 1977, the Bank bureaucrats could no longer ignore the facts: ". . . there is doubt as to the seriousness of the Government's commitment to land reform, which may have decreased if anything. . . ."[20]

While the Bank reconciled itself to the preservation of the status quo in the countryside, it was extremely upset by the regime's profound hesitation in applying the IMF-World Bank plan to eliminate the national entrepreneurial class by dismantling the protectionist barriers on which it depended for survival.

While the "legislative obstructionism" of this class, as the Bank termed it,[21] had been clipped with the abolition of Congress, its power remained substantial enough for Marcos to retain a healthy respect for it. Indeed, concerned by his increasingly narrow base of support, Marcos hoped to neutralize the local industrialists for as long as possible. Consequently, the regime's industrial policy began to deviate from the Bank's prescription. While providing foreign export manufacturers with the attractive incentives demanded by the Bank, the government made no substantial moves to withdraw the tariff mechanisms sheltering the import-substitution sector. Indeed, the strike ban and controls on labor organizing, intended principally as bait for foreign investors in export industries, were also seen as a way to neutralize, if not win over, the national industrialists, whose factories were also covered by the repressive labor decrees.

This political compromise was, in the Bank's view, undermining the strategy of drawing most of industry's resources into labor-intensive export manufacturing. Pressure mounted on the regime to bring down the tariff walls, with the Bank handing down the ultimatum at the 1979 meeting of the Consultative Group. An undesirable "dualism," the government was warned, had developed in Philippine industry between the export-oriented sector and the highly protected home-market sector.[22] It was time for the regime to undertake a "fundamental restructuring" of the economy.[23]

The Crisis of Export-led Growth

It is eloquent testimony to the tenacity of bureaucratic tunnel vision and bureaucratic perversity that the Bank was stepping up the pressure on the Marcos regime to restructure the economy—that is, go all out for a strategy of liberalization and export-led growth—at a time when international economic developments had seriously undermined the rationale for that model.

Three conditions had to be present for this strategy to succeed. The first was the maintenance of favorable prices for export commodities and stability in the prices of imports. The second was continued economic growth in the key export markets—the advanced capitalist countries of the West and Japan. As McNamara put it:

> There is a strong—almost one-to-one—relationship between changes in the growth rate of OECD [developed] nations and that of the oil-importing nations. This is not surprising. Exports to OECD countries constitute 75 percent of total exports of those nations. A diminished growth rate in the OECD nations translates very quickly into reduced demand for the developing nations' exports leading in turn to a reduced capacity to import, and hence to lower growth rates.[24]

The third key condition was a nonprotectionist world trading atmosphere.

By the second half of the 1970's all these conditions had ceased to exist. The "stagflation" taking hold of Western economies exacerbated the traditionally erratic behavior of primary commodity prices. In 1975, the prices of the three top Philippine foreign exchange earners—sugar, coconut and copper—fell sharply from the boom prices of 1973 and 1974. After growing by 30 percent, from $1.9 billion to $2.7 billion, between 1973 and 1974, the value of exports dropped by 15 percent, from $2.7 billion to $2.3 billion, between 1974 and 1975.[25] The decline was especially dramatic in the case of sugar, the second largest foreign exchange earner: from a high of $766 million in 1974, the value of sugar exports plunged to $216 million in 1978.[26] This plunge led to the bankruptcy of hundreds of sugar operators and a drastic weakening of the political position of the sugar barons—traditionally the strongest interest group within the country's ruling bloc.

But while the value of the Philippines' exports plummeted, that of its imports continued to skyrocket, reflecting the extent to which multinational giants controlling the production and marketing of these products had distorted "free market" price mechanisms. Thus, largely due to the manipulation of international oil prices by the Western oil companies taking advantage of OPEC's effort to increase its share of the income from oil, the value of Philippine oil imports rose by 450 percent, from $166 million in 1973 to $907 million in 1978.[27] At the same time, the prices of capital-intensive machinery and transport equipment, largely determined by monopolistic Western and Japanese producers, rose almost threefold, from $469 million in 1973 to $1.3 billion in 1978.[28]

Caught in the squeeze of plummeting primary commodity exports and skyrocketing industrial raw material and equipment imports, the Philippine economy saw its trade balance swing from a surplus of $290 million in 1973—the one bright year of the martial law period, when still-expanding exports cushioned the effects of the great oil price hike of that year—to a ballooning deficit of $1.3 billion in 1978.[29]

The main threat to the viability of export-led growth, however, lay in the protectionist trend in the advanced capitalist economies. Rising protectionism in these countries was a response not only to the inroads made by Japanese durable goods imports, but also to rising imports of light manufactures from the Third World—the very commodities that the Bank exhorted the developing countries to produce.

The Philippines was, in fact, already hard-hit by protectionist measures. Most damaging, in the Bank and IMF's view, were the barriers being erected against the "nontraditional, labor-intensive manufactures" like garments, which was regarded as the "cutting edge" of export-led industrialization. In two years alone, 1978 to 1980, the IMF identified at least 33 barriers erected against Philippine exports, mainly textiles and garments, in Australia, Canada, the Common Market, Japan, the U.S., and five other advanced countries.[30] The Bank was not, of course, oblivious to this development. As one 1979 industry paper admitted: "The quotas imposed on imports of Philippine garments by the U.S., Australia, the EEC, and Canada have not been a severely limiting factor, but as the exports expand, their pressure will become more severe."[31] The agency was not, however, prepared to draw the appropriate lesson—for that would have meant, among other things, dumping the model of export-led industrialization for the Third World which it had only recently enshrined as the new doctrine of development economics, the latest panacea of growth.

The Debt Trap

Clinging to an export-oriented growth strategy in the face of shrinking export markets is the key explanation behind the swift deterioration of the external position of the Philippine economy. The rapidity of this collapse took IMF and Bank bureaucrats by surprise. The Bank strategy had envisioned the deficit in the current account (the current account consists of trade in goods and such items as shipping, tourism receipts, insurance, and remittance from citizens abroad) to stay below $1 billion annually between 1976 and 1985. "Actual events have deviated somewhat from these expectations,"[32] World Bank Vice President Shahid Husain admitted at the 1979 Consultative Group meeting. The deficit passed the $1 billion mark in 1976, $2 billion in 1980, and was expected to hit $3 billion by 1983.[33]

The heavy inflow of foreign loans needed to bridge the yawning deficit threw early Bank projections of the rise in the country's external debt way off the mark. Estimated by a 1976 report to reach $11.4 billion in 1985, the external debt actually passed $11 billion in 1981 and was conservatively estimated by a 1980 Bank report to hit $19.3 billion in 1984.[34] At the December 1979 Consultative Group meeting, concerned delegates were told that the magnitude of debt-service payments would push the debt-service ratio (ratio of export receipts to loan repayments) to 22 percent in the mid-eighties[35]—above the commonly accepted "danger threshold" of 20 percent and far above the 14 to 15 percent projected earlier by the Bank.[36] The best terms that the government could get in "restructuring" or rescheduling talks with its creditors would still have it laying out at least $9.5 billion in the period 1983-85 alone[37]—a task that one Bank analyst described as "possible but not probable."[38] The regime thus found itself in a situation not unlike that of the typical Filipino tenant farmer; it had to go deeper in debt to pay off installments of the already existing debt.

Consequently, the country's escalating debt requirements pushed it into even greater dependence on the resources of the IMF and World Bank. Almost every year during the 1970's, the Philippines was under some "stand-by" lending program of the IMF—giving it the distinction of being one of the few Third World countries to complete not just one but several IMF-directed programs. "In the process," noted the *Asian Wall Street Journal,* "The IMF began supervising a wide variety of Philippine economic decisions."[39] Indeed, by mid-1980, the Philippines owed the IMF almost $1.0 billion, making it the Third World country most indebted to the agency and second only to the United Kingdom in overall indebtedness.[40] As for the World Bank, its claim on the total external debt rose to 9 percent in 1980 and was conservatively expected to reach 13 percent by 1985.[41]

The powerful influence that both agencies had over the country's external economic position, however, did not spring solely from their large claims on Philippine debt. Perhaps even more important was the "good credit risk" status that they stamped on the regime. As the Bank put it, "The Government regards the IMF's role as essential not only for the large volume of resources provided, but also for the reassurance on economic management provided to private sources of finance."[42]

Such reassurance was, indeed, needed by U.S. bankers by the end of the 1970's, when it was estimated that the Philippines, together with Argentina and Taiwan, accounted for about 10 percent of the capital loaned out by the nine largest U.S. banks to developing countries.[43] By early 1981, U.S. banks held about $4.2 billion of the country's burgeoning $12.3 billion external debt.[44] In the opinion of the Bank and the IMF, these figures indicated that U.S. creditors were dangerously overexposed in the Philippines, as they were in the Third World in general. This led the Bank to conclude that "it would probably be necessary for the Philippines to draw an increasing share of its private source external capital from non-U.S. sources such as Japan, Europe and OPEC."[45]

The Japanese, however, balked at this proposition. Noting that the 22 percent debt-service ratio projected for the mid-eighties was above the commonly regarded danger threshold, they warned, "The established figure of debt service now seems sufficiently high and may even tend to rise . . . if export receipts grow less than expected in the 1980's. We therefore consider that a cautious and reserved attitude toward this point should remain warranted."[46]

The Japanese posture appeared to prefigure an international credit crunch in the early 1980's for the developing countries, particularly the heavily indebted ones like the Philippines. Whereas non-American banks had stepped up their lending when U.S. banks slowed their pace in the mid-seventies, by the latter half of the decade, according to a Morgan Guaranty Report, "Japanese and European banks were also showing tendencies of slackening their pace of lending . . . partly motivated by concerns of excessive growth of international lending and portfolio concentration . . . ."[47] The report warned that "while banks will continue to play an important role . . . in financing balance-of-payments deficits in the 1980's, their share will and should diminish."[48]

The implication of these trends was an even greater role for the IMF and the Bank in keeping the Philippines afloat—and the Marcos regime alive. For, no matter how serious the external debt situation of the Philippines became, the IMF, World Bank, and international private bankers apparently saw no other alternative but to maintain the financial lifeline to the dictatorship. Refusing the regime more loans carried the prospect of almost certain default on external debt. And that development, bankers feared, could very well spark a chain reaction among similar debt-ridden countries. It could also lead to the fall of Marcos and the rise of a new government which might, among other things, repudiate the country's debts. That this scenario was a nagging worry among Bank bureaucrats was evident in a 1980 economic review: "The fundamental creditworthiness risk is political, relating to the possibility of a sharp deterioration in the quality of economic management under a different political regime."[49]

The path of export-led growth, traveling as it had to through local resistance and an inhospitable international economic climate, had led the Philippines into the debt trap.

Foreign Capital Hesitates

In November 1981, Marcos told the American business community in Manila, "My country subscribes to the free enterprise system in which American business thrives best."[50]

With such assurances, proclaimed throughout the martial law period, one would have expected multinational corporate investment to flood the Philippines. Foreign investors, however, remained cautious. Foreign capital flowing into the Philippines throughout the 1970's was considerably less than that flowing into neighboring Singapore, Taiwan, Hong Kong, or South Korea. Capital flows are extremely difficult to calculate because of the secrecy that pervades the transfer of funds by multinational corporations. Nonetheless, IMF and World Bank figures suggest that the *net inflow* of foreign capital into the Philippines between 1973 and 1979 came to a minuscule $87 million.[51]

This small amount of fresh investor capital entering the Philippines did not mean that foreign investors were getting less influential and active. On the contrary, the Bank estimated that in 1980, investment by foreign firms came to 500 percent more than the annual average for the 1970's.[52] What this seeming contradiction suggests is that, reluctant to bring in fresh capital, foreign firms were financing new investments mainly from their local profits or borrowings from domestic capital sources. Indeed, U.S. corporations, according to one study, borrowed $1.1 billion from local sources between 1973 and 1977.[53]

There were several reasons behind the reluctance of multinational firms to commit fresh capital. One was the perception of political instability. Consistently, business surveys showed the Philippines tagged by executives as one of the least attractive countries to invest in. A major uncertainty, noted a widely consulted *Business International* report, was the "succession in the event of Marcos' death or incapacitation."[54] Marcos, investors feared, had been unable to "institutionalize authoritarianism" to the same degree as had, for example, Lee Kuan Yew in Singapore or the Brazilian military, and this failure could lead to a choatic struggle for the throne once the central figure of the New Society coalition passed from the scene.

An even greater worry was what Frost and Sullivan, the "political risk" analysts, speculated would be a "regime change" in the near future.[55] With Marcos' dismantling of the political bases and networks of the elite opposition, left-led nationalist movements like the National Democratic Front (NDF) had emerged as the only viable opposition forces. Foreign investors' concerns about the direction of economic policy if the opposition took over were not idle, according to the World Bank:

> The nationalist position of Marcos' opposition commits them to support nationalist legislation, even at rather high economic costs. If not, the precarious interclass coalition cemented by the nationalism issue would be jeopardized. An industrial program based on foreign investment would in all likelihood come under attack.[56]

But foreign investors' hesitations did not spring solely from political concerns. A major factor alienating multinationals was the increasingly capricious character of official policy toward business and the favoritism displayed by the government toward Marcos' powerful cronies.

The cronies, acting as front men for Marcos in many instances, exerted monopoly control over key sectors of the Philippine economy including the sugar and coconut industries, two of the country's top foreign exchange earners. While the practical tactics of the crony capitalists were mainly directed at local Filipino competitors, they were nevertheless regarded warily by foreign business. Although Marcos' friends had direct tie-ups with particular multinational investors—for example, one assembled Toyotas while another grew bananas for the agribusiness giant, United Brands—the powerful position they had carved out as procurers of presidential favors, manipulators of government policies, and dispensers of multimillion dollar government contracts created a great deal of uncertainty in business affairs. The normal "greasing of the palms" of petty bureaucrats that had been a fact of life during the premartial law period became an object of nostalgia for foreign businessmen who now had to raise multimillion dollar payoffs. "This country's becoming as bad as Indonesia"—became a common complaint among U.S. businessmen who regarded the Philippines' southern neighbor as the ultimate in corruption.

Wariness turned into exasperation when the cronies' antics began to hurt big U.S. corporations like Ford, General Motors, and General Electric. In the opinion of many in the foreign business community, the time had arrived for Marcos to put his friends in their proper place as junior partners of foreign capital. Speaking through a prominent Filipino industrialist with tight links to the multinational corporations, U.S. business warned Marcos that capital would not enter the country "unless the administration demonstrates in unequivocal terms that it is prepared to abandon its failed policy of favoritism and to start dealing a fresh deck and an even hand."[57]

In the eyes of U.S. investors, however, the tactics of the crony capitalists were a minor irritant compared to the rising militancy of the long-repressed working class.

The People Resist

The Workers' Movement. Urban workers had been designated as the key victims of the Bank-prescribed development strategy since the centerpiece of the program was cheap labor. Foreign investors would sink capital in export industries attracted by the bait of cheap labor. The victims, however, chose not to submit passively, and it was resistance from workers and other impoverished classes that emerged as the chief obstacle to the World Bank-Marcos effort to refashion the economy to serve foreign capital more effectively.

By 1979, Philippine labor was priced at an average of 49 cents per hour.[58] This was considerably cheaper than in Singapore, Hong Kong, Taiwan, and South Korea—the Philippines' chief competitors in labor-intensive light manufacturing. To achieve this dubious status, the regime had strictly implemented the Bank-prescribed policy of wage repression which forced down the real wages of unskilled workers by over 30 percent and those of skilled workers by over 25 percent in the 1977-78 period.[59]

The regime drove down wage levels by banning strikes, preventing the emergence of free labor unions, "coordinating" labor through a government-sponsored national labor federation, and imprisoning, torturing, or murdering dissident labor leaders. Repression, however, had its price—increasingly bolder resistance among workers who felt they had nothing to lose. Disoriented and fragmented in the early years of martial rule, workers began to militantly regroup in the mid-seventies under the leadership of organizers affiliated with the National Democratic Front. Despite government repression, a wave of strikes swept factories in the Metro Manila area following an historic confrontation between labor and the management-government combine at the La Tondeña Distillery in the summer of 1975.[60] By 1979, the strike wave had rolled across Manila Bay and threatened the privileged sanctuary of export-led industries, the Bataan Export Processing Zone in Mariveles. When workers struck the Ford Body Stamping Plant in the Zone, the alarm went off in foreign business circles, for it signified that the capitalist nirvana offered to foreign investors by the regime and the Bank was about to vanish.

The government attempted to contain the workers' movement by establishing periodic "tripartite" negotiations among labor, business, and the regime to set wages and prices. Yet the pressure from the grassroots was so strong that Marcos' hand-picked labor bureaucrats in the Trade Union Congress of the Philippines (TUCP) were forced to take relatively militant positions in the talks. The regime was pushed into granting wage raises, but these concessions immediately drew the fire of the IMF, which warned the government to take a firm line against wage increases because they were fueling inflation.[61] The government's desultory attempt to pacify labor also provoked the powerful American Chamber of Commerce to denounce "unwarranted government intervention in wage setting."[62]

Faced with these pressures, the regime shifted to a strategy of selective concessions to divide labor. Workers in the export industries, it was decreed, would get only a fraction of the wage raises and cost-of-living allowances granted to workers in the nonexport sector. The export sanctuary, in other words, was to be preserved at all costs.[63] From the perspective of the Bank, the differential wage policy, indeed, served an additional purpose: allowing wages to rise in the import substitution sector of industry constituted one more nail in the coffin of the "inefficient" Filipino manufacturers.

The handwriting, however, was already on the wall. In May 1980, the May 1st Movement (KMU), a powerful, one-million strong independent labor federation, was born, laying to rest the illusion that the government-controlled TUCP was the legitimate voice of the Philippine working class. It was only a matter of time before militant trade unionism made significant inroads into the export sanctuary and eroded the foundation of the Bank's industrialization strategy.

Confrontation in the City. As workers rebelled against the cheap-labor strategy, the Bank found itself facing opposition from another quarter, the urban poor. The cause of the controversy was a World Bank-funded "urban-upgrading" project in Manila's Tondo district—reputed to be Asia's biggest slum. The project, begun in 1976, sought to convince residents of the Tondo Foreshore area, a reclaimed strip of land off Manila Bay, to rent their lots; about 4,500 families would then be relocated to new "upgraded" sites in an adjoining area.[64] Motivating the plan was the government's program of turning most of the

Tondo Foreshore area into an industrial park with port facilities for multinational corporations.

In its feasibility studies, the Bank did not reckon with a grassroots residents' organization named ZOTO, a veteran of militant opposition to government efforts to relocate the urban poor. Though most of its top leaders had been arrested—and some tortured—by the regime, ZOTO was able to delay the Bank project and contain its most repressive aspects. ZOTO employed a strategy of combining nonviolent mass protests with efforts to sow division between the government and the Bank and between the Bank and prospective bilateral donors such as the West German government. The organization also made effective use of contacts in international church circles to create what the Bank acknowledged was an effective worldwide support network for the slum dwellers.[65]

By 1979, almost all components of the project were strained by cost overruns, delay, and low morale. Worse, an official West German mission condemned it as " authoritarian in implementation" and hardly meant to benefit its intended beneficiaries.[66] Moreover, ZOTO's example became a rallying point for communities resisting World Bank-funded urban upgrading schemes elsewhere in the Philippines. The local government of Cagayan de Oro City in Mindanao, for instance, came out in strong opposition to a similar scheme in 1980—provoking a move by the regime to unseat the mayor and a World Bank threat to withdraw future assistance to the city.[67]

Defeat in the Highlands. If the Tondo urban poor were able to stall a Bank project, the tribal minorities of northern Luzon managed to stop one—and a fairly important one at that. How ironic that one of the most sophisticated international financial institutions would be handed its worst setback by preindustrial tribal groups in the highlands of Northern Luzon!

A Bank "prefeasibility study" had identified 3,400 square kilometers in northern Luzon as the best site for what was trumpeted as the Philippines' most ambitious hydroelectric project:[68] a gigantic four-dam complex to harness the power of the Chico River to serve the needs of distant Manila and its multinational firms. One hundred thousand people of the Bontoc and Kalinga tribes would have to be relocated from their ancestral lands. But when the Bank advanced the project to "feasibility-grade level" in 1974, the "statistics" came to life.

As in the case of the Tondo slum dwellers, the Bank did not reckon with the strong communal ties among the Bontoc and Kalinga, nor with their ability to muster widespread international support from environmentalists, church groups, and solidarity organizations.[69] Yet there was an added vital ingredient that the Tondo residents lacked—the threat and eventual resort to armed resistance. In addition to mass assemblies and acts of civil disobedience such as lying in front of bulldozers, the Kalinga, in particular, began to rely on the presence of the New People's Army (NPA), the military arm of the Communist Party of the Philippines. As government security forces filled the area to impose the will of the Bank and the government, troops and survey teams were ambushed. This sparked the deployment of more military units, including the 60th Constabulary Battalion, notorious for such terrorist tactics as beheading its victims, which it had used in the brutal effort to contain the Muslim rebellion in the South.

By 1976, the Chico River Dam site was a battleground. With basic security for survey and construction teams impossible to provide, the project was effectively stalemated. By 1979, Bank reviews had eliminated all references to the Chico feasibility study. And by October 1981, Prime Minister Virata quietly admitted, "One of the original four dams . . . will not be built because the people are against it."[70]

It was a silent retreat, but this did not detract from the fact that the Bontoc and Kalinga had accomplished something exceedingly rare in the Third World: the Bank's withdrawal in the face of popular resistance. Chico, therefore, was not just a local victory. Chico was, indeed, the equivalent of the Tet debacle in Vietnam for the World Bank development offensive in the Philippines.

Because of its immense symbolic value, the tribal resistance carried enormous significance for communities resisting development from above. A visitor wrote the following account after talking with the people of Pantabangan, in Central Luzon, who had been uprooted by a Bank-funded irrigation project and again faced displacement by a Bank-financed corporate tree plantation:

> "Before we believed promises," explains an elderly man. "We were ignorant and naive about what was happening to us." His son continues, "But this time, if the government tries to take over our land, we will fight for it." The threat is far from empty. For the people of Pantabangan are learning from the Chico victories. One of the govern-

> ment engineers working on the new project had already been sent an NPA (New People's Army) black ribbon—a warning to leave or else. . . .[71]

But like the American generals in Vietnam, World Bank technocrats refused to draw the real lessons from the people's resistance. The Chico experience triggered an internal World Bank assessment of Bank policy for tribal minorities threatened by development programs in the Philippines, Brazil, and other parts of the Third World. As in many other instances, the concerns of a number of lower level bureaucrats were sidestepped by the Bank's senior officials. The conclusion of the final version of the report, *Economic Development and Tribal Peoples,* showed that the Bank was more concerned with pleasing the Philippine and Brazilian dictatorships than with respecting the rights of tribal minorities:

> It is not Bank policy to prevent the development of areas presently occupied by such [tribal] peoples. . . . Assuming that tribal people will either acculturate or they will disappear, there are two basic options: the Bank can assist the Government either with acculturation or with protection in order to avoid harm.[72]

Salvaging the Strategy

By the end of the 1970's, the unraveling of the World Bank strategy in the Philippines could no longer be ignored by the Bank and the IMF. In recognition of this fact, Michael Gould, the bureaucrat most identified with the faltering effort, was replaced in late 1980 as head of the Philippine program office. If any doubts remained that the program was in deep trouble, they were banished by the report of the high-powered "Poverty Mission" that visited the country in 1979.[73] The group came back with a number of stunning conclusions.

Foremost among these was the fact that between the early 60's and 1975—an era dominated by Marcos—the real income of Filipinos had dropped "in both urban and rural areas, in all regions, and practically all occupations."[74]

For the Bank, the finding was particularly worrisome because, as the 1980 Country Program Paper put it, "whereas military-dominated government in, for example Thailand or Korea, has been justified on the basis of credible external threat, martial law in the Philippines has been justified considerably on the basis of its benefits for the poor."[75]

More disturbing, however, was the mission's assertion that the key factor behind what it termed the "startling" 50 percent decline in the real wages of urban workers in the period studied was the more than 60 percent devaluation of the peso imposed by the Bank and the IMF in 1970[76]—the move that had constituted the second salvo in the effort to "liberalize" the Philippine economy. In arcane economese, the mission argued that the devaluation move had made investment in industry less attractive and pushed capital instead into agricultural export production. The fall in real wages, then, was an inevitable consequence of the resulting stagnation of the industrial sector.[77]

The assertion immediately provoked opposition from World Bank higher-ups for it confirmed all too bluntly the human costs of the strategy of liberalization and export-led growth it had imposed on the Philippines. Not surprisingly, it was excised from later versions of the *Poverty Report*.

The mission's conclusions were doubly disconcerting because they came at a time that the Bank and the IMF were issuing their ultimatum to the Philippine government to dismantle the protectionist system at the December 1979 meeting. Bank bureaucrats were determined to impose their dogmatic prescription for economic growth, despite accumulating evidence calling it into question.

At this meeting, the regime capitulated completely, promising "to take the difficult and often painful decisions to dismantle some of these protective devices, and thus to promote a free and competitive system."[78] In other words, the national industrialists who had until then given the regime their cautious support were finally to be cast adrift.

Awarding the carrot after brandishing the stick, the IMF approved two loans totaling $654 million to help bridge the alarming trade deficit. In justifying the loans, the IMF announced: "The Philippine Government adopted a new economic and financial program in support of which the present standby arrangement has been approved . . . the authorities have placed emphasis on export promotion, and have recently introduced fiscal incentives and other measures to encourage exports."[79]

The main vehicle for the industrial reform was a "structural adjustment loan" of $200 million from the World Bank. In contrast to previous "project loans," this credit was a *program* loan: it involved restructuring the industrial sector through tariff reform, formulating more attractive incentives for foreign investors and export producers, and planning more export-processing zones where multinational firms enjoying tax breaks could relocate to gain access to cheap Filipino labor. The scope of the loan and the power of decision making it gave the Bank was immense. As Bank Vice President Shahid Husain confessed to the *New York Times*, "These *structural adjustment* loans do go to the heart of the political management of an economy. We will have to approach them with humility."[80]

Yet even as it forced the Philippines to burn all bridges to its industrial past, Bank bureaucrats were not totally detached from reality. At the Executive Board meeting of September 16, 1980, which approved the structural adjustment loan, the Bank staff admitted that "the benefits resulting from export expansion would depend on the economic and trade restrictions in industrialized countries. If the environment turned out to be more adverse than projected, then the ultimate benefits under the adjustment program would be reduced. . . ."[81]

More Strong Medicine

Radical industrial reform was the key element in the Bank and IMF's cure for the deteriorating economy. But there was more strong medicine prescribed by the two agencies. One was scrapping the regime's much publicized plan to initiate eleven massive industrial projects. The other was taking the traditional IMF tonic to cure balance-of-payments imbalances: devaluation. Confronted with both demands the regime evinced half-hearted opposition.

The eleven big capital-intensive projects—which included a steel plant, a petrochemical complex, and a copper smelter—had been unveiled by Marcos in late 1979 as a desperate effort to gain some legitimacy as an economic nationalist. Planned by some technocrats worried about the virtual absence of a heavy industrial base for the economy, the $6 billion package obviously clashed with the Bank's efforts to push industrial investment into export-oriented, labor-intensive manufacturing.

It is not surprising then that the Marcos plan provoked the Bank to issue the stern warning that many of the projects "do not harmonize well with the policy reforms."[82] The government retreated and promised that the projects would be implemented only if they were "found viable by rigorous economic analysis."[83] But what finally killed Marcos' desperate dream was the cold shoulder given to most of the projects by prospective financiers who had learned of the Bank's veto.

Devaluation, prescribed by the IMF for quick relief from mounting balance-of-payments pressures, was a more difficult pill for Marcos to swallow. The regime knew the consequences would be as disastrous, if not more so, as those triggered by the devaluation of 1970. Devaluation would almost certainly bring about a sharp increase in the country's inflation rate, which stood at 20 percent in 1980, and an equally sharp downward push on the sagging growth rate, which had already fallen from 5.5 percent in 1979 to 4 percent in 1980. With the recession driving more than 21,000 business establishments to bankruptcy and knocking 56,000 workers from their jobs between May and December 1980, many officials in the government resisted the devaluation prescription as "unacceptable."

But the Bank and the IMF were undeterred, for they had more than just a quick fix to the external deficit in mind. Devaluation was one more weapon to be deployed against the national entrepreneurs: by raising the peso prices of imported raw materials, intermediate goods, and machinery, devaluation would hopefully drive many of them into bankruptcy. Thus the Bank warned the regime that it had only two alternatives: a "moderate" devaluation of the peso or default.[84] The latter was clearly an unacceptable solution in view of the chaos which would result.

A compromise was finally arrived at which took into consideration the political difficulties of the regime. A large one-shot devaluation like that of 1970 was rejected in favor of a gradual devaluation through a "floating exchange rate," whereby the value of the peso was pegged to the movement of a basket of foreign currencies, in particular the dollar. The regime, in other words, had been given the choice of giving the economy the quick massive blow of the guillotine or suffocating it gradually with a garrote—and it opted for the latter. Beginning in August 1980, the peso was gradually but deliberately devalued, though not without resistance from some Central Bank officials, including Governor Gregorio Licaros. In January 1980 the exchange rate stood at P7.4 to $1; by early 1982 it had deteriorated to P8.3 to $1.[85]

The Crisis Deepens

In the midst of these efforts by the World Bank and the IMF to salvage the badly faltering economy, bombs began to go off in government buildings and Marcos-associated businesses in the summer of 1980. Planned and put into motion not by radical opponents of the Marcos regime, but by disgruntled elements of the local business elite and traditional political opposition, the bombing campaign was rapidly suppressed by Marcos' U.S.-trained security forces. But the short-lived wave of violence nevertheless struck a deep chord of fear in the high commands of the World Bank and the IMF. It seemed to foreshadow a process they had recently witnessed in Nicaragua—the upper-class opposition embracing violent methods and linking up with the left.

Fearful that the planned January 1981 meeting of the Consultative Group might become a bombing target, the Bank and the IMF shifted it from Manila to Paris.[86] More importantly, World Bank Vice President Shahid Husain, under instructions from Robert McNamara, ordered a secret study of political developments in the Philippines to assess future Bank and IMF activities in the country. The study was considered so sensitive that it was placed under the control not of the Philippine program division, but of William Ascher, a visiting staff member of the Bank's key Central Projects Division and a leading "political risk" analyst from John Hopkins University. In preparing his special assessment of the Marcos regime, Ascher was assisted not only by the Bank's East Asia division but by private commercial bankers with wide operational experience in the Philippines.[87]

The Ascher Memorandum was submitted to the World Bank's top management on November 6, just two days after the election of Ronald Reagan. The 14-page report painted a vivid picture of an inept dictatorship sinking into an economic swamp and edging toward political disaster. The Ascher report warned that the Marcos administration was marked by increasing instability "which could result in the lifting of martial law under a parliamentary system in which President Marcos, even if initially situated as Prime Minister, would have serious difficulty remaining in power, or a military government."[88]

Of special concern to Ascher was the alienation of Filipino industrialists from the process of "structural adjustment":

> . . . the elimination of protective tariffs and special subsidies has led to great dissatisfaction within the industries targeted for "streamlining." Therefore, in the Philippines, where the additional element of strongly perceived favoritism to Marcos' personal friends has created

> considerable resentment, the local business community has several mutually reinforcing reasons to try to undermine the policy directions of the current government.[89]

Deepening the fears of the Bank management was the apparent participation of some business figures in the Manila bombings. But the most alarming development, in Ascher's view, was the nationalist position to which the national industrialists were being pushed, in common with other forces in the political opposition. Nationalism, his report noted, "is the general appeal of the opposition's attack on Marcos' policy" and "anti-American sentiment is its most immediate and growing manifestation."[90] It warned that "the inflow of foreign investment has been portrayed by critics as American recolonialization."[91]

Rounding out the picture of unmitigated failure, the report confirmed the trend of increasing poverty and inequality that the *Poverty Report* had brought to light eleven months earlier:

> . . . there is an almost universal perception in the Philippines that income distribution is deteriorating. . . . The political implication of this perception of a worsening distribution of income has been, as one might expect, to detract from the popularity of the Marcos administration and to bring into question the sincerity and competence of the "New Society" program, which was to bring greater economic equality to the Philippines by stripping away the political and economic power of the "oligarchy." Marcos' justification of martial law . . . is weakened by any evidence that the martial law arrangement cannot reverse the trend of income concentration.[92]

The Marcos regime, the Bank had finally come to realize, was a political albatross. But the dilemma it faced was that nationalist policies were likely to be implemented by all of the three alternatives it saw to the dictatorship—a government dominated by young nationalist officers; a parliamentary coalition; or a revolutionary situation dominated by the New People's Army and the mass-based National Democratic Front.[93]

None of these "scenarios," to use Ascher's term, had any room for the Bank's trusted agents, the technocrats, who were seen as less "adoptable by a succeeding administration that either rejects the liberalization strategy or shies away from being associated with it."[94]

Such then were the political parameters within which the Bank advanced its perhaps final attempt to salvage the government with which it had become irrevocably intertwined.

Direct Rule

The Marcos regime paid for the structural adjustment loan from the World Bank and the two IMF balance-of-payments support loans by handing over even broader policy-making powers to the two multilateral agencies.

What remained to be devised was the political mechanism through which that power would be exercised. In the first half of 1981, Marcos lifted martial law while retaining the dictatorship and carried out other cosmetic moves suggested by the World Bank and the U.S. government. In the middle of the year, the mechanism for the virtual direct rule of the World Bank was set in place: a cabinet dominated by technocrats and headed by the Bank's most reliable agent, Prime Minister Cesar Virata. This elite body was to be responsible principally to the Bank and the Fund—an understanding that Marcos expressed when he told the international press that he intended to be a "French-style president," standing above the political fray and letting the technocrats have a free hand in directing the economy.[95]

The cabinet, as noted earlier, was mandated with four tasks by the Bank and the Fund:

- to salvage the Bank's multibillion dollar investment in the Philippines;
- to complete the World Bank-IMF program of liberalization, export-led industrialization, and foreign investment;
- to act as the guarantor for the payment of the Philippines' huge $15 billion external debt; and
- to discipline the president's cronies and put them in their place as junior partners of foreign capital.

The new cabinet, in short, represented a major step toward direct colonial rule. This was bitterly clear to most politically aware Filipinos. Even some of the president's most trusted allies, like chief propagandist Teodoro Valencia, felt obliged to join, in rhetoric at least, the rising crescendo of nationalist criticism of the latest twist in the system of neocolonial control:

> The government's worst enemies are on the side of the President. They are the ones sinking the economy to

> please the Americans. . . . Only the small-fry Filipinos will be left to suffer the consequences of the decisions made in the midst of crisis. After we go under, they can always go to the IMF and the World Bank as officers. . . . Insistence by the President that his economic advisers can never be wrong will be his undoing.[96]

Washington's Seal of Approval

Valencia and others in the New Society coalition realized, of course, that direct rule through the technocrat cabinet was the pill that all of them had to swallow to retain the economic backing of the U.S. government and U.S. capital. This support was immediately and enthusiastically extended by the new Reagan administration.

The World Bank reform program, the Reagan administration told Congress, was "worth the pain" that it might cause the Philippine government.[97] The Reaganites' enthusiasm for the program was partly to be explained by the fact that they were themselves in the process of applying to the American economy the traditional IMF formula for "sanitizing" Third World economies. But more important was the radical right's opinion that, in contrast to some of its programs elsewhere in the Third World, the World Bank structural adjustment strategy in the Philippines served as a good example of how multilateral aid should be used—with no humanitarian claptrap and for the direct and immediate benefit of U.S. economic interests.

The support for the liberalization and stabilization program must, of course, be seen in the broader context of the strategic affinity that the Reaganites have with the Marcos regime and other right-wing authoritarian governments in the Third World. With the ascent to power of the American radical right, the old ideology of missionary democracy previously employed to justify U.S. intervention was definitely shelved in favor of a new rationale built on hidebound conservative principles. Support for repressive elites like Marcos, Somoza, and the Shah, asserts Reagan's chief foreign policy ideologist, UN Ambassador Jeane Kirkpatrick, is justified because:

> . . . the fabric of authority unravels quickly when the power and status of the man at the top are undermined or eliminated. The longer the autocrat has held power, and the more pervasive his personal influence, the more dependent a nation's institutions will be on him. Without

> him, the organized life of the society will collapse, like an arch from which the keystone has been removed.[98]

Though a bit late in coming, the Kirkpatrick Doctrine is the political rationale that complements the economic rationale for authoritarianism—"technocratic modernization"—that the World Bank has been quietly espousing and putting into practice all along.

Conclusion

By the end of 1981, economic conditions in the Philippines were significantly worse than they had been eleven years earlier when the Bank launched its first major effort to refashion the Philippine economy. The country was over $15 billion in debt to foreign creditors and virtually bankrupt. According to the latest IMF report, servicing the external debt alone would require $2.3 billion alone in 1982 and $3.1 billion in 1984. And, to the dismay of even the most pessimistic business forecasters, the debt service ratio went way past the danger point, hitting 23 percent of export earnings in 1981 and expected to climb to almost 30 percent in 1983. The twin devils of stagnation and inflation had virtually choked off growth. The number of families living in absolute poverty had increased significantly. The Bank had tossed over $2.6 billion into what it billed as a cure consisting of an ambitious development effort, but that money had gone to finance an ill-conceived rural development program, liberalization, and export-led growth that proved worse than the disease.

By the end of the decade, key sectors of Philippine society were in open revolt against the World Bank's massive presence and influence. And in the face of this popular resistance, the Bank abandoned what little remained of the antipoverty elements of its strategy and concentrated on what had been its underlying strategic goal all along: the tighter integration of the Philippine economy into an international economy dominated by U.S. capital. The World Bank cabinet imposed on the Filipino people in 1981 was the culmination of this decade-long process to more completely subordinate their country to external forces with interests which, it became clear, were antagonistic to theirs.

CHAPTER THREE

Containment in the Countryside

The Crisis in the Countryside

"Rural development," carried out with the assistance and advice of the World Bank, was promoted as a major focus of the revolutionary change promised by the Marcos regime to justify the imposition of martial law in September 1972. The centrality of the rural development program was determined by the gravity of the economic and political crisis to which it had been hurriedly put together as a response. This crisis had several causes: the rapid expansion of commercial export agriculture, backward agricultural technology, and the antiquated system of land tenure in the food crop, subsistence sector.

The Impact of Export Agriculture. By the early 1960's, the "land frontier" in the Philippines had reached its limit.[1] With very little new land available for cultivation in the Philippines, expansion in large-scale commercial farming could only come at the expense of the food crop, subsistence sector. Cultivated land devoted to rice declined from 3.2 million hectares in 1960 to 3.1 million hectares in 1970.[2] In the early 70's, export agriculture continued its relentless advance, with the amount of land devoted to sugar, coconut, and other commercial crops increasing by 650,000 hectares between 1970 and 1976.[3] By the end of the decade, over 30 percent of the country's 10 million hectares of cultivated land was planted in export crops like sugar, coconut, pineapple, and bananas.

The expansion of export agriculture was not a purely spontaneous process sparked by international demand for tropical commodities. It was, in fact, part and parcel of the strategy of "export-led growth" promoted by the Marcos regime and the World Bank. This strategy deliberately hitched economic development in the Philippines to the locomotive of expanding demand in the advanced capitalist markets of Japan and the West. Because foreign investors brought in capital, possessed superior technology, and maintained well-developed international marketing systems, they held a privileged position in this economic strategy. As Del Monte officers explained it, the expansion of the firm's Philippine operations "was a response to an ongoing program of the Philippine Government to promote national and foreign investment in . . . exports."[4]

By the mid-seventies, the pineapple plantations of Del Monte and Castle & Cooke (Dole) on the island of Mindanao had grown to 35,000 hectares and employed some 20,000 workers. Even more remarkable was the expansion in commercial banana production. Triggered by a rising demand for tropical fruit in Japan and the discovery that the loamy, alluvial, and well-drained soil of southeastern Mindanao was perfect for growing bananas, the industry spread rapidly and became, almost overnight, one of the country's top foreign exchange earners. By 1978, banana exports came to $84 million, 15,000 hectares were planted in bananas, and 20,000 workers and contract growers were dependent on the industry.[5]

There was, however, an underside to the prosperity of large local and foreign growers: the major cost of the expansion of export agriculture was the misery it imposed on thousands of smallholders dispossessed of their lands either by outright landgrabs, land title frauds, or their forced or voluntary entry into strictly regimented contract growing or "associate producer" arrangements with the agribusiness giants.[6] This increasing impoverishment of the now landless rural poor rapidly raised the social tinderbox temperature of the countryside. In addition, as hundreds of thousands of hectares of cultivated land were turned over to sugar, coconut, pineapple, and bananas, export crop expansion contributed to the growing inability of the country to be self-sufficient in staple foods. Between 1960 and 1972—twelve years of rapid export-crop expansion—rice imports rose from $2 million to $34 million.[7]

Land Tenure, Productivity, and Class Conflict. In assigning blame for the crisis in Philippine agriculture, the World Bank and other development agencies focused on the backward technology and low productivity of the Filipino smallholder. Hesitation in adopting advanced mechanical or biological technology did, indeed, contribute to low productivity in the food-crop sector. But this hesitation was often justified. For many peasants the glittering promise of the Green Revolution was more than offset by the soaring costs of fertilizer and chemical inputs necessary for higher yields and by the low resistance of the "miracle seeds" to tropical diseases and weather conditions. This peasant stubbornness was rooted deep in the knowledge that most of the benefits of the new technology would accrue not to the tiller but to the landowner.

By the beginning of the 1970's, the Philippines had one of the highest land tenancy rates in Southeast Asia: an estimated three million of the country's food producers were tenant farmers. Many were required to turn over 50 percent or more of their yields to the landlord.[8] Together with the highly inequitable control over land came highly inequitable access to credit and irrigation facilities. Tenants, gouged by landlords for much of their produce, were also victimized by usurers charging interest rates as high as 100 percent per year. Usurers were often the very same landlords. Irrigation facilities were also usually controlled by the landed rural elites, and the exorbitant fees they charged for water constituted one more mechanism for squeezing the tenant farmer.

Displaced and proletarianized by export agriculture and trapped by an oppressive and obsolete land tenure system, the Filipino peasantry, silent since the defeat of the Huk Rebellion in the early 1950's, began to throb once again with political activism in the late sixties. In the sugar fields of Negros and Panay Islands, sugar workers forged the National Federation of Sugar Workers despite massive landlord opposition and repression. Throughout Luzon and Mindanao, groups of smallholders began to affiliate with the Federation of Free Farmers, which advocated land reform and more cooperative production arrangements. In Central Luzon, the traditional bastion of rural rebellion, peasant organizations affiliated with the Marxist underground held demonstrations and marches for land reform. But the most significant development, and the most alarming in the eyes of the authorities, was the birth of the New People's Army (NPA), the armed wing of the Philippine Communist Party, in March 1969. The NPA swiftly resumed the armed peasant revolution which had been aborted in the early 1950's. By the early 1970's, the NPA had created the beginnings of a base area among peasants in the Cagayan Valley in Northern Luzon.

Rural Development as Pacification

The World Bank strategy of rural development was formulated in the early 1970's by Robert McNamara as a *political* response to this rural volatility in the Philippines and other Third World countries. As defense secretary to both John Kennedy and Lyndon Johnson, McNamara had confronted and been defeated by the mobilized peasantry of Vietnam. The priority of the political concern was evident in his speech at the IMF-World Bank annual conference in September 1973 in Nairobi, where he unveiled the new World Bank development thrust: "The real issue is whether indefinite procrastination [in land reform] is politically prudent. An increasingly inequitable situation will pose a growing threat to political stability."[9]

McNamara's program of preemptive reform was described by a development specialist close to the Bank as a strategy of "defensive modernization" which

> if successful, will create a smallholder sector closely integrated with the national economy. Bank projects will encourage subsistence farmers to become small-scale market producers. With economic ties to other sectors, the farmers will be loath to link their interests to those not yet modernized and will hesitate to disrupt the national economy for fear of losing their own markets.[10]

Rural development, in other words, aimed to create a stratum of kulaks, or small capitalist producers, who would serve as a social cushion by absorbing and defusing pressures from the masses of tenant-farmers, landless peasants, and rural workers below.

What McNamara was offering the poor of the Third World was *not* a program that would come to grips with the root cause of rural disaffection: the unequal distribution of wealth and power. As he explained to the World Bank's Board of Governors in 1974, the new strategy would "put primary emphasis not on the redistribution of income and wealth—as justified as that may be in our member countries—but rather on increasing the productivity of the poor, thereby providing for an equitable sharing in the benefits of growth."[11] An even franker expression of the Bank's intention not to disrupt the status quo was provided by the agency's *Rural Development Policy Paper*:

> It may frequently be desirable to design a project so that all sections of the rural community benefit to some degree. In some countries, avoiding opposition from the powerful and influential sectors of the community is essential if the program is not to be subverted from within. Thus, in some cases where economic and social inequality is initially great, it is normally optimistic to expect that more than 50 percent of the project benefits can be directed toward the target groups; often the percentage will be considerably less.[12]

McNamara's rural development strategy, in essence, was nothing more than an updated version of the old, discredited "trickle down" approach to development—an approach which the Bank claimed to have abandoned by the early 70's. To ameliorate poverty, the Bank proposed to increase the access of poor smallholders to critical technological and economic inputs, provide some benefits to the richer sectors of the community to keep them happy, and have everybody share the larger cake created by increased production and productivity. On paper, increasing productivity, mitigating poverty, and maintaining the rural power structure might have appeared to be reconcilable objectives. In reality, they became contradictory objectives that eventually tore apart the World Bank-Marcos effort to stabilize the Philippine countryside.

Components of the Rural Development Effort

The World Bank's rural development program in the Philippines is one of the largest in the Third World: between 1973 and 1981, the Bank committed about $1 billion—or over 40 percent of total lending to the regime—to rural development. This sum was spread out over 26 projects ranging from large-scale irrigation to rural credit schemes, from highway construction to land settlement. Yet the agency's participation in Philippine agricultural development cannot be measured simply by the projects it funded, for the Bank played a major advisory role in the government's key programs, land reform and the *Masagana 99* credit program. In the following pages we shall examine the key items in this joint development effort.

Land reform, the regime's most ambitious rural program, was proclaimed shortly after the declaration of martial law in September 1972. Though the Bank's involvement in the program was limited to advice, encouragement, and financing of a few associated projects, the centrality of land reform gradually dawned on Bank technocrats. They realized that the government's failure to alter the rural power structure was nullifying, if not subverting, the whole range of rural projects promoted by the Bank, all aimed at raising productivity.

The World Bank's participation in the *Masagana 99* program—a nation-wide credit scheme to facilitate the "Green-Revolution"—was minimal in terms of finance but substantial in terms of advice and encouragement. For Bank technocrats, the *Masagana 99* was decisive since the success of their own projects was predicated on the widespread adoption of advanced techniques of rice agriculture (riziculture) As we shall see, *Masagana 99* was a qualified success in terms of increasing production and productivity. But as an anti-poverty effort, it was a massive failure: the rapidly escalating costs of fertilizers and other inputs of high technology riziculture propelled thousands of tenants into financial crisis.

Irrigation accounted for close to half of all Bank funds committed to the Philippines for rural development, but the capacity of the irrigation projects to ameliorate poverty was undercut by the lack of any serious effort to alter prevailing patterns of social inequality. The Bank's same narrow focus on productivity also undermined special Bank-financed projects aimed at the smallholder, such as rural credit, tree farming, and land settlement schemes.

Our study of the World Bank rural development effort will conclude with what turned out to be the most significant aspect of rural development, a thinly disguised counterinsurgency program to frustrate the growing revolutionary forces in the countryside. This effort consists of "new style" projects called "Integrated Area Development" (IAD) schemes. Integrated Area Development concentrated financial resources on several interrelated efforts, from land titling to infrastructure building, within a specific province or island. As we shall see, with the failure of the Bank's antipoverty efforts elsewhere, the repressive aspect of rural development came to the fore in the IAD projects which were transformed into vehicles for the counterinsurgency campaigns of the Marcos regime.

Land Reform: The Promise and the Reality

Upon the declaration of martial law in September 1972, land reform was proclaimed the cornerstone of the New Society. The World Bank reacted enthusiastically to Marcos' promise to alter the feudal system of land tenure and applauded the government for "vigorously" carrying out the program.[13] Support from the Bank itself, however, came mainly in the form of advice and encouragement. Direct financial assistance from the Bank was limited to three credits: a $16 million loan to assist land reform beneficiaries through the Land Bank, the government body that received amortization payments from peasant beneficiaries; a $35 million loan to the Ministry of Agriculture to modernize the extension system (delivery of technical services to peasants) supporting land reform and other services; and a $15 million credit to the Ministry of Agrarian Reform to assist participants in a complementary program of land settlement.

But the actual land reform, which affected only a miniscule portion of the targeted beneficiaries and worsened the lot of landless peasants, did not merit the fanfare trumpeted by the regime and the enthusiasm expressed by the World Bank. From the outset, the land reform program excluded three million hectares planted in commercial export crops and another 920,000 hectares devoted to fruit and root crops.[14] The exemption of these lands was dictated by the World Bank and the regime's strategy of "export-led growth"; foreign and local agribusinesses were considered vital foreign earners whose operations should not be disrupted by the social turmoil of land reform. What appeared to be a legitimate economic argument, was, of course, mainly a sophisticated justification for the fact that the regime would not dare to harm the interests of groups that constituted its key political support.

The land reform was to involve only 1.8 million hectares of rice-and-corn land and one million peasants. However, this already limited number of beneficiaries was suddenly cut by two-thirds in the mid-70's when the regime decided that landlords owning between 7 and 24 hectares of land could retain 7 hectares of their holdings.[15] (In the Philippines, as in other Southeast Asian countries where the land/person ratio is very small and agriculture is labor-intensive, a holding of 7 hectares is a very large parcel.) The average landholding is only 1.5 hectares. 396,000 tenants tilling

730,764 hectares were finally declared eligible for "Operation Land Transfer." Those tenants within the 7-hectare retention category, estimated at about 609,000, were instead to have their tenure shifted from share tenancy to leasehold (fixed rent and a written contract).[16]

As of mid-1979, very little land had actually been transferred to eligible tenants. Some 242,000 tenants, the regime boasted, had received certificates of land transfer (CLT's).[17] These pieces of paper, however, were not land titles but merely constituted a declaration of the tenant's eligibility to receive land. CLT's, in other words, "qualified" the tenant to become an "amortizing owner" paying for the land in 15 annual installments before he got full title to it. But even before this cumbersome process could get underway, the Land Bank, which received the peasant's payments, had to have already paid the landlord a substantial portion of his compensation in cash and bonds. The value of this compensation reflected, in most cases, the superior bargaining power of the landlord.[18] As of mid-1979, seven years after the proclamation of the reform, only 70,315 tenants tilling 134,666 hectares had started the process of amortizing ownership. To label these lucky few as "owners" was to engage in euphemism, for as one Bank official observed: ". . . without timely and adequate credit and inputs the recipients of Certificates of Land Transfer often remain beholden to their traditional landlords who continue to supply the essential inputs. Many so-called beneficiaries of the land reform program continue to pay rent or share crop."[19]

The process of amortization was, indeed, so onerous that most peasants defaulted on their payments. As one Bank memo warned early on in the program:

> . . . it has been reported that among the 20,000 or so tenants who have payments due, the collection rate has been only about 20 percent. In a sense, this is not surprising given the high degree of tenant indebtedness in the Philippines. . . . While it is not surprising that the present rate is only 20 percent, the possibility exists that it may not rise much above that level.[20]

Peasants who were forced to default on their payments risked losing their land to the government, which, in time, became the country's largest landowner. By the end of 1980 effective owners, or those who had received "emancipation patents" for their lands, came to a meager 1,700 tenants.[21]

Even before that date, however, the failure of the land reform had become obvious to the Bank's Philippine specialists. In 1978, a confidential survey revealed that the program had stalled owing to "(a) incomplete records of land titles and land rights; (b) lack of dynamic leadership within the principal agencies; (c) inefficient management and shortage of trained manpower; and (d) opposition to the land reform program by landlords, coupled with lack of power on the part of DAR [Department of Agrarian Reform] to enforce the reform legislation."[22]

Dale Hill, the Bank's agricultural loan officer for the Philippines, traced the crisis to Marcos' lack of "political will" to confront the landlord class: "Land reform is not amenable to halfway measures. Either the landlord owns the land, or the tiller does. To make that radical change requires more commitment and energy than the Marcos administration has yet been able to demonstrate."[23] What Hill could not fully understand, however, was that expecting Marcos to seriously pursue the reform was tantamount to asking him to cut his own throat. For while the small and medium landlords might not have been as critical to the regime as the big agribusiness interests, they were certainly vital sources of support. Their support became even more critical as the regime's increased repression and continued failure to deliver prosperity spawned popular alienation in the countryside.

The World Bank's controversial *Poverty Report,* in fact, suggested that not only had the land reform not accomplished its professed antipoverty goals, but it also appeared to be contributing to greater inequality in the countryside. Many tenants, the report noted, were forcibly evicted by landlords trying to take advantage of the loopholes in the land reform laws.[24] It also observed that many of the limited number of beneficiaries "have actually become landlords . . . and have consolidated quite considerable holdings."[25] Subleasing arrangements between the better-off beneficiaries and poorer or landless peasants were beginning to proliferate, leading to the incipient formation of a kulak class that was simultaneously more prosperous than their fellows and more attuned than traditional landowners to efficient capitalist production. As envisioned in the Bank's rural development strategy, kulaks were, in fact, being created but not in the numbers and not in the context of increasing all-around prosperity promised by Bank rhetoric.

The Marcos land reform was publicized not only as a question of land transfer but also as a process of improving the lot of tenant farmers. But the cooperative system (*Samahang Nayon*) that was to serve as the political framework of the reform hardly got off the ground. The purposes of the *Samahang Nayon* or "pre-cooperative" of land reform beneficiaries were, instead, subverted by local elites. As one study of representative pre-cooperatives conducted for the U.S. Agency for International Development revealed, many *Samahang Nayon* had been captured by landlords, powerful politicians or opportunistic bureaucrats manipulating their office for commercial gain.[26] In a forthright assessment, one World Bank consultant asserted that officially sponsored organizations like *Samahang Nayon* had never genuinely served the rural poor because they had never been meant to empower them in the first place:

> Because of the threat and the localized successes of . . . radical movements, the Philippine government and national elites are extremely fearful of genuine, grassroots organization and participation. This is why government agencies and elites themselves have resorted to the tactic of introducing organizations of their own design. In this way, they hoped to preempt the emergence of uncontrollable rural organizations as vehicles for the implementation of government programs, as well as for the convenience of government bureaucracies. As such their real functions and capabilities are limited by the purposes for which they were organized. Most of them, not surprisingly, exist only on paper. What kind of meaningful participation do they provide? No comment.[27]

The unraveling of land reform confronted the Bank with the specter of the whole range of its rural development projects going down the drain. Questions were increasingly raised at the Bank's Executive Board about the implications of the failing program for the income-distribution impact of the Bank's massive irrigation effort.[28] Bank-funded projects directed at smallholders, such as the Second Rural Development Project (Land Settlement), complained one Board member, were being stymied by the slow pace of the reform.[29] Ironically, one frustrated Bank official was reduced to hoping that "recent press reports (both in the U.S. and the Philippines) on the activities of the New People's Army in Central Luzon . . . would translate itself into more effective implementation of the program."[30]

Reacting to these concerns, some staff members proposed that the Bank involve itself more directly in the land reform program in the hope that this "might allow it to have an influence on a program of major importance to low income farmers."[31] Another asserted, "It is my belief that we cannot go on much longer with our agricultural program in the Philippines without contributing to the government's efforts in the field of agrarian reform."[32]

But the only real alternative to Marcos' brand of reform was, as Dale Hill had realized, one that would drastically alter the balance of power in the countryside. Yet the Bank shrank from recommending such a move, and, as an alternative to the discontent and confusion created by Marcos' halfway measure, it eventually proposed *stepping back*: "Some former tenants, and other potential tenants," stated the *Poverty Report*, "were not really ready for a shift in tenure status; they need and prefer the protection of the landlord, who is also their creditor, particularly for insurance against bad harvests." Indeed, it complained that agrarian reform contributed, "in many areas [to] disruption of productively healthy landlord/tenant relations."[33] In short, the World Bank, frustrated by Marcos' faltering effort but frightened by the political and social whirlwind that would come with a more radical agrarian reform, ended up spouting the archaic argument that landlords had been using all along to oppose any kind of land reform.

Masagana 99: Credit and Calamity

Along with land reform, *Masagana 99* (M99), a nationwide credit program, was projected by the regime as a pillar of Marcos' agrarian revolution. When it was launched eight months after the declaration of martial law in May 1973, the dictator declared: "With the program—the integrated, intensive agricultural program—we stake the very nature of constitutional revolution. So if we cannot bring about a firm foundation among our farmers (for the farmer is the foundation of all societies), the entire experiment will fail. . . ."[34]

Masagana 99 was presented to tenant farmers and smallholders as a package: a low interest, no collateral credit system tied to the use of high yielding rice seed varieties, fertilizers, pesticides, and herbicides. Patterned after the Puebla Project in Mexico, M99 was viewed as a way of bringing the Green Revolution to smallholders.[35] Part of its appeal lay in the tantalizing prospect it offered of achieving greater productivity and providing benefits across the board without resorting to drastic measures which would alter vested social inequality. A report by Bank technocrat Dale Hill asserted, "One of the most attractive things about M99 was that it could do all this without antagonizing any part of the population in the same way other programs (particularly land reform) did. With *Masagana 99*, 'everyone appeared to be a winner.' "[36]

Although Bank support came in the form of advice and financial support for credit projects for small farmers which supplemented M99, Bank operatives felt that they had a great stake in the success of the larger program as well. As one confidential 1974 report put it, the success of Bank-supported and other government rural development programs "will depend on increased use of high-yielding seed varieties, fertilizers and agrochemicals, and the provision of adequate credit and other supporting services."[37]

The regime had a more immediate stake. As Marcos himself stated at the time of its launching, "*Masagana 99* is a program of survival."[38] To offset the popular alienation triggered by the massive repression that accompanied the imposition of martial law, the regime needed a program that would yield fast results—something dazzling to validate the rhetoric of authoritarian development. "*Masagana 99*'s capacity to buttress the fledgling authoritarian Marcos regime," asserted the Hill report, "was just as important as its capacity to produce rice. In 1973-74, rice was the critical commodity, but political survival was the key issue."[39]

Initially a pilot project administered in two provinces by the International Rice Research Institute (IRRI), M99 was suddenly expanded to 43 provinces and hundreds of thousands of peasants. The poorest smallholders, however, were never included, and at its height in late 1974, only 36 percent of all small rice farmers participated in the credit program.[40] As one Bank report observed, "There was some bias against the smaller farmers in that credit was not extended to very small farms because these farms were mainly subsistence and would not generate sufficient income to repay the loan."[41]

Masagana 99 was accompanied by a major propaganda blitz involving the services of the American advertising firm, J. Walter Thompson, a drive to coerce or cajole rural banks to participate in the scheme, and efforts by government-financed fertilizer and pesticide dealers to cash in on the effort.[42]

The outcome was perhaps the most spectacular crash of a rural development scheme—an event made all the more painful for Marcos because he had publicly staked his regime's legitimacy on its success. The culprit, according to one Bank report, was the high cost of the new rice technology: "With the higher investment the program requires, a low harvest will not provide enough for both adequate farm income and repayment of M99 debt."[43] For instance, in one province studied, tenant farmers involved in the concurrent land reform program had an average yield of only 63 cavans (a dry rice measure of 42 kilograms, the common marketing unit of dry rice) of rice. This was well below the minimum yield of 80 cavans needed to enable them to simultaneously shoulder the costs of M99 and make amortization payments for their lands.[44]

Another report underlined how the "survival program" hurt the agrarian bureaucracy: "Concentration of effort on programs such as *Masagana 99* and *Masagana Maisan* [the corn credit program] has been particularly disruptive to the functioning of the country's agricultural extension service."[45]

Most disastrously affected, however, was the rural credit system. Indebtedness to rural banks, noted a January 1980 Bank review, had become so widespread that farmers "now regard arrears as an uncontrollable community hardship akin to natural calamity."[46] Out of about 500,000 loans in mid-1977, 366,000—worth $93 million—were in arrears. The government's solution to debt collection was to have Philippine Constabulary troops threaten peasant households to pay up immediately, or else.[47] Rural banks were in a parlous state by the late seventies, with the grave financial constraints created by M99 forcing 500 participating banks to drop out of the credit system altogether. The World Bank was forced to conclude:

> The use of credit as the incentive for participation has had a high cost in terms of unrecovered capital, the serious effect on the financial conditions of lenders and borrowers alike . . . . The impairment of the financial capacity of rural banks—and many borrowers—and the detrimental impact of the program on the credit attitudes of both, have jeopardized the ability of agricultural credit to serve longer-term production objectives in the Philippines.[48]

In desperation, the Bank recommended a new tactic. Rather than lending directly to farmers, the government should make arrangement with "informal creditors"—i.e. the usurious traders and merchants who for centuries have plagued Filipino tenant farmers with their 100 percent interest rates. In the sanitized language of the Bank:

> Within the context of credit programs, appropriate measures should be explored to preserve the benefits of informal credit at lower cost to the borrower; for example, relatively more attractive terms could be considered for bank lending to traders and merchants rather than directly to farmers, with covenants concerning use of proceeds by traders/merchants.[49]

Euphemism could not disguise the fact that, in the face of the disaster created by M99, the World Bank was advocating a return to the traditional village usurer—just as its fear of a more radical land reform led it to justify the paternalistic role of the landlord. In both cases, fear of the peasant discontent spawned by halfway measures led the Bank right back to a hesitant reiteration of support for the status quo.

Masagana 99 and the High-Technology Treadmill

Though it was a clear failure as a credit program for smallholders, M99 could, however, boast of one "success": it hooked thousands of tenant farmers into an allegedly more productive—and clearly more expensive—rice-growing technology dependent on escalating inputs of inorganic fertilizers, pesticides, and herbicides. "The drastic reduction in production credit which has taken place as a result of default in repayment," one report pointed out, "has not reduced the use of cash inputs such as fertilizer and pesticides. Between 1975 and 1977 new M99 credit declined by 80 percent while fertilizer consumption increased by 12 percent. . . ."[50] This, the Bank noted with approval, was the main virtue of M99: "The persistence with which the program has been pursued is a major factor in the widespread adoption of new rice technology throughout the economic spectrum of Filipino farmers. Increases in rice production and fertilizer consumption are notable successes."[51]

Contrary to the Bank's rosy projection, however, riziculture was by 1981 in a state of crisis in the Philippines. That the Bank contributed to this crisis is clear. Through such schemes as the Second Rural Credit and Third Rural Credit Projects, discussed below, the Bank promoted mechanization, a labor-displacing process in a labor-surplus country. Likewise, it was one of the major forces behind the indiscriminate spread of high-technology, chemical-intensive agriculture.

The Fertilizer Fix. The new rice technology spawned by the development of high yielding rice varieties (HYV's) in the late 1960's, has created severe problems for Philippine agriculture, including the loss of soil fertility through the massive application of petroleum-based fertilizers, such as urea. This compound, which the Bank projects will make up 69 percent of consumption of nitrogen-source fertilizers by 1985, lacks the sulfur present in traditional sources abandoned by farmers who switched to HYV's. In the Philippines and other Asian countries, sulfur deficiency is already limiting production.[52] Massive fertilizer application has also led to zinc losses which have put more and more farmlands out of production. As a result, many soil scientists are suggesting a return to natural nitrogen sources.[53]

The Bank ignores these trends in its prescriptions for Philippine riziculture. Instead, in a 1980 memorandum, it recommended *doubling* the rate of application of nitrogen—mainly urea—from 35 kilograms per hectare to 60 kilograms and *quadrupling* phosphate use from 8 kilograms to 30 kilograms per hectare.[54]

The dependence on petroleum-based fertilizers to which programs like M99 have pushed rice farmers has placed their economic fate in the hands of the local fertilizer oligopoly. This particular oligopoly is composed of six major producers and distributors, the largest of which is Planters Products, Inc. (PPI). PPI is a good example of the workings of "bureaucrat capitalism"—the use of public agencies for the accumulation of private wealth—in the Philippines. Controlled by Marcos interests through Agriculture Minister Arturo Tanco, Jr., who sits on its board, PPI enjoys a government subsidy and is also one of the five local distributors of imported fertilizer. In classic cartel fashion, PPI and other distributors set prices and divide up the market under the direction of the government's Fertilizer and Pesticide Authority.[55]

Most fertilizer is now imported—a fact that has had a tremendous impact on the economic viability of the Filipino rice farmer. During the oil crisis of 1973-74, for instance, world fertilizer prices quadrupled from $4 a bag in 1973 to $17 in November 1974.[56] This blow, according to the Bank, was hardly mitigated by the desultory 35 percent increase in the support price of rice decreed by the government,[57] and it certainly contributed to the massive default on M99 loans among smallholders.

With urea costing $200 per ton by late 1980 and expected to go higher, high-technology riziculture has also been a factor in the deterioration of the external position of the economy. In 1976, urea and other fertilizer imports came to $21 million.[58] In 1980, the foreign exchange drain represented by fertilizer imports was projected by the Bank to quadruple to $87 million. By 1985, the drain is expected to nearly double the 1980 figure and reach $164 million.[59]

Thus, the dependence on rice imports characteristic of the early 1970's has merely been transformed into dependence on Green Revolution inputs. While the country is now exporting rice, this condition is likely to be evanescent, subject to the vagaries of the international market that have savaged the Philippines' other primary commodity exports, such as sugar and copra. The demand for fertilizer inputs, however, is relatively unresponsive to price changes, or "inelastic," to use the orthodox economist's phrase, and its inexorable growth is likely to become an increasingly heavy burden on the balance of payments.

The Pesticide Threat. Like fertilizers, pesticides are an integral component of the high tech package, and promotion of pesticide use has been a Bank priority. The agency complains that current pesticide application by rice farmers is unsatisfactory, averaging only P60 ($8) per hectare, or less than 20 percent of the "plant protection element" of P338 ($45) in the *Masagana 99* package.[60]

"This clearly reveals that a major development effort is needed for GOP [Government of the Philippines] and the private pesticide companies to promote a reasonable level of protection for the rice crop . . .,"[61] states the Bank. Given the growing health and environmental hazards of indiscriminate pesticide use promoted by the international pesticide cartel, this recommendation is most irresponsible.[62] It is all the more dangerous when one realizes that, as Weir and Schapiro discovered in their 1980 classic of investigative journalism, *Circle of Poison*, "the Bank staff does not include a single pest-control expert to advise on pesticide use in its agricultural projects."[63] Bank practice consists of "giving a government a bulk loan for 'chemicals' and not specifying the specific pesticide."[64]

Pesticide abuse is becoming a major problem in Philippine agriculture. Bayer and Pfizer, two of the biggest international dealers, import two extremely hazardous substances, malathion and methyl parathion—the latter considered 60 times more toxic than DDT.[65] Reports from the banana plantations of Castle & Cooke in Mindanao reveal numerous cases of pesticide poisoning caused by the lack of protection of workers from the substances they come in contact with.[66] These workers were forced to petition the company to stop heavy spraying after it was discovered that dangerously low oxygen levels induced by exposure to pesticides made them more susceptible to disease.[67]

As in the case with fertilizers, pesticide promotion by agencies such as the Bank has pushed Filipino peasants into dependence on a cartel. A description of this monopoly is provided by a Bank report: "The industry is dominated by local affiliates of foreign manufacturers, with the exception of PPI (Planters Products Inc.) which, in addition to being the largest fertilizer marketer, is also one of the largest in the pesticides field."[68] As the Bank reported, PPI, Shell, and Bayer control 60 percent of the market, with the rest shared by Hoechst, Union Carbide, Warner Barnes, Monsanto, Dupont, Cyanamid, and Velsicol.[69] *Almost all of these firms—which the Bank encourages to join with the government to promote more intensive pesticide use—have engaged in the international trade and dumping of dangerous pesticides.*[70]

Like the fertilizer industry, pesticide manufacturers and distributors enjoy a cozy relationship with the government. In 1972, they established the Agricultural Pesticides Institute of the Philippines (APIP), which the Bank describes as "an influential, active body, which has a close working association with the related government bodies."[71] Moreover, the fertilizer monopoly has very close ties with the pesticide cartel. At the start of the M99 program, they carried out a joint operation which effectively gouged the smallholder "beneficiaries." According to the Hill report, this scheme "was a fertilizer-pesticide tie-up, which was meant by dealers to coerce farmers into buying chemical products without controlled prices. When farmers came to pick up fertilizer with the chits, dealers told them that they were required to buy certain chemicals (with cash) to obtain fertilizer."[72]

To conclude, M99 and the Bank-supported high technology riziculture that accompanied it, unleashed a typhoon of "modernization" in the Philippine countryside that drove thousands of tenant farmers into financial degradation and bankruptcy. Squeezed by mounting arrears and skyrocketing fertilizer prices, threatened with fertilizer-induced soil exhaustion and pesticide poisoning, it is no wonder that Filipino peasants have come to look at *Masagana 99* as a "natural calamity," to use the Bank's own description. The beneficiaries of the new rice technology may include some kulaks or operators who can consistently maintain high yield levels, but, as the Hill report admits, these are the peasants "who least need a program like M99."[73]

The real beneficiaries of Green Revolution programs like Masagana 99 were revealed by the Bank's *Poverty Report*: "Some of the benefits of the new technology were captured by small rice farmers in the 1970's, but a disproportionate amount has probably gone to landlords, farmers with irrigation, relatively large or progressive farmers, owners of inputs, and creditors."[74] In this list of elite beneficiaries, one must underline the fertilizer and pesticide cartels for whom M99 and Bank-supported projects promoting high technology agriculture have been valuable subsidies.

Irrigation: The World Bank and the Politics of Water

Visitors to the Philippines during the seventies were often impressed by the scope and pace of dam building in the countryside—an active atmosphere that evoked the 1930's TVA era in the U.S. The World Bank was heavily involved in this activity; about $450 million, or half of the Bank's total lending for agriculture and rural development, went to eight massive irrigation projects. These included the huge Pantabangan Dam in Central Luzon and the Magat River Multipurpose Dam in Northern Luzon, which the government described as "the biggest project . . . to tap the country's water resources."[75] To justify the vast financial commitment, the Bank claimed that about 85,000 persons would benefit from the projects—"most of them smallholders."[76]

Reality, however, contradicted the rhetoric. Acting under World Bank advice, the Marcos government in 1975 increased the charges for irrigation water from P25 per hectare to P100 per hectare for wet season rice and from P35 per hectare to P150 per hectare for dry season rice.[77] The hike was needed, the government claimed, to cover the costs of the project. This move did not, however, satisfy the Bank: "These new fees will . . . cover the operating costs, but do not really help cover capital costs."[78] But Bank technocrats could not escape the implications of the steep price rise for irrigation water: a 1978 review of agricultural services asked the rhetorical question: "Have small farmers been priced out of irrigation schemes by the 400% rate increases of 1975?"[79]

The Bank's agricultural specialists also began to realize that Bank-financed irrigation projects could not just be imposed on rural communities and automatically benefit smallholders. Seeking to explain why the expected level of rice production did not materialize from the Upper Pampanga River (Pantabangan) Project, a key Bank-funded irrigation effort, one technocrat wrote:

> The provision of infrastructure in rural areas is the most straightforward method for the government to promote economic development. . . . The Bank and the government have pumped more money into irrigation investment in the last few years than any other infrastructure affecting rural development. . . . The easy part is to put up the hardware and run it; the hard part is to get effective agricultural support services into place. . . . Everybody knows agricultural supporting services are poor in the Philippines.[80]

Even more troubling than the inadequate support services was the fear that the irrigation program might not be benefiting the rural poor, for whose welfare the big dams had been promoted in the propaganda of the regime and the Bank. "The Bank's irrigation program has expanded rapidly," stated a 1979 secret memorandum, "and questions are increasingly raised in the Bank's Board and elsewhere about the effects of these large investments on income distribution."[81]

Watering the Rich. Why these questions had become increasingly urgent becomes understandable if we examine the circumstances surrounding one major Bank irrigation project, the Chico River Irrigation Project. The project received $50 million from the Bank, and work on it began in 1976. 8,000 families—4,100 tenant farmers and 3,950 owner operators—were to benefit from the program, claimed the project appraisal report.[82] The unstated assumption behind this claim, however, was that land reform and other measures promoting social equality would be implemented in the project area, the lush Cagayan Valley of Northern Luzon—an area where Defense Minister Juan Ponce Enrile controlled major agribusiness interests.

But while work progressed on the dam project, land reform did not. A Catholic Church agency investigating land tenure conditions in the Cagayan Valley in 1978 discovered that peasants were deeply in debt to the *Masagana 99* credit program and had not benefited from land reform:

> Notwithstanding the supposed conversion of tenanted farms into leasehold a long time ago, farmer leasees still have to pay rents as high as 35 cavans per hectare per crop season [out of average yields of 40-50 cavans]. Sharecropping on a 50-50 basis is still being practiced in many places.[83]

Indeed, the Church agency claimed that "land reform *in reverse*" had taken place in the Valley:

> The government's corporate rice farming program . . . has resulted in the transfer of 1,151 hectares from small farmers to large mechanized farms owned by Manila corporations. On top of this, rice and corn lands are being converted to sugar plantations to supply the newly established Cagayan Sugar Corporation . . . . Already 4,015 hectares have been converted to sugar production and more land is needed.[84]

The Chico River Irrigation effort is scheduled to be completed in 1982. But as early as the mid-70's, Bank bureaucrats could not help realizing that ultimately, its beneficiaries would be big landlords and big agribusiness interests of Cagayan Valley, many of them linked to Defense Minister Enrile and to Ferdinand Marcos himself.[85]

Uprooting the Poor. While Bank technocrats in Washington fretted over their irrigation dams, the local inhabitants grew to fear them. For most Filipinos, in fact, the World Bank is now commonly associated with the uprooting of people through projects such as the Pantabangan Irrigation Dam in Central Luzon, the Tondo "slum upgrading" effort in Manila, and the proposed Chico Hydroelectric Dam Complex in Northern Luzon. Projects such as these have created the popular image of the Bank as Marcos' willing partner in repression and endowed it with a local reputation worse than that of the CIA.

The Pantabangan Dam has now become a good example of how not to build an irrigation dam. Financed by the Bank to the tune of $34 million, the project sought to tap the waters of the Pampanga River to irrigate 83,700 hectares of agricultural land and generate electricity for the Luzon grid. Considered a prestige project by the Marcos government, which was looking for powerful symbols for its martial rule, "Asia's biggest dam," as the regime billed it, was constructed at breakneck speed and opened ahead of schedule in February 1974.

Speed, however, had its costs, and it was the people of the region who paid the price. The absence of a serious environmental impact study was an oversight that led to "grave damage to the surrounding watershed," according to a leading Filipino consultant to the Bank.[86] Other investigators visiting the area in 1978 asserted that "erosion around the reservoir is almost certainly due to the disruption of the area's ecological balance. . . ."[87] Even Prime Minister Virata was forced to concede that, because of the project, "some slopes of watershed are barren."[88]

Even more serious, however, the relocation plan for the 14,000 citizens displaced by the dam from their good farmlands and "abundant natural resource base" turned out to be a social disaster. The assistant manager of the Pantabangan project admitted that the relocation program was plagued by the lack of preparation of the resettled population for new livelihoods, inadequate farm lots and poor soil, poor domestic water supply, and soil erosion.[89] "Despite promises, no land came to the people except for desolate mountainsides," noted one post mortem report.[90] Nor did the jobs promised by the National Irrigation Administration materialize. Houses provided by the government were left unfinished, and 100 of these slid down the mountain because of soil erosion. Food rations promised by the government came in very irregularly. Many members of this once relatively contented community have been reduced to dependence on meager doles from private aid groups for their very existence.[91]

Lowlanders who were completely ignorant of the upland way of life, the resettled people of Pantabangan had no choice but to turn to upland farming. This involved essentially a wholly different way of life—an immense cultural change for which the project planners had shown no sensitivity. Most cruelly, as the displaced community struggled with mountainsides that cracked with dryness, they received not a drop of water from the dam that had displaced them.

A World Bank loan signed in July 1980 carries with it the prospect that the displaced people of Pantabangan will be pushed off their farms once more and forced to begin their lives anew on even higher hills. This time a World Bank-funded corporate tree plantation will take their place. The reason for the plantation? To prevent further erosion of the hillsides and thereby slow down the siltation of the poorly planned Pantabangan Dam.[92] The people of Pantabangan, in other words, are ensnared in a Kafkaesque process set in motion by short-sighted technocrats in far away boardrooms.

Undermining the Smallholder: Three Case Studies

Irrigation, the largest investment in the Philippine countryside, was also the World Bank's most spectacular fiasco. The same phenomenon of smallholder-directed projects ending up with consequences drastically different from those they had been ostensibly designed to promote was repeated in the Bank's smaller projects.

The experience of the *Second Rural Development Project* illustrates the pitfalls of working through governments that have no serious commitment to rural change. Backed by a $15 million loan from the Bank, this project aimed to provide infrastructural, organizational, technical, and credit support to three settlements on public lands inhabited by 13,000 families in Mindanao and Capiz.

A very basic condition for the implementation of the program was the granting of land titles to the settlers. However, government institutions, such as the key implementing agency, the Ministry of Agrarian Reform (MAR), were strongly biased against titling small settlers. "The procedures and requirements for a settler to apply and receive title for the land he tills," complained the Bank, "are extremely complicated, and require actions and approvals by many agencies, so much so that applications are hopelessly bogged down somewhere along the line. The net result is that many settlers simply give up."[93]

The key rural credit component of the project was to be implemented with the participation of rural banks, but the latter "would not grant loans from their own capital to settlers without a land title."[94] Thus, in November 1979, two years after the start of the project, a supervision mission concluded, with alarm and frustration that:

> Rural Development II . . . has been apprehensive of a worrisome prospect that the majority of the project settlers may remain ineligible for rural credit; the project rural credit component may not be consummated; without credit the settlers may not be able to adopt the extension packages and cropping systems

being developed under the project; and the project objectives may not be fulfilled.[95]

Exasperated Bank bureaucrats attacked the Ministry as "notoriously weak," asserting that it "lacks dynamic leadership and effective management."[96] This did not, however, help the project "beneficiaries," who, like the people of Pantabangan, were trapped in a bureaucratic labyrinth.

Lack of commitment to change and bureaucratic blundering undid the Second Rural Development Project. In the case of the *Smallholder Tree Farming and Forestry Project,* however, the implementing agencies could not be faulted for inertia. This effort was sabotaged by something else: the Bank's insistence that the richer sectors of the rural community, in order to be "neutralized," had to be incorporated into rural development projects.

Supported by a Bank loan of $16 million, the Tree Farming Project had two major components. The first consisted of supervised credit and technical services for tree farm development by smallholders on 28,600 hectares of marginal lands. The second was the development of 3,000 hectares of trial pine plantations in Abra Province. Leafmeal, fuelwood, charcoal, and pulpwood were to be produced under marketing contracts with private companies.

One year after the start of the project a Bank mission evaluating the tree farming component complained: "By early September, approved loans and those being processed covered 51 percent of areas targeted for 1979, but the majority of these loans were not made to the target smallholder population."[97] Regarding the 1,168 hectares of committed area for which information was available, "It is made up of 58 tree farms only, averaging 29 hectares in size. This is seven to eight times the area of the target size stated in the appraisal report (about 4 hectares) and about five times that of the revised . . . target (six hectares)."[98] It concluded that "response from genuine smallholders has been weak up to now and the vast majority of the present areas approved consists of medium size holdings or parts of large holdings . . . . Many of them are owned by absentees living in provincial cities or in the capital."[99]

The subversion of the program was traced by the Bank to the smallholders' lack of proof of ownership or legal possession of land.[100] An even greater problem suggested by the Bank supervision papers was that the implementing agency, the Development Bank of the Philippines (DBP), was acting as an agent of large landed interests. The DBP's effort to undermine the original intent of the program was exemplified by its recommendation that the following be included as qualified borrowers under the program: corporations, in addition to individual firms, cooperatives and farmers associations; participating firms without any limitations in hectarage; and other interested processing/industrial plants that will utilize firewood/charcoal as fuel in line with the government effort to find alternative sources of energy.[101]

In response, the Bank stated in alarm that "approval of these uses would change the character of the loan agreement . . . ."[102] However, it gave the DBP an out: "In practice, it may not always be easy to uphold the above principle and the cases would have be decided individually by the Bank manager."[103]

Church sources claimed that the pine plantation component of the project had become an out-and-out subsidy for Cellophil, a giant private logging venture integrated with pulp and paper manufactures owned by Marcos' crony, Herminio Disini. The 3,000-hectare Abra pine plantation project, financed by the Bank, turned out to be merely a part of a larger project targeting 33,000 hectares for plantation development, carried out as a joint undertaking between the implementing agency, the Bureau of Forest Development, and Cellophil.[104] Tree farming was, in turn, but one component of the firm's operations, which had won the right to exploit 200,000 hectares of virgin pine forests in the area—a process that now threatens to uproot the Tingguian national minority from its ancestral lands.[105]

The failure of the *Third Rural Credit Project* is even easier to explain. While the Bank uttered the ritual words about smallholders, they were, in fact, excluded from the start by the project's objective: to spread mechanization by providing credit for tractors.

Financed by a $22 million loan from the Bank, the credit program was instituted to promote "farm mechanization, transport and other equipment; fisheries and livestock development, as well as cottage and agroindustries."[106] 8,000 people—"mainly small and medium-sized farmers"—were to benefit from the project.[107]

Promoting mechanization as a way of benefiting the rural poor in a labor-surplus country like the Philippines is, in itself, a contradiction. As the Bank's "project performance report" admitted, "evidence has emerged from recent surveys to confirm that under particular circumstances adverse social conditions [from mechanization] do occur."[108] Still, 86 percent of project funds went to financing purchases of machines, especially four-wheel tractors.[109]

Contrary to the Bank's proclaimed intention to funnel credit to smallholders, the Bank aimed at farmers cultivating between two and ten hectares, obviously because of the scale requirements of tractors. In the Philippines, where most farms are 1 to 2 hectares, most farmers in the 2 to 10-hectare range are clearly medium-sized or large landlords. Indeed, the Bank performance report conceded that "no particular effort was made in general to reach the small farmers . . . loan terms, risk and cost servicing may have been a factor in this development."[110] More explicitly, it asserted that:

> Distribution of project funds among subloan categories was still weighted in favor of tractors and imported power tillers purchased by larger and medium-size farmers. The same trend was observed in fisheries and livestock projects: their scales were much larger than the models prepared and appraised for small farmers. Rural banks in general did not give due consideration to identifying those smaller farmers who were viable but were traditionally rejected as lacking in creditworthiness.[111]

With the stress on machine purchases and creditworthiness, the number of direct beneficiaries eventually came to only 4,500 farmers—or merely 57 percent of the initial target of 8,000.[112] Moreover, a significant number of them were commercial crop operators raising sugar.

The encouragement to mechanize provided by the project, in fact, turned out to be disastrous for a great number of beneficiaries, whether big, medium, or small farmers. The project was implemented between June 1974 and May 1977, a time characterized by a steep rise in the price of oil followed by a slump in the sugar industry. For sugar landlords, these events "rendered their investment unviable."[113] As a consequence, they could not repay their loans to the project. Indeed, the sugar slump became so severe that "some borrowers have rejected rescheduling and requested repossession of tractors and disposal of other collateral offered to rural banks."[114] As for the rice farmer, the project evaluation concluded:

> the investment was not really profitable. The price of the tractor had increased faster than the increase in the paddy price of rice . . . so the rice farmer was in a situa-

tion where his income from the farm could no longer amortize the cost of the tractor.[115]

Instead of assisting farmers, the Third Rural Credit Project became, in effect, a massive subsidy for the foreign manufacturers of tractors. The foreign manufacturers had become quite adept at turning World Bank projects to their advantage after their experience with a previous credit effort, the *Second Rural Credit Project*, which had also promoted mechanization.[116] This earlier scheme had enabled them to rake in handsome profits when the prices of imported farm machinery skyrocketed after the World Bank-imposed devaluation of 1970. Buoyed by this experience, these interests were ready for the Third Rural Credit; they launched a campaign to inform farmers of the availability of the tractor loans and even went to the extent of assisting applicants prepare loan documents.[117] The industry made a killing at the expense of all classes of farmers; in a two-year period, 1973-75, the price of tractors skyrocketed by 89 percent.[118]

Financing Counterinsurgency

By the late 1970's, it was crystal clear to most World Bank officials that the joint antipoverty effort in the rural Philippines had collapsed. It is not surprising, then, that the repressive facet of rural development, so well concealed earlier by the Bank's rhetoric, gradually came to the fore as the World Bank became a participant in the regime's "Integrated Area Development" (IAD) programs. The IAD programs were thinly disguised military counterinsurgency schemes to contain the explosive expansion of the revolutionary New People's Army. The NPA had, by 1980, created 26 battle fronts in the countryside and operated in 41 of the country's 71 provinces. The rural crisis, in other words, was turning into a revolutionary situation approaching that which existed in Vietnam in the early sixties.[119]

Integrated Area Development. Integrated Area Development (IAD) is one of the government's main vehicles for counterinsurgency. This strategy consists of delivering a "development package" that ostensibly offers inhabitants of a region a coherent set of services ranging from "security" and medical assistance to road building and technical agricultural aid. The concept is very close to the Bank's "new style" approach promoted by McNamara. Formulated in the early 70's as a response to the growth of armed resistance in the countryside, IAD programs were aimed at four priority areas: Cagayan Valley in Northern Luzon, the principal base area of the NPA; the Bicol region in Southern Luzon, the key expansion area of the NPA in the period 1971-74; the island of Samar in the Eastern Visayas, where the NPA began organizing in force in 1974; and Mindoro, a large southern island regarded by the authorities as a potential area for NPA expansion.

The Bicol River Basin Development Project in northern Luzon was the test case of the IAD approach. The Marcos regime enlisted the support of USAID (U. S. Agency for International Development), which proceeded to pour about $15 million into "one of the major centers of insurgency in the post-World War II period."[120] In addition to projects that were ostensibly geared toward increasing agricultural productivity, the project sought to upgrade approximately 200 kilometers of feeder roads and 1,000 linear meters of bridges in an area that one foreign correspondent described as "better guerrilla country than Isabela [Cagayan Valley] . . . mountains, good cover, bad roads where there are any at all, and above all, abundance of food."[121]

Road building was clearly meant to facilitate the logistical mobility of the Philippine Army, then conducting a major search-and-destroy operation in the area.[122] Security and development were seen as so integrally related, according to a Filipino World Bank consultant, that "military officers head up key positions even in the rural development component of the Bicol River Basin project."[123] The IAD effort appeared to pay off in the short term. According to a USAID assessment in 1979, " . . . the Bicol is one area in which insurgent behavior declined rapidly after the declaration of martial law. With an influx of foreign assistance, this has led to impressive gains in infrastructural improvement and the provision of government services."[124]

Encouraged by its apparent success in Bicol, the regime next targeted Mindoro and Samar, this time with commitments of financial and organizational support from the World Bank and the Australian government.

Supporting PANAMIN in Mindoro. The Mindoro Integrated Area Development project, begun in 1975, was described by the Bank as an effort to increase farm incomes and improve living standards by providing water services, port construction and road building, certified rice seed, rat control, schistomiasis preventive measures, and financial assistance for the 20,000 Manggyan families, the island's indigenous tribal group.[125] Among the participating agencies were the Civic Action Group of the Philippine Army, a key counterinsurgency unit,[126] and the Presidential Assistant on National Minorities (PANAMIN),[127] headed by Marcos' crony, Manda Elizalde.

PANAMIN was assigned the role of administering the Manggyan outreach component of the project. Its tasks, supported by World Bank funds totaling $600,000, included dispensing medical assistance and agricultural inputs and constructing an access road. More important, PANAMIN was to "grant legal titles for ancestral lands traditionally used by these communities. . . ."[128]

The project had hardly begun, however, when PANAMIN decided to shelve the land-titling process. "Rather than titling Manggyans on their ancestral land," reported one correspondent, "PANAMIN seeks to establish new reservations for Manggyans and have PANAMIN hold title to the land, leasing it to the tribespeople."[129]

It is not surprising that the original intent of the program was thus subverted. Under the leadership of Marcos' well-heeled associate, Manda Elizalde, PANAMIN achieved the reputation of being the government's counterinsurgency arm for national minorities. As one review of PANAMIN's activities put it, "PANAMIN . . . has no intention of helping tribal Filipinos acquire title to their lands. PANAMIN policy is to secure reservation areas which it then administers as government property. This way, PANAMIN has full control not only over these lands but also over tribal Filipinos."[130]

In its internal documents, PANAMIN makes no attempt to conceal its security objectives in dealing with tribal groups like the Manggyans:

"With the success of the antisubversive campaign in the cities, the subversives now will seek sanctuaries secure from government forces. The remote areas inhabited by the tribes offer many heavens [sic]." It continues: "It would be tragic if the enemies of the Republic succeeded simply because no one else reached the minorities first . . . . Fundamental to the effort is *getting to them first—ahead of the subversives*. This means an immediate effort to expand our personal contact with all the tribes and a longer range program to address their problems and convince them the government way is best."[131]

The reservation system, to which PANAMIN channeled World Bank funds in Mindoro, is seen as an ideal system of extending military control because it enables the agency "to assist the military in the organization of home defense units in areas where such organizations are required in connection with security programs."[132]

The Bank and Pacification in Samar. Samar is the third largest island in the Philippines and one of the poorest. IAD planning for Samar began in 1974, when signs of revolutionary activity appeared on the island. In 1976, the Samar Integrated Rural Development Office was established and negotiations for financing the program began with both the Bank and the Australian government. The Marcos regime was running against time. According to one estimate, between 1976 and 1979, the New Peoples Army in Samar grew to a force with 500 men under arms and a mass base of 200,000 farmers.[133] To counter the spectacular growth of the guerrillas, 9,000 troops in ten battalions were dispatched to the island. The arrival of the Philippine Army began a reign of terror, murder, and rape—a continuing episode vividly described in the reports of such human rights groups as the Task Force Detainees.[134]

During this military buildup in 1979, the Australian government made a formal commitment to finance the IAD project and the final touches were being put to the proposed World Bank subproject. The Australian input, centered in northern Samar province, was viewed as complementary to the Bank effort. "The project," stated a Bank press release, "is part of the overall development plan for the island and complements separate projects being assisted by the Governments of Japan and Australia."[135] The World Bank-financed component of the overall project, asserted the Bank project document, "would give a degree of emphasis to Eastern Samar, the most isolated of the three provinces, and would avoid duplication of efforts."[136]

The Australians, eager to tighten their political and economic ties to the Marcos regime, were clear from the start about the political, counterinsurgency intent of the Samar IAD project. The most important portion of the Australian subproject was the construction of a 68.5-kilometer feeder road on the northeast coast of the island. Significantly, this was the area where the NPA was strongest. The strength of the revolutionary forces had consequently drawn the presence of the military's notorious 60th Constabulary Battalion, whose trademark was to behead and collect the ears of its victims. The battalion's mobility, however, was restricted by the absence of a viable transportation network. In a confidential memo of the Australian Development Assistance Bureau, leaked by World Bank sources, the military relevance of the proposed feeder road was baldly stated:

> The Far East coast of northern Samar, i.e., the Mapanao-Gamay-Lapinig area is at present entirely isolated from the rest of Northern Samar with access limited to oceangoing pump boat when weather permits or to foot travel. It is thus almost impossible for authorities to provide adequate education, health or *security* services in the area. *As a consequence, even though construction of the road would be difficult and expensive and perhaps not strictly justified by economic argument, it is intended that an early start be made on this portion of the East Coast Feeder, regardless of economic priorities.*[137]

The World Bank component of the project began in late 1980. It consisted principally of an effort to modernize the port of Catbalogan and improve 230 kilometers of the Coastal Road[138] of Eastern Samar—an area occupied by four battalions engaged in relentless "antisubversive" operations. Military atrocities were common in the wartorn area, and according to the International Commission on the Militarization of Samar, a delegation of international human rights activists sponsored by Philippine religious groups, "free fire zones" were being created. "In free fire zones, any nonmilitary person is shot on sight. The victims are often farmers who have not received word that their farm is now so designated," the Commission reported.[139]

The presence in Eastern Samar of two military engineering battalions was further evidence that the World Bank project was being implemented in the context of an overall military plan. These battalions were occupied in "building roads and airstrips which have a primarily strategic value."[140] Throughout the island, notes one firsthand report, "the regime has been pushing the construction of many large ports for the boats of the Philippine Navy, airstrips for the planes of the Philippine Air Force, and highways for the quick movement of troops."[141]

The counterinsurgency implications of the Samar project disturbed many at the middle and lower levels of the Bank staff. "Don't think we're blind," one middle-level staffer commented in an interview. "How could anyone fail to see that the Samar stuff had military potential, with all the news about a military buildup in 1979?"[142] He revealed that on two separate occasions in 1979—at a "decision-meeting" in mid-April and again at the key Executive Directors meeting in December—some staff members articulated concerns about the military relevance of the project. But just as McNamara handled lower level staff dissent and questioning about the Vietnam War when he headed up the Department of Defense, these concerns were sidestepped by higher-ups. They countered with the standard argument about the "political neutrality" of Bank projects.[143] One of the Executive Directors, however, was said to have questioned "whether this was in fact an RD project designed to benefit the poor with nearly all that money going to road building and port improvement."[144] The question was, of course, rhetorical, for the Bank's stabilization effort had been left with no other recourse but repression.

Conclusion

By the end of the seventies, the picture of the Philippine countryside was marked by glaring contrasts.

The country was exporting rice, after decades of being a chronic rice importer—yet the vast majority of Filipinos were eating less than a decade earlier.

Agricultural growth was averaging 5 percent a year—yet, according to the Bank, the number of families living in absolute poverty increased by 23 percent between 1965 and 1975.[145] Government sources were forced to admit that the trend continued in the second half of the decade: the real income of rice farmers declined by 53 percent between 1976 and 1979.[146]

The World Bank *Poverty Report* provided the explanation for the paradoxical results of the rural development effort it had pushed with the government:

> A substantial portion of agricultural growth . . . was concentrated in activities known to have substantial commercial content, and one could therefore argue that the benefits from the high level of agricultural growth may not have reached substantial numbers of the poor.[147]

If there is a phrase that captures the essence of this process wracking the Philippine countryside, it is "growth with immiserization."

The World Bank could perhaps find some comfort in the fact that a small stratum of kulaks, or small capitalist farmers, had emerged—a stratum which served as the medium for the instutionalization of more "efficient," more capitalistic relations of production in the countryside. But the political stability that this stratum potentially brought was dissipated by the even larger mass of discontented smallholders plunged into the ranks of the rural proletariat by the same process of "modernization." In addition, this kulak stratum was itself rendered unstable by the tendencies of modern capitalist agriculture: those who started from a more advantageous land and capital base and were more efficient in applying the new HYV technology left the others behind. As capitalist farmers, they stood at the vanguard of an inevitable process of land reconcentration. The dynamics of this process are described by Alain de Janvry, who draws from the experience of smallholder capitalism spawned by rural development efforts in Latin America:

> . . . peasants who successfully modernize need to amplify the scale of their operations and make use of hired labor power to meet agrarian costs and effectively compete against the well-established commercial sector. And in this, land is only available from the worse off peasants. As a result, successful implementation of rural development projects effectively negates their very purpose.[148]

In the face of failure, Bank officials began to engage in self-justification suspiciously similar to that offered by many generals for the U.S. defeat in Vietnam: "We went in to help the South Vietnamese. But we couldn't do anything if they refused to help themselves." As the Ascher Memorandum saw it, the failure in the Philippines was entirely the responsibility of the government: "The government has shown little administrative effectiveness in attacking the problem of rural poverty at the grassroots level."[149] Indeed, it accused the regime of "little improvement . . . in even attempting rural development projects."[150]

But the excuse would not wash. As the foregoing survey has shown, the Marcos government's "ineffectiveness" was only part—the superficial part—of the reason why rural development collapsed. The deeper explanation lay in the Bank and regime's common assumption that rural development would concentrate on raising smallholder productivity without substantially altering the prevailing patterns of political and economic power in the countryside. Removed from the day-to-day dynamics of putting a contradictory strategy into effect, some World Bank technocrats could afford to adopt a sanctimonious attitude and criticize government bureaucrats for not being more "determined" and "effective." But when the Bank seriously pondered the implications and consequences of a less timid approach to rural problems, it, too, shrank back from them. And the Bank was trapped by its own rhetoric. As we have seen, the

Bank eventually ended up reluctantly justifying the continued existence of landlords and usurers.

The failure of rural development in the Philippines, then, was principally a failure of a common strategy shared by the technocrats of both the World Bank and the Marcos government. Perhaps the most appropriate epitaph for this debacle was provided by none other than a consultant to the World Bank:

> In short, rural development strategies to date have failed to provide meaningful benefits to those rural Filipinos most in need of them. Underlying all the rhetoric, concerns for production, control of rural discontent, and maintaining the support for elites are still paramount, as circumstances of most rural Filipinos continue to erode rapidly, perhaps already in an irreversible direction.[151]

CHAPTER FOUR

Counterinsurgency in the City

The Urban Crisis

In the Philippines, as in most Third World countries, the crisis of the countryside has triggered an equally profound crisis of the city. Increasingly desperate conditions in rural areas have sparked a massive migration of people to the cities—a movement that shows no signs of abating. The dimensions of this crisis are captured in the urban sprawl that is Metropolitan Manila. With its six million people, this megalopolis dominates the country, standing out like the swollen head of a sickly infant, to borrow Che Guevara's classic description of Havana at the time of the Cuban Revolution.

The explosive growth of the Philippine urban population from both natural increase and in-migration is reflected in the statistics: whereas the national population is growing by 2.8 percent a year, the urban population is increasing by 3.5 percent.[1] As of 1975, 14.3 million Filipinos—one third of the population—lived in urban areas. That figure is expected to triple by the end of the century.[2]

With the capacity of industry to absorb new workers remaining practically unchanged, most of the recent entrants into the urban labor force have been forced into very low paying and irregular service jobs.[3] While this has given government statisticians an excuse to exclude most of the urban poor from the category of unemployed, the economic situation of slumdwellers is nothing but wretched. The typical urban laborer, notes the Bank, is employed on a part-time basis and makes P10 (or $1.40) a day.[4] In 1978 a worker's income was only two thirds of what it was in 1970[5]—a fact that reflected the general decline of living standards during the martial law period.

Such conditions of employment have contributed to a state of extreme poverty for a substantial number of city dwellers. According to one Bank report:

> The 1977 urban poverty income estimated for the Philippines was P1877 ($250) per person per year. 39 percent of families in urban areas and 80 to 90 percent of families in slum areas of major cities have per capita incomes below this level. In Metro Manila, 35 percent of the population, or about 2.1 million people, live below the poverty level; they account for 30 percent of the urban poor in the Philippines.[6]

The crisis of the Philippine city is perhaps most graphically communicated by the burgeoning slums of squatter settlements, where about 25 percent of all Filipino urban dwellers live in tin and cardboard shacks. In Manila, according to the Bank, the percentage is even higher: 30 percent, or 1.8 million, of the city's population are squatters.[7] Even this figure is an understatement; according to a West German Government study, 34 to 40 percent of Metro Manila's population in 1979 were squatters.[8]

These settlements of the urban poor, such as Tondo in Manila—reputed to be Asia's biggest slum, exhibit not only the worst housing conditions in the Philippines but also some of the highest concentrations of malnutrition and disease. A 1975 survey discovered that infant mortality in Tondo was 130 per 1,000 live births—compared to 68 to 80 per 1,000 for the country as a whole.[9] The slum area of Macabalen in Cagayan de Oro City in the south has a gastroenteritis mortality rate ten times higher than that of the surrounding region.[10]

Shantytown life, however, has another face. The very conditions of adversity that slum dwellers confront has forced them to create communities. As one of the most experienced students of the urban poor in the Philippines writes:

> The sense of community reminiscent of village life persists in many a new urban neighborhood cluster, fostered both by social and economic necessity in face of unresponsive urban institutions, as well as by sheer tradition. The very density that breeds quarrels and fights among neighbors also encourages helping relationships. Living in the vicinity of one's transplanted ethnic or language group . . . or occupation group allows bonds of reciprocal service and friendship to flourish.[11]

It is this other communal face of shantytown life that has become increasingly exasperating to the elites who control the economic conditions which perpetuate slums.

Counterinsurgency and Centralization

The World Bank saw the urban poor as both a promise and a threat. A promise, because they made up the pool of cheap labor for export industries. The justification advanced for urban projects, therefore, rested partly on their supposed contribution toward "increasing the productivity of the poor."[12] Thus the staff appraisal report for the Third Urban Upgrading Project for the Philippines asserts:

> The government places a high priority on increasing employment and productivity in view of . . . the high level of skills, education and low comparative wages of Philippine labor which should enable it to expand exports, especially for the sectors of small machinery, consumer products, and crafts. These objectives will become increasingly important as urbanization absorbs the surplus rural workforce. . . . The project is designed to support this objective in Metro Manila.[13]

But it was fear of the explosive mixture of poverty and rising expectations which principally determined the Bank's stance toward the urban poor. As with its rural development strategy, containment and counterinsurgency were the primary objectives of the Bank's urban program. McNamara expressed this frankly when he laid out the strategy at the annual IMF-World Bank conference in September 1975:

> Historically, violence and civil upheaval are more common in cities than in the countryside. Frustrations that fester among the urban poor are readily exploited by political extremists. If cities do not begin to deal more constructively with poverty, poverty may well begin to deal more destructively with cities.[14]

McNamara's concern was echoed in the Ascher Memorandum's discussion of the Philippine urban situation:

> While the population shift to the cities (particularly Metro Manila) has created a much larger labor pool to fuel industrial expansion, the constellation of urban

> unemployment, urban slums, and labor unions of growing size has shifted government concern considerably toward the metropolis and away from the countryside.[15]

The Bank warned that "a politically sensitive economic strategy cannot ignore the fact that it is in the urban areas where the level of political awareness is highest and the possibility of *new* sources of disruption the greatest."[16] Urban housing projects such as those being jointly pushed by the Marcos regime and the Bank, admitted the memo, were meant "to palliate urban dissatisfaction."[17]

The Bank's counterinsurgency concerns were reflected in its contribution to the process of centralizing political authority and management in Manila. Just as the Bank had hailed the advent of martial law on the grounds that it gave the executive "absolute power in the field of economic development," so did it favor the creation of a centralized Metro Manila government for the sake of "administrative efficiency," to better control the restless slum dwellers.

The political and administrative centralization of the region's seventeen separate cities and municipalities must be viewed as part of the general concentration of political power which both led up to and later was promoted by the declaration of martial law. Moves to centralize metropolitan police services were started in the late 60's with the assistance of the USAID Public Safety Program.[18] Immediately after the declaration of martial law, pliant local officials were used to stage the infamous "referenda" of January and June 1973, which retroactively legitimized Marcos' assumption of dictatorial powers in September 1972. Local mayors were instrumental in forging the network of *barangay*, ward leaders who acted as the "grassroots eyes and ears" of the regime. Police services were formally integrated in March 1974, under the control and supervision of the Philippine Constabulary.[19] In the view of the regime and its foreign advisers then, a Metro Manila Government was the natural culmination and linchpin of the process of regional power concentration.

After a World Bank team visited the Philippines in July and August 1973, the agency's pressure on the government to create a metropolitan administrative body escalated.[20] Indeed, it reached the point that Onofre Corpuz, a top Marcos development technocrat, was compelled to warn against restructuring political authority in Metro Manila simply "because it is required by the World Bank."[21]

The Bank's impatience and the reasons behind it were articulated by a mission that visited the city in the summer of 1975:

> Several draft decrees concerning the creation of a Metro Manila Government are under consideration. Whatever the ultimate form of the government body, it will be several years before the Metropolitan Government can effectively manage the affairs of the metropolitan area. In the meantime, there is no single agency that is assessing development needs and priorities within Greater Manila.[22]

Finally, on November 1975, the government fell in step with the Bank and created the Metropolitan Manila Commission (MMC) governing four cities and thirteen municipalities. The function of MMC was, according to the Bank, "to establish strategic policy and coordinate infrastructure planning for the area and supervise the administration of local services."[23] Later that month, during staff preparations for a Washington visit by First Lady Imelda Marcos, McNamara was briefed to tell her: "The Bank strongly supports the establishment of a Metropolitan Manila Government and stands ready to assist the Government with technical assistance and financing to tackle questions of organization and management, fiscal policy, programming and budgeting."[24]

Megalopolis and Megalomania

While its objective was *technocratic* centralization, in actuality the Bank promoted greater personal concentration of power in Marcos' hands. This became very clear when Marcos appointed his wife Imelda as governor of the area, the Philippines' most prosperous region. The power and functions of the Commission were to be exercised by the First Lady "pending its full constitution."[25] All local officials in the area were to be appointed by President Marcos, and the power to levy and collect revenues was transferred from local governments to the Commission.[26]

The Bank thus aided in destroying the few remnants of local checks on central authority that still existed after the declaration of martial law. Perhaps the realization that it had fostered Marcos' personal accumulation of power in the name of technocratic efficiency made the Bank uneasy about the appointment of Imelda Marcos. "Mrs. Marcos,"

Bank bureaucrat Gregory Votaw briefed McNamara, "has identified herself with a few showcase projects, which we consider ineffective and which are a bit of a joke among knowledgeable Filipinos."[27]

The Bank had good reason to distrust Imelda's appointment, for her overriding concern was not technocratic administration but the creation of an expensive, extravagant, and grandiose domain to bolster her influence and match her regal self image:

> In Mrs. Marcos' vision, Metropolitan Manila would extend south and east of its present boundaries—as far south as Tagaytay City incorporating the urbanized towns of Cavite and Laguna . . . and as far east as the Pacific Ocean coast of largely undeveloped Quezon Province.[28]

The forbidding foothills of the Sierra Madre Mountain Range 50 miles east of Manila did not discourage Imelda from dreaming about reaching the Pacific so that "Manila will . . . have access to two great bodies of water—the Manila Bay port receiving ships sailing in from the China Sea, the Infanta port directly receiving ships coming in from the Pacific.[29]

There was a darker side to this megalopolitan megalomania. The Bank considered the burgeoning slum dweller population the most urgent and complex urban problem. Imelda, on the other hand, had a simple answer: demolition and relocation. For the governor of Metro Manila, squatters were simply an eyesore—an obstacle to "beautification" and the creation of "a modern city" complete with financial center, an area for hotels and restaurants, an embassy enclave, high-class restaurant areas . . . and other appurtenances of luxury living, Florida style.[30] Only the middle and upper classes and tourists really figured in Imelda's vision—and this showed in her construction priorities. In her effort to make Manila a tourist center on a par with Hong Kong, $300 million were sunk into nearly a score of luxury hotels. Several million more went to building the monumental Convention Center, designed to host international conferences, and the Cultural Center complex, where western personalities, such as ballerina Margot Fonteyn and classical pianist Van Cliburn, performed for Manila's well-to-do.

Toward Manila's urban poor, Imelda displayed a mixture of paternalism, contempt, and fear. Her attitude was captured in a classic statement: "We are very lucky in our people. It takes so little to make us happy. The smiling faces of slum dwellers, for example, never cease to astonish me. It is for us who are a little better off to see to it that they keep these smiles, and that they should have reason to smile."[31]

Not surprisingly, Imelda blamed the housing shortage on the urban poor themselves. They should not have come to Manila in the first place, she asserted, "without knowing exactly where they're going to live."[32] Low-cost mass housing was distasteful to her on a fundamental philosophical level: "Why do I build a Heart Center or a Convention City instead of urban mass housing?" she asked rhetorically. I believe we just can't do that. I don't believe in building houses for everyone because I don't want our people to be mendicant. . . ."[33]

With her vision for Manila completely at odds with the needs of the urban poor, Imelda's commission responded to the squatter problem in several ways. White fences were built around shantytowns to prevent foreigners and tourists from seeing squatters.[34] Forced relocation, however, was the preferred solution. One of the more notorious cases of the bulldoze-and-uproot technique occurred during preparations for the Miss Universe Pageant in 1974, when squatter shacks housing an estimated 100,000 people along the parade route were demolished. Equally sensational was the removal of 60,000 squatters to "beautify" the city for delegates to the IMF-World Bank Conference in Manila in October 1976.[35] While the international financiers met in Imelda-style luxury, the squatters were relocated to remote sites twenty miles outside the city.

A World Bank confidential report offered the following explanation for the failure of the government's method of dealing with the urban poor:

> Until recently, Government responded to Manila's problems by resettling squatters on four sites at the edge of the metropolitan area. Results have been poor, largely because inadequate consideration was given to employment opportunities, which resulted in the resettled squatters returning to the city core area; moreover, even the resettlement program has touched only a small number of the urban poor.[36]

The failure of relocation forced frustrated regime officials to periodically threaten the imposition of the "Return to the Province Program." Under this scheme, rural families would be prevented from migrating to Manila. This would be accomplished by providing current residents of the city with identity cards to distinguish them from those that the government regarded as intruders. According to one high official, the government would "see to it that the family really boards the boat or the bus going home."[37] In essence, the Marcos regime sought to implement an embryonic pass system like South Africa's, but with class replacing race as a criterion for residence and occupation.

The government did not, however, dare to apply the program. By the mid-1970's, popular resistance had simply become too strong.

Popular Resistance and Palliatives

ZOTO, or Zone One Tondo Organization, spearheaded this resistance. Forged in the struggle against evictions in the late 60's and early 70's, ZOTO is a federation composed of 113 organizations, each focused on a specific issue, from eight adjacent shantytown areas. In the mid-70's, ZOTO joined similar federations from Magsaysay Village and Barrio Magsaysay to form a superfederation, Ugnayan. This body soon attracted the affiliation of federations from Navotas and Malabon which had been created in response to the common threat posed by arbitrary government actions.[38]

By 1976, the confrontational protests of ZOTO-Ugnayan had attracted not only assistance from Philippine church groups but also international attention. In a widely circulated statement presented at the United Nations Conference on Human Habitat in Vancouver in May 1976, ZOTO-Ugnayan informed the world that its goals were modest but vital:

> The peoples' organizations in Tondo have worked hard to attain security and freedom from harassment for the squatters there. They have continually fought against government efforts to eject them and to demolish their neighborhoods, not because the neighborhoods are so beautiful but because there is no other place to go where they can be near their jobs and afford housing.[39]

Faced with such resistance, the government responded with repression and some token efforts at "mass housing." For the most part, these government housing projects were expensive, middle-class oriented, and ineffective. For instance, a 526-family model housing project, *Kapitbahayan* (Neighborhood), build by Imelda in Dagat-Dagatan adjacent to the Tondo Foreshore, was criticized by ZOTO as setting rental rates at levels "which no squatter will be able to afford."[40] The World Bank secretly agreed: "It is our judgment that the . . . project will in fact provide housing and a level of services not affordable by slum dwellers or squatters, but we have not expounded this view fully to the government."[41]

Imelda Marcos' approach to mass housing later evolved into a program with a typical acronym, BLISS, or *Bagong Lipunan* (New Society) Sites and Services Program. BLISS envisioned the development of settlements characterized by mixed income levels, an "emphasis on employment," and a "degree of self-sufficiency." In practice, however, BLISS settlements turned out to be copies of the showcase *Kapitbahayan* project with its heavy middle-class bias. In confidential documents, the World Bank made short shrift of Imelda's claims that BLISS projects were directed at the poor:

> The Metro Manila BLISS presently consists of four-story walk-up apartments costing P75-90,000 per unit excluding land and infrastructure and affordable to low-income families only on the basis of substantial subsidies. Based on the MMA [Metropolitan Manila Area] income distribution . . . the high investment cost and considerable cross-subsidy required would rule out this approach to providing shelter for lower income groups on an extensive scale.[42]

Slum Upgrading: The World Bank's Alternative

To both relocation and Imelda's expensive housing projects, the World Bank counterposed a strategy of "slum-upgrading *in situ*." Slum upgrading was promoted as a novel approach to mass housing that consisted of "reblocking" or physically regularizing squatters' residential sites, providing basic housing infrastructure and access to water and electricity, then renting or selling the sites to the beneficiaries. What the Bank did not mention in its propaganda was that it had pirated the approach from ZOTO-Ugnayan, which had drawn up a similar alternative to the government's relocation plans in the early 1970's.

As formulated by the people of Tondo, slum upgrading was a more humanitarian approach than relocation. As reformulated by the World Bank, however, humanitarian rhetoric coexisted with hard capitalist economics. On the one hand, the Bank claimed that slum-upgrading projects were directed at "very poor people";[43] on the other hand, they were economically predicated on "recovery of full costs from the beneficiaries . . . ."[44] This was a major contradiction but it was something the Bank confidently ignored in the mid-1970's as it sought to persuade the Marcos regime to adopt slum upgrading as its general approach to mass housing.

The government, however, did not readily accept the Bank's prescription because as one memo put it, it involved "a radical departure from existing practices."[45] What finally changed the regime's mind was a series of mass actions staged by ZOTO-Ugnayan challenging the relocation strategy.[46] But although it was accepted by technocrats close to the Bank, such as Alejandro Melchor, Marcos' executive secretary,[47] the new approach was viewed with suspicion by Melchor's archenemy, Imelda Marcos. This conflict between Bank-backed technocrats and Imelda precipitated a division in the government's housing program. Imelda eventually created her own fiefdom, the Ministry of Human Settlements, which carried out showcase middle-class-oriented projects, while the Bank virtually fathered the National Housing Authority (NHA). When, under Bank pressure, the NHA was founded by merging a number of existing government housing agencies in the summer of 1975, a World Bank mission sighed, "The creation of the NHA was a long overdue and welcome move. . . ."[48]

In an attempt to shut Imelda out of the NHA, the Bank's almost full control over the agency was written into the terms of the contract of the First Urban Project, the upgrading of the Tondo Foreshore area. Reading the covenant, it is difficult to believe that the Bank regarded the agency as part of a sovereign government. Thus, Article IV, Section 1 reads: "The Borrower [the government] shall cause NHA at all times to carry on its operations, manage its affairs, plan its future development and maintain its organization and its financial position all in accordance with appropriate town planning and financial and administrative practices and under the supervision of experienced and competent management."[49] Section 2 is even more specific in asserting the Bank's authority: "The Borrower shall cause NHA: (i) to maintain in employment on a full-time basis: a deputy to the general manager, an officer responsible for financial planning, an officer responsible for general administration and an officer responsible for project development . . . (ii) to afford the Bank a reasonable opportunity to comment on the qualifications and experience of the candidates before making any designation to such positions except that of officer responsible for financial matters. . . ."[50]

With its chosen instrument securely under the command of a military technocrat, Gen. Gaudencio Tobias, the World Bank went to work on Tondo, the Bank's first urban-upgrading effort in the Third World. As with so many of its other projects, the Philippines was to serve as guinea pig.

The Tondo Fiasco

The Relocation Question. "Upgrading is accomplished with an absolute minimum of relocation," asserts a Bank policy paper by Edward Jaycox, former director of the Bank's Urban Projects Department.[51]

In practice, however, The Tondo project directly contradicted this policy: this model project involved the relocation of about 4,500 squatter families[52] to provide space for the expansion of international port facilities servicing foreign multinational firms. The Bank claimed that it was not encouraging displacement because it was not financing the international port expansion,[53] which was being partly funded by the West German government. Such denials were unconvincing, however, since the government had always seen squatter relocation and port expansion as two components of the general redevelopment plan for the Tondo Foreshore area.

Of the 4,500 families to be relocated, 2,000 were to be provided sites in the adjoining area of Dagat-Dagatan. Those who moved into the Foreshore *after* the project began in 1976, estimated at 2,500 families by 1980, faced relocation to the distant site of Dasmarinas, Cavite.[54] Those not targeted for relocation, about 160,000 persons, were supposed to benefit directly from the "reblocking" and upgrading of their residential sites and access to newly provided water, electricity, and health services.

Pricing Out the Poor. Relocating thousands of individuals constituted a major political and logistical problem. Equally formidable was the task of convincing the remaining residents of Tondo to pay rent for sites they had occupied for years. "Many Tondo residents feel very strongly about the question of land ownership and tenure," warned one Bank memo. The Tondo Foreshore area "is mostly inhabited by squatters, who, after years of residence feel entitled to full legal ownership at a nominal price compared with the current market value of the land."[55] In fact, residents had already been given the *legal right* to purchase their sites by legislative acts passed in 1956 under the premartial law Republic. Republic Act 1597, later amended to Republic Act 2438, for instance, "provided for the subdivision and sale of part of the Tondo Foreshore area at P5 per square meter, a fraction of the current market value."[56]

For the Bank, this earlier legislation smacked of a "giveaway," and that grated against its nature as a bank. A Bank mission in the summer of 1975 therefore proposed: "Due to past governmental promises and conflicting legislation on the subject of land tenure in the Tondo area, a Presidential Decree apparently will be required to implement any proposal."[57] In November, following the Bank's recommendation, the Government issued Presidential Decree 1314 repealing the premartial law acts and requiring residents to lease their sites from the NHA under 25-year leases at the rate of $6.40 per month for a 48-square-meter plot. Those who wished to buy their lots could do so only after five years of leasehold, when the sites would be sold at their market value at the time of purchase.[58]

The presidential decree provoked angry resistance in the community. ZOTO denounced the arbitrary revocation of the previous laws and asserted that the proposed rental rates would not be affordable to most Tondo residents. A West German government mission investigating the possibility of bilateral aid to the project in 1979 bluntly contradicted the World Bank's claim that rental rates could be afforded by 75 percent of Tondo residents. According to the mission report, authored by urban expert Dieter Oberndorfer, the actual figure was much lower, around 30 percent:

> Taking into account that according to official statistics 38 percent of the Tondo Foreshore population lives below the "nonstarvation" level . . . it seems highly improbable that this 38 pecent of the population can pay the rents foreseen by the NHA. The number of households which cannot afford the rental to be paid after the reblocking has been completed must be even much higher. Looking at the data available on income distribution . . . only 30-40 percent of the squatter households *can afford* to

> pay regularly the rents foreseen under PD 1314; this means that 60 to 70 percent cannot pay the rentals.[59]

The provision in the presidential decree requiring the eviction of any resident who was in arrears of three months rent was especially onerous, the report added, since "About two-thirds of the households have highly irregular sources of income: as a result they will have great difficulties to pay their rent *regularly* on a monthly basis as required in PD 1314 . . . ."[60]

Confronted with the detailed German critique, the Bank's Urban Division Chief Anthony Churchill was forced to admit that "Survey data on income are notoriously poor whenever squatters are interviewed about their monthly earnings."[61] But Churchill made an even more damaging concession: "The government's provision of shelter for the urban poor with which the World Bank has been associated benefited fewer people than ultimately need assistance, and cannot necessarily benefit the very poorest segments of society."[62]

Nonetheless, cost recovery from beneficiaries had to be maintained as a principle since, Churchill argued:

> A policy of housing subsidy for the poor which does not contain a repayment element, requiring comparable repayments among residents of a given new or upgraded settlement would, we believe, eventually be unworkable and socially deceptive in the communities to which assistance is directed.[63]

In short, housing would only be provided to those who could afford it. Despite their differences in approach, there was a meeting of minds at this basic philosophical level between the World Bank and Imelda Marcos.

A middle-level Urban Division official with considerable experience in upgrading projects in Asia, Africa, and Latin America expressed the proposition more candidly than Churchill: "The Bank is a bank, so the emphasis on cost recovery. But generally, our experience has been that the poverty focus and cost-recovery components of Bank projects contradict each other. Personally, I would be for straight subsidization of upgrading projects."[64]

In many ways, he continued, basic affordability is not the issue. "It's simply difficult to demand rent from people who're not used to paying rent for their sites. When the Bank comes in with an SIR [Slum Improvement and Resettlement program], what you get is a 'Thank you effect.' But it'll be difficult to convince them to pay for water services and other improvements because they have other priorities. They'd rather spend on better food than rent. In Tondo and other places, we've constantly come up against the reality that poor people and the Bank have different priorities."[65]

Denying Democracy. The "affordability" question was not, however, the only one that incensed Tondo residents. The slum dwellers were irate about the way they were excluded from making decisions about their homes and lives. While the urban projects policy paper stated that in upgrading projects, it is "essential that they [the beneficiaries] participate in the decisions in planning and implementing the project,"[66] the Tondo project was marked by a high degree of authoritarianism in both planning and implementation.

The West German mission, in a blistering assessment, concluded, "One of the causes of the slow progress of upgrading . . . has also been the lack or almost total absence of genuine cooperation and communication between the implementing authorities and the squatters." Key in the World Bank's plan to get the community "involved" were the government's *barangay*, or ward leaders. The Germans, however, found that *barangay* leaders:

> were not very effective in their official role as a communication agency for informing the population on the overall planning and implementation procedures of NHA and vice versa informing NHA on local conditions, basic needs, and aspirations of the people . . . [A]bout 50 percent of the *barangay* officials did not even know the existence of three possible different options for reblocking despite . . . the fact that all *barangay* officials were informed by sheets handed out to them by the NHA. These sheets contained all the relevant information on reblocking and explained the possible three options. The ignorance of the *barangay* officials can only be explained by a high degree of carelessness for the lot of the people affected by the various upgrading measures. Other studies show that the *barangay* officials consider themselves to be implementing agents of the authorities and only to a very limited degree as representatives of the people.[67]

In his confidential response, Urban Division chief Churchill admitted that "many *barangay* chairmen were confused in the beginning stage of the project and in some cases pushed more expensive options over ones cheaper to *barangay* residents."[68]

But expecting the Bank to promote democracy was perhaps asking for the impossible as the middle-level urban division officer cited earlier conceded: "Tondo reflected a more general problem." He continued,

> Except in one-party states like Zambia, where the government has some grassroots organization, we haven't been successful in generating community participation. It's just something we're not structured to do. We've even tried working through voluntary organizations. We even tried to get a religious group involved in El Salvador, but they hesitated to work with us.[69]

The people of Tondo themselves had no illusions. The government, they knew, wanted to shut out community groups like ZOTO from the decision-making process. As a 1977 Bank assessment confirmed: "The issue [of community participation] is made more difficult because the NHA considers ZOTO/Ugnayan to be antigovernment and does not want to enhance their credibility in the community."[70] They also knew that, though it might be more liberal than the regime, the Bank itself was an authoritarian institution that was fundamentally unsympathetic to democratic control.

"The War of the Flea". The regime's principal method of excluding critical voices from decision making was the periodic repression of ZOTO-Ugnayan and its sympathizers. At a "People's Conference" called to air popular grievances about the Tondo project in 1976, 7,000 residents were arrested. ZOTO leaders were periodically driven underground. Many, unable to escape the clutches of the authorities, were subjected to torture. One of the unlucky ones, a frail woman in her forties, told a human rights investigating mission of "nine straight hours of interrogation and forced 'Russian roulette' after her arrest."[71]

The most notorious case of government brutality was that of popular ZOTO president Trinidad Herrera. Arrested by security forces in April 1977, Herrera was subjected to weeks of imprisonment without trial, electric shock torture, and sexual indignities, out of which she emerged "able to merely sit and stare blankly with tears rolling from her eyes."[72] Herrera's tribulations did not end with torture. To calm the international controversy created by the incident, the government staged a showcase trial for two of Herrera's military torturers. The accused were declared innocent by a military court which strongly implied that Herrera had inflicted torture marks on herself.[73]

Faced with such savage repression, in 1977 the community opposition shifted from mass protests to more indirect, but equally effective, ways of slowing down the project. Threatened by two big bureaucracies, the Bank and the regime, ZOTO-Ugnayan resorted to the time-honored tactic of divide and conquer. By demanding alternative, cheaper reblocking plans and closer community consultation at each stage of the upgrading effort, the organization was able to sow division between the hardline government authorities and the more liberal Bank staff.

The consternation of the Bank over the methods of ZOTO-Ugnayan is evident in a confidential Bank memorandum. On the one hand, it asserts that "as far as Bank staff are concerned, relations with all community groups, including ZOTO-Ugnayan, have been good; during one of the missions, ZOTO even referred to the Bank as its 'hero.' "[74] On the other hand, the Bank was worried that "the exact position toward the Project of some of the more radical groups within the area, such as ZOTO-Ugnayan, is unclear at this time. They seem to be supportive when Bank missions discuss the project with them but on other occasions they are alleged . . . to be lobbying against the project."[75]

The "War of the Flea," as the Vietnamese would call it, succeeded to some degree. A government threat to unilaterally set the price of rent, for instance, was stopped when fishermen used their boats to "blockade" the waterfront entrance of the presidential palace on the Pasig River.[76] Indeed, the community prevented a definitive setting of rent for the upgraded sites. Reblocking, checked by close community surveillance, became what the Bank described as a "time-consuming process."[77] As of late 1979—more than four years after the launching of the Tondo project—only 25 percent of the reblocking was complete.[78] A World Bank mission registered its frustration that for most of that year, "no significant progress has been achieved."[79] Moreover, "practically all the contracts under the project have had serious time overruns."[80] In August 1980, another Bank mission gloomily projected that the conclusion of the project would have to be set back about a year and a half, from March 1981 to September 1982.[81]

The vicissitudes of the project sparked sharp internal conflicts within the Bank. Gregory Votaw, director of East Asia and Pacific programs at the Bank, was fired by McNamara in 1977 under pressure from the Marcos government.

Regime officials were enraged by Votaw's meeting with representatives of ZOTO-Ugnayan during the IMF-World Bank conference in Manila in October 1976.[82] The Bank's urban division began to divide into those "who felt we're in a hell of a mess here and wanted to withdraw" and others "who admitted we made major mistakes but wanted to hang tough. They saw it as a learning experience."[83]

The World Bank and the Government have made it clear that they intend to complete the upgrading and relocation effort. As one Bank officer put it, "There was no question all along that senior management was backing those who wanted the Bank to stay in there. My own opinion is that we made mistakes, but hell, admit them and go on with the project. The alternative is the bulldozer and that's worse. Of course, there's the question of bad press. But if Tondo proved anything, it's that we can survive international headlines."[84] Thus, the slum dwellers' resistance had its limits. The most that the community has been able to accomplish is slowing down the project and softening its most repressive aspects.

Upgrading for the Upper Crust. When the project is finally completed, a new period is likely to begin in the history of the Tondo Foreshore Area: its transformation into a middle-class community. World Bank officials, in their more candid moments, now see this development as inevitable. One official of the Bank's Urban and Regional Economics Department admitted:

> In Tondo and everywhere else, in terms of accessibility, the original assumption was that all the beneficiaries were poor. But we now see that a wide range of income groups—including the top 30 percent of Manila—are among the beneficiaries. So we always find that lots of people getting the project benefits are quite wealthy.[85]

Putting the best possible interpretation on an outcome that directly contradicted the Bank's initial rhetoric, he rationalized that the presence of upper-income groups would make the Tondo Foreshore "an economically dynamic area."[86]

A foreign consultant attached to the NHA was more blunt:

> The intentions of these projects are excellent. . . . But there is no way that the lowest or marginal income groups will receive all the benefits intended. It's inevitable that the higher-income groups, though still fairly poor—higher and lower is all relative—will buy out the

> lowest once the improvements have been made. The poorest families will be unable to maintain the payments and find it profitable to sell out. The laws are set up to prevent these transfers, but laws like this are circumvented all the time. . . . I think these people will be back in the shacks in five or ten years. But the program is still a good thing. At least, it's expanding the development of needed housing.[87]

The final outcome of the World Bank's urban strategy in the Philippines is thus indistinguishable from the results of Imelda Marcos' "beautification projects": removal of the poor from the choice parts of the city. The difference lies only in the means of reaching this end: in place of the First Lady's method of coerced and immediate dislocation, the Bank offers indirect and gradual uprooting, accomplished with the indispensable assistance of the real estate market.

Urban II: More of the Same

Undeterred by the popular resistance spawned by the Tondo project, the Bank launched another urban assistance project in 1979, Urban Development II. The project had two key components. The first was the creation of 8,600 plots for squatters in the Dagat-Dagatan area adjoining the Tondo Foreshore for families displaced by the international port expansion. The second major component of Urban II was the upgrading of slums and the provision of lots to the urban poor in three other cities, Cebu, Davao, and Cagayan de Oro.

The project, the Bank once more claimed, "would be addressed to the provision of basic needs for the lowest-income families."[88] According to the Bank, 6,000 of the 8,600 lots in Dagat-Dagatan would be "targeted for families below the poverty level and would be affordable by these families,"[89] while the other 2,600 would be reserved for middle-income families. In the three other cities, "some 85 percent of families whose lots are improved and 90 percent of those receiving new lots" were regarded as being in the urban poverty group.[90]

The Disappearing Poor. But even as it made these confident assessments, the Bank was contradicting itself. The key project document admitted in a footnote that "The urban poverty figure for Manila is the subject of considerable uncertainty."[91] Indeed, another major and damaging admission is buried in the text: even the smallest lots in the

Dagat-Dagatan project would be too expensive for the poorest 10 percent of the Metro Manila population.[92]

The Bank sought to downplay this concession, saying breezily that

> most of the lowest income families in each project site are transients or families who are currently renting individual rooms from the primary occupants of the lot. While it would be impractical to provide separate lots for all such families, they would benefit substantially from improved conditions in the project areas.[93]

However, this assessment ignored the very basic economic law that with "improved conditions" would come higher rents and eviction for those who could not afford them.

Critics like the West German mission immediately took issue with the Bank's calculations. After a detailed examination of available income distribution figures, the Oberndorfer Report ripped apart the Bank's assumptions and projections. The lowest-priced 600 of the 8,600 lots, it asserted, were unaffordable not only by the poorest ten percent but by the lowest fifteen percent of the Metro Manila population.[94] Indeed, 50 percent of the lots were "definitely not destined for the urban poor," and 30 percent could be afforded only by the upper 30 percent of the population.[95] The mission acidly concluded: "It is questionable whether this group, the upper 30 percent of the Metro Manila population, should be accommodated in a so-called low-cost housing project for the urban poor, a project which will be heavily subsidized by public funds and foreign loans."[96]

The Oberndorfer Report immediately went to what it saw as the root of the problem: "It seems that the income data on Metro Manila for 1979 used by . . . the World Bank are extremely inaccurate for the lower 50 percent of the population." It added: "The source of the . . . World Bank data on the Metro Manila income distribution for 1979 could not be found"[97]—a statement that stopped just short of calling the Bank's data base fabricated.

But the German analysts were only scratching the surface. For the real lesson that the Bank had learned from the Tondo project was that cost recovery from the poor, not to say the poorest of the poor, was an impossible undertaking. *The inclusion of middle and upper-income groups as beneficiaries was the key to making the projects "viable" by the Bank's standards.* As one NHA staff member frankly admitted:

> . . . the middle income group is where we make our money. This is where we provide individual detached housing programs, joint ventures with the private sector, etc. We make money on these programs. The low-income and marginal-income projects—we don't make money here. The cost of normal government services provided here in fact are not recovered from the beneficiaries.[98]

Cultivating Anomie. The affordability issue was not, however, the aspect of Urban II that provoked the harshest comment from the Germans. They reserved this for the plan to distribute housing sites through a public lottery announced in the media. This system of selection, warned the report:

> will have high negative social side effects. . . . The urban poor will be placed in an environment in which they cannot rely on the help of friends and relatives. They will not be embedded in a familiar social fabric in which traditional norms will regulate life. Numerous examples show the disastrous social consequences of socially amorphous housing projects based on a western individualistic philosophy alien to most underdeveloped countries.[99]

The Germans failed to realize, however, that the lottery idea was not some short-sighted bureaucrat's mistake. For the Tondo project had impressed on both the regime and the Bank the consequences of a "familiar social fabric." Individualism, anomie, and social stratification had come to be regarded by these two authoritarian institutions as important weapons to be deployed in the effort to control the urban poor.

Confrontation in Cagayan de Oro

The controversy over Dagat-Dagatan was soon superseded by a more explosive situation in Cagayan de Oro, in Northern Mindanao.

Cagayan de Oro was one of the regional cities targeted for slum upgrading under Urban II. 11,000 of its 34,200 shantytown dwellers, claimed a Bank report, would benefit from improved services, while another 6,000 would get new lots.[100]

The Bank's choice of Cagayan de Oro was dictated not only by the needs of urban pacification. The agency also saw the city as an ideal future site for an export-processing zone, a tax-free haven where multinational firms could relocate to take advantage of cheap labor. The reasons given to the city by a Dutch consultant to the Bank was that it was a "typhoon-free city, with cheap electricity and cheap labor."[101] Urban II, then, was partly designed to "improve the productivity of the poor" for the benefit of prospective foreign investors.

The project began in 1979 after the Bank and the Marcos regime agreed on an arrangement whereby the local government would take major responsibility for executing the project under the supervision of NHA. The city would also pay a major portion of the cost of the project.[102]

But a major hitch developed in the Bank's scheme for Cagayan. In the local elections of January 1980, Aquilino Pimentel, Jr., was elected the city's new mayor, decisively unseating the regime's candidate. Pimentel was one of the few anti-Marcos mayors placed in office by voters in elections characterized by widespread fraud and terrorism on the part of Marcos loyalists. The new administration closely scrutinized the Bank's plan for the city. In June, the City Council passed a resolution asking NHA to relieve the city of responsibility for the project.

Fiscal Drag. Mayor Pimentel argued that a variety of factors, including inflation, had pushed the city's contribution up to $8 million. "Considering that Cagayan de Oro has an annual budget of only P30 million [$4 million]," argued Pimentel, "this constitutes a tremendous fiscal burden." The terms of the contract, said Pimentel, "are clearly onerous, especially since we have to fill other needs than paying for a project designed to benefit only a small number of residents."[103]

The city, however, had more than just fiscal considerations in mind. Pimentel maintained that the majority of the so-called beneficiaries of the new upgraded lots would end up being evicted. "Many of these poor people even now default on the P5 to P20 they pay to rent their current dwellings. How does the Bank expect them to make the P120 monthly payments to rent their upgraded sites?" He added: "In fact, a lot of these people were surprised when I told them that they were going to have to pay for their new sites. They thought they were getting it all for free."[104]

Internal Bank documents confirmed the mayor's fears. "The investment requirements of the proposed project are significant in relation to existing capital works in progress in these cities particularly in Cagayan de Oro and Davao," admitted one memo.[105] To pay for its contribution to the project, the city would have to borrow funds from the National Housing Authority, but "the present borrowing capacity in relation to existing debt in Cagayan de Oro is inadequate, under present procedures, to accommodate project requirements."[106]

Lending substance to the mayor's prediction that most of the "beneficiaries" would not be able to afford rent on their upgraded sites—and that he might be forced to evict them—was the Bank's stern warning: "The final viability of these projects will depend in part on efficient collection procedures. NHA and local governments must be prepared to enforce contract agreements with beneficiaries in cases of default."[107]

Destroying Dissent. Imposing a tremendous fiscal responsibility on the city and saddling squatters with the threat of eviction, according to Pimentel, was not the solution to the urban problem. "We have ways of doing it more cheaply," he claimed, "for instance, by giving the squatters the land."[108] Views like this, together with Pimentel's advocacy of strong environmental controls and his opposition to the plan to establish an export processing zone made him a marked man in the eyes of the government and the Bank. Thus, it was not surprising that he received a telegram from NHA chief General Guadencio Tobias warning him that he was "criminally liable, because it is a crime for government officials to encourage squatters."[109]

The city's request to withdraw from the project disturbed Bank officials, prompting a mission headed by Caroline Sewell of the East Asia urban projects division to investigate the project in the summer of 1980. The mission strongly sided with the central government in the dispute, informing Washington that Cagayan de Oro's decision to seek withdrawal "was apparently triggered by overwhelming political factors and by private parties with vested interests."[110] The substance of the City Council's position was ignored.

Fearful that Cagayan's posture might set a precedent, both the regime and the Bank resorted to threats. NHA chief General Tobias recommended expelling Pimentel from office. Carolyn Sewell warned Pimentel that unless the city fell into line, future Bank loans would be difficult to come by.[111] The conflict climaxed in July 1981: President

Marcos ousted Pimentel from office, citing the Mayor's opposition to the project as one of the reasons for his action. But the move backfired. Ten thousand citizens of Cagayan de Oro staged the biggest demonstration in the history of the city to support the Mayor they had elected to office with 75 percent of the votes cast in the 1980 elections. Marcos backed down and ordered Pimentel reinstated.[112]

Confrontation in Washington. The mayor was not intimidated. In late August 1981, he brought the fight against the World Bank project to the agency's headquarters in Washington, D.C. "Maybe the World Bank also wanted to see me ousted," Pimentel told officials at a meeting on August 30, 1981.[113] "We don't have a position on that," Steven O'Brien, head of the Philippine division, responded nervously.[114] At the same meeting, Bank officials admitted they had no updated figures on the costs and other economic impacts of the project. Even more startling was their lack of knowledge of the mayor's objections to the project. These had apparently been bottled up by the NHA and the Sewell mission.

Confronted firsthand with Pimentel's arguments, O'Brien was forced to concede:

> We embarked on something that looked quite good three or four years ago. Since then a number of things have changed, like increased costs of land and materials—all of which have produced a set of circumstances which we now have to reconsider. We should reexamine our basic assumptions and current facts for anticipating costs and benefits. If the project is too expensive, then we should scale down costs.[115]

But while O'Brien seemed willing to review the project, Inder K. Sud, urban division chief for Asia and the Pacific, resorted once more to threat: "This may have an effect on future projects for the city."[116] Pimentel replied: "We can't be quiet on this just because future projects will be threatened."[117] At a press conference following the meeting with Bank officials, Pimentel was even more defiant: "They cannot silence my opposition. If any World Bank project goes against the interests of the people of Cagayan de Oro, I will oppose it."[118]

How far Marcos and the World Bank will tolerate Pimentel's opposition remains to be seen. What has especially worried them both is the fact that the example of Tondo has evoked similar efforts to resist dictatorial authority in other cities. Pimentel was raising the same themes of inexpensive housing, humanitarian concern, and democratic control that the people of Tondo had popularized. Yet, there was also something disturbingly novel in Pimentel's opposition. While the Bank could understand opposition from the urban poor, it was quite surprised to see that a member of the traditional elite such as Pimentel would take the lead in opposing a Bank project. The confrontation in Cagayan de Oro, the Bank could not fail to see, was a manifestation of the "multiclass opposition" to the World Bank strategy that the Ascher Memorandum had warned was developing.

Full Speed Ahead

The Bank urban program in the Philippines, however, lurches on with a momentum that is seemingly impervious to the unpopularity it has elicited. The Third Urban Project, which finances upgrading in thirteen poor communities in Metro Manila, was launched in 1980. Two more big programs are scheduled to begin between 1982 and 1985. "The time is now ripe," declare Bank bureaucrats, "to expand the [Tondo] approach on a program basis to address all the large slums and squatter areas."[119] For the urban poor, this sounds like a threat, not a promise.

Conclusion

As with its rural development program, the underlying concern of the World Bank's urban development effort was the pacification of a restive population. With its emphasis on control, the Bank promoted the centralization of metropolitan power in the hands of the executive, building on the earlier efforts of agencies such as USAID.

From its pacification perspective, the Bank realized the brutal relocation efforts of the regime were counterproductive. Yet the Bank's alternative housing program, slum upgrading, suffered from a number of major contradictions. While Bank rhetoric claimed that the projects were aimed at the very poor, the Bank's principle of full cost recovery from beneficiaries effectively priced out not only the very poor but the "ordinary poor" as well. The social consequences of Bank projects, therefore, were indistinguishable from those associated with the First Lady's middle-class-oriented housing schemes. To explain results strikingly different from the Bank's initial rhetoric, technocrats quietly dropped claims about benefiting the very poor and began to articulate the concept of building "economically dynamic areas" to justify the inclusion of upper-income groups as beneficiaries of slum-upgrading schemes.

While Bank rhetoric paid lip service to democratic participation in project decisions, the upgrading efforts were actually implemented in a highly authoritarian fashion by government bureaucrats. Though it tried to project a more liberal image than the regime's, the Bank was itself a highly authoritarian institution that recoiled against democratic controls on its projects. This institutional preference for authoritarian control was clearly revealed when the Bank actively joined the regime in a highly dictatorial effort to destroy the opposition to the upgrading scheme in Cagayan de Oro.

In almost every instance, then, the Bank's pacification objective was contradicted by its dogmatic adherence to cost recovery and other principles of capitalist finance and by its distaste for democratic decision making. The result was that, by the end of the 1970's, the Bank was inexorably associated with the government in the popular mind and multiclass urban opposition had been forged in opposition to its program.

CHAPTER FIVE

Export-Oriented Industrialization: The Short-Lived Illusion

Perhaps the key reason the World Bank sanctioned the imposition of martial law in 1972 was the unprecedented opportunity it created to effect fundamental changes in Philippine trade and industrial policies along lines prescribed by the Bank. Martial law, in the view of one secret Bank assessment, "provided the government with almost absolute power in the field of economic management,"[1] and, thus, would clear away the political obstacles to the implementation of a new strategy hailed by the Bank as "the second phase of Philippine industrialization."

Prodded by the Bank, the IMF and international business interests, the martial law regime gradually instituted a new set of fiscal, trade, and financial reform measures aimed at fostering the growth of "export-oriented industrialization" (EOI). The new formula represented a dramatic departure from the program of "import-substitution industrialization" (ISI) promoted by the government during previous decades, by redirecting the focus of Philippine industrial production away from a limited domestic market toward a seemingly limitless global market.

The Bank's EOI prescription was, however, hardly unique to the Philippines. Indeed, its application in the Philippines and in many other Third World countries during the 70's was most often justified by its earlier "successes" in South Korea, Brazil, and Taiwan. As the documentation in this and the two following chapters reveals, the successful replication of the EOI formula in the Philippines was to be completely undermined by several flaws in the economic and political assumptions built into the plans of its promoters. Indeed, by the time the Marcos regime established the foundation of the Philippine "export platform," the global economic conditions essential to its success had ceased to exist.

The first part of this chapter examines the dynamics of the struggle which erupted around the drive of the multilateral agencies and foreign business to dismantle the import-substitution structure in the 1960's, prior to the imposition of martial law. The focus of the second part is the World Bank-Marcos effort to erect the scaffolding for export-oriented industrialization in the early and mid-1970's. The final section analyzes the internal and external contradictions which torpedoed the strategy at the end of the decade.

Import Substitution and the Debate on Philippine Industrialization

From the late 1940's to the early 1960's, the Philippines experienced what many economists now regard as the "golden age of manufacturing." In response to a drain of foreign exchange, the Philippine government instituted import and foreign exchange controls that discriminated against "nonessential" manufactured imports. These controls effectively undermined the free trade regime that was supposed to prevail between the U.S. and the Philippines under the Bell Trade Act, a law imposed on a recalcitrant Philippine Republic at the time of independence in 1946.

More importantly, the import and exchange controls spawned, almost by accident, a vibrant consumer goods industry that filled the demand for scarce light-manufactured imports, such as processed food, textiles, and shoes. Supplemented by a tariff system in 1957, the controls spurred a rate of industrial growth that averaged 12 percent annually between 1950 and 1957. By 1960, almost 20 percent of the country's net national product originated in manufacturing.[2] The controls also created a national manufacturing elite with a vital stake in maintaining the protected market. This pattern of "industrialization by accident" was similar to the experience of Latin American countries, where industrial sectors developed to make up for the shortfall in imports triggered by the Great Depression and the Second World War.

By the 60's however, Philippine industrial growth based on "import substitution" was stagnating. Declining growth combined with the capital-intensive character of much of the manufacturing sector resulted in a leveling off of manufacturing employment. The number of people employed in manufacturing in 1969—1.3 million—was practically the same as in 1963.[3] The serious implications of this decline sparked a heated debate over the future of Philippine industrial policies, with left and right unable to agree on anything except that import-substitution industrialization was in crisis.

The Nationalist Critique. The left and nationalist groups, inspired by the towering figure of the late Senator Claro M. Recto, put forward a critique which evolved along the following lines:

1. Import substitution might have created a national entrepreneurial elite, but it was a very fragile one. Lacking expertise and access to advanced technology, many Philippine industrialists were shunted onto the route of manufacturing U.S. brand-name commodities under stringent royalty agreements with U.S. firms. Indeed, some entered outright into joint ventures with foreign investors.[4]

2. The fragility of the local industrial elite was paralleled by the weakness of the manufacturing sector. For the most part, Philippine firms produced light manufactures, such as shoes, textiles, and processed foods, and finished consumer goods. The intermediate-goods sector was slight, and a capital-goods industry was nonexistent. The fundamental reason for the failure of "backward linkages" (i.e., basic industries which provide the necessary inputs to the consumer goods industry) to develop was the very limited size of the internal market. And the market was limited because of a highly skewed distribution of income. With a mere five percent of the population controlling as much as 25 percent of the national income in 1970, income inequality in the Philippines was the worst in Southeast Asia.[5]

3. The failure to develop industrial sectors producing intermediate goods, capital goods, and industrial raw materials pushed the manufacturing sector to ever-growing dependence on imports of these inputs. Thus ISI aggravated the very condition that import quotas and exchange controls had initially set out to remedy: the hemorrhage of foreign exchange for imports. While exports and imports were roughly in balance in 1960, the trade deficit soared to $257 million in 1969. The key items widening the deficit were machinery and vehicle imports, the value of which rose by over 100 percent from 1960 to 1969.[6]

4. Import-substitution industrialization, stressed the nationalists, was *not* nationalist industrialization. The failure to accompany protectionist measures with nationalist controls on investment encouraged many U.S. firms, in particular food processors such as Procter and Gamble and pharmaceutical manufacturers such as Mead Johnson, to set up shop in the country. By doing so, they were also protected by import controls and tariffs from their U.S. and international competitors. By the late 60's, U.S. firms had a strong position in the manufacturing sector, with assets totaling at least $520 million.[7] Total U.S. investment in the country, including that of oil, agribusiness, and mineral-extraction enterprises, was estimated to be between $1.5 and $2 billion. Indeed, total U.S. investment in the Philippines accounted for about 60 percent of all U.S. investment in Southeast Asia.[8]

From the nationalist perspective, such a dominant U.S. presence was of dubious value, since instead of bringing in capital, U.S. corporations were in fact pumping it out. A landmark study of 108 U.S. firms, for instance, revealed that 84 percent of the capital they invested in the country in the period 1956-65 was raised from domestic sources, and only 16 percent—including reinvested profits made in the Philippines—came from the U.S.[9] Moreover, most U.S. industrial establishments in the Philippines did not contribute to genuine industrialization because they amounted to no more than assembly plants for commodities whose key inputs were produced elsewhere in the network of the global corporation.[10]

This diagnosis of the roots of industrial stagnation also suggested the cure: "nationalist industrialization." This prescription, which came to be most clearly articulated by groups on the left of the nationalist coalition, consisted of: tighter controls on foreign investment, including nationalization; stronger protection for Filipino-owned industries; the extension of ISI to the intermediate and capital-goods sectors; and massive income redistribution—through land reform and other egalitarian measures—to create a market big enough for sustained industrial growth.[11]

The View From the Right. ISI also came under attack from the right—from business ideologues of the American Chamber of Commerce, conservative neoclassical economists holding court at the elite Jesuit-run Ateneo de Manila

University, and technocrats trained in U.S. Ivy League schools. From the conservative perspective, the protectionism that made ISI possible also encouraged "inefficiency" in industry and imposed costs on Filipino consumers by depriving them of access to cheaper and better foreign commodities. Moreover, protectionism was regarded as the stalking horse of nationalist restrictions on foreign investment, which they considered the "strategic factor" in industrial development.

"Liberalization" became the right's response to the left's call for nationalist industrialization. Liberalization meant, first and foremost, the dismantling of the protectionist barriers to imports. It also signified a strong effort to attract foreign investment. As the vice president of the Philippine-American Chamber of Commerce put it: "What is needed for a long-term solution is to speed up industrialization by increasing the inflow of foreign capital. This can come about only if the Filipinos will intensify their efforts to attract capital."[12]

Not surprisingly, all this came out of the ordinary textbook of neoclassical economics. But while the right was short on substance, it was long on power, representing as it did the interests of U.S. capital and the U.S. state.

Caught between these divergent options advocated by left and right was the economically fragile but politically influential group of national entrepreneurs spawned by ISI. Attracted by the protectionist elements of the nationalist program, they felt, at the same time, threatened by the populist calls for radical income redistribution. But as foreign capital, through its local allies in the Philippine ruling elite, launched its determined effort to liberalize the economy, the national industrialists were forced to edge closer and closer to the nationalist alternative.

Dismantling the ISI Structure: Round 1

The Philippines got a taste of just how devastating the deceptively named program of liberalization could be in 1962. Pressured by U.S. investors seeking freer repatriation of their profits and U.S. exporters frustrated by protectionist obstacles, the U.S. government forced President Diosdado Macapagal to abolish import and exchange controls.[13]

To accomplish this, the U.S. used the good offices of the World Bank and the IMF. By the early 60's, the IMF had become the preferred instrument to impose liberalization in a neocolonial international order. The rationale for this was articulated at a high-level roundtable of U.S. officials and businessmen:

> As the Filipinos deal more with international organizations like the IMF, World Bank and the Asian Development Bank (ADB), they will learn to address economic problems more realistically and accept the contraints on economic behavior that are required for participation in the international economic community.[14]

To offset the flood of foreign exchange expected to leave the country in the form of repatriated profits and investments, the IMF forced the devaluation of the peso by almost 100 percent relative to the dollar. Devaluation was based on the expectation that "cheapening" Philippine agricultural and raw material exports in the international sector would increase the volume of exports and foreign exchange earnings from these commodities.

The impact on the country was severe. Between 1962 and 1964, Philippine workers saw their real wages decline by 10 percent.[15] While big agricultural exporters, such as the sugar landlords, reaped windfall profits from devaluation, the nascent Filipino entrepreneurial class found itself in a very precarious position, facing a 100% increase in the peso cost of their imported inputs and repayments on foreign loans.[16] An estimated 1,500 Filipino entrepreneurs were driven into bankruptcy.[17] Many of those who survived were forced into joint ventures with foreign capital.[18] The inevitable economic slowdown helped depress the growth of manufacturing from the 11-12 percent average annual growth of the 1950–57 period to a mere 5 percent annually throughout the 60's.[19]

Nonetheless, the tariff structure on Philippine imports, first erected in 1957 and revised at the time of decontrol, continued to provide a degree of protection to import-substitution businesses—a degree that was clearly unacceptable to the World Bank and the IMF. This dissatisfaction was later reflected in an industrial policy paper that complained: "Although the strict import restrictions prevailing in the 1950's were gradually decontrolled in the early 1960's, they were replaced by a highly protected tariff system . . . policy reform in the 1960's did not alter the bias of the incentive system in favor of import substitution."[20] Indeed, the bitter events of 1962 turned out to be merely the first salvo fired by the IMF-World Bank conglomerate in the cause of liberalization.

The Genesis of the EOI Model

By the late 60's, pressure from the World Bank and the IMF to liberalize was again mounting. This time, however, the call for liberalization was coupled with the promotion of an alternative to inner-directed nationalist industrialization: "exported-oriented industrialization."

The inspiration for the new model for Third World development that congealed Bank doctrine in the 70's was provided by Brazil and South Korea. The cutting edge of the "Brazilian Miracle" in the late 60's was an almost sevenfold increase in exports of manufactured goods, mainly to advanced industrial countries, between 1968 and 1973. At the center of the export drive were labor-intensive commodities such as shoes, Brazil's most spectacular export, which went from $2 million to $200 million in only seven years.[21]

The "South Korean Miracle" was equally impressive. As one World Bank consultant associated with this "miracle" glowingly described it, "With real GNP rising about 10 percent a year in the one-and-a-half decades following the policy reform of the early sixties, [South] Korea was one of the star performers of the world economy. Rapid economic growth was achieved under an export-oriented strategy that led to increases in the value of exports of goods and services at approximately 27 percent a year."[22]

Fixated on growth rates, World Bank planners tended to downplay the institutions that were a prerequisite for the "successes" in South Korea and Brazil: the systematic depression of wages and a military state dedicated to, among other things, disciplining labor. The underside of the Brazilian miracle was revealed in the national income accounts: while the real income of the lowest 40 percent of the population remained practically stagnant between 1960 and 1970, that of the top 5 percent increased by over 80 percent. Moreover, the share in the national income of 95 percent of the population declined from 73 percent to 64 percent.[23]

But herein lay the beauty of export-oriented industrialization to World Bank planners: industrial growth could be divorced from significant expansion of domestic markets since production was essentially geared toward the markets of advanced industrial countries. The specter of underconsumption that had appeared to Keynesian technocrats as an insurmountable barrier to economic development seemed to be exorcised. Indeed, in such a scheme, a significant expansion of internal demand would be a *negative* signal, reflecting significant rises in real wages that might make a country's exports less competitive in world markets and discourage foreign investors. For technocrats, restricting wages was not difficult to rationalize: someone, after all, had to pay the costs of industrial development.

For Third World technocrats, EOI's attractiveness resided in the fact that it allowed them to espouse rapid domestic industrialization—long the province of nationalists—while at the same time advocating liberalization and hospitality to foreign investors. For liberals in international development agencies, EOI also provided a sense of liberation from traditional neoclassical development theory and policy, which had relegated Third World economies to the roles of hewers of wood and drawers of water—that is, raw material and agricultural exporters—with the rationale that it was to their "comparative advantage" to remain such. Industrial growth for the Third World could now be promoted in a way that did not disturb but, in fact, complemented the prevailing international economic power structure. For, after all, those who stood to gain the most from cheaper light manufactured exports from the Third World were the advanced countries, and the main beneficiaries of cheap Third World labor were Western and Japanese multinational firms.

The shift from a conservative, defensive perspective on Third World industrialization to a liberal, activist one was evident in the World Bank. There Robert McNamara enshrined EOI as doctrine in the early 70's: ". . . special efforts must be made in many countries to turn their manufacturing enterprises away from the relatively small markets associated with import substitution toward the much larger opportunities flowing from export promotion."[24]

EOI in the Philippines: The Beginnings

When Marcos became president in 1966, he recruited from the private sector a team of high-powered technocrats trained in U.S. business schools and economics departments to set up the institutional framework of EOI in the Philippines.

Two major pieces of legislation, the Investment Incentives Act of 1967 and the Export Incentives Act of 1970, were pushed through the Philippine Congress as a preliminary attempt to "rationalize" investment. These laws represented a delicate balancing act: while "crowded" consumer goods industries were "reserved" for Filipinos, attractive incentives for export manufacture and for intermediate and capital-goods production were provided for foreign investors.

In 1969, legislation was passed creating the "Export Processing Zone" (EPZ) in Mariveles, Bataan across the Bay from Manila. The EPZ was modeled on the highly successful Kaohsiung "export platform" that opened in Taiwan in 1966. Kaohsiung had been promoted as a "package" combining a concentration of cheap labor, duty-free raw material and intermediate goods imports, corporate tax holidays, accelerated depreciation rates on fixed assets, permanently subsidized infrastructure, and ready-made buildings for rent or purchase.[25] Multinational firms were attracted to Kaohsiung because it "substantially facilitated (and thus lowered the cost of) obtaining all the technical and fiscal benefits required to promote the reexport of intermediate goods after the addition of value in the form of (mainly) unskilled labor."[26] This important advantage was enhanced by the fact that many industrialized nations, including the United States, did not impose tariffs upon reentry of processed intermediate goods except for the value-added portion of the product.[27] Even with tariffs on the value-added component, multinationals still came out farther ahead with Third World labor than if they relied on the assembly of finished products by high-cost domestic labor.

But Marcos' technocrats did more than legislate incentives for export production and establish a Philippine Kaohsiung. They spearheaded a propaganda offensive for the program of export-led industrialization, liberalization, and foreign investment. Leading the offensive was Gerardo Sicat, head of the National Economic Council and trained at the Massachusetts Institute of Technology. Sicat's basic posture was perhaps best captured in his assertion that "at this stage of development, it doesn't concern Filipinos who controls the resources and economy of our country."[28] Sicat's *bete noire* was the class of national industrialists whom he attacked as a group "who essentially considered it their vested right to exploit the domestic market."[29] Sicat also downgraded what he called "modern labor laws" and called for the "liberalization"—i.e. lowering—of the minimum wage.[30]

Dismantling ISI: Round Two

The IMF and the World Bank, however, were not content to leave the conflict between EOI and ISI at the level of debate. In early 1970, they carried out another drastic intervention in the direction of liberalization. This time, the two agencies took advantage of the fact that Marcos had dried up the government's foreign exchange reserves in his successful attempt to buy his second presidential election victory in 1969. Left without resources to cover the mounting trade deficit and service external debt, Marcos desperately turned to the IMF and the World Bank. He knew very well what they wanted—devaluation—and what this would mean. Earlier, during his campaign, he had promised that "we have no intention of devaluing the peso because we would be hitting our low-income groups, especially daily wage earners and employees with monthly salaries."[31]

Campaign promises notwithstanding, Marcos received an IMF standby loan of $37 million and the IMF and the World Bank got their more than 60% devaluation of the peso. The move jacked up the inflation rate from 1.3 percent in 1969 to 14.8 percent in 1970 and, as the World Bank admitted, fostered "a slower growth of GNP" throughout the early 70's.[32] Later, a World Bank mission admitted that the devaluation was the single most important factor responsible for what it termed a "startling" 50 percent decline in the real wages of workers between 1960 and 1975.[33]

As in 1962, the devaluation wreaked havoc on Filipino entrepreneurs. They were suddenly faced with a 31.4 percent rise in the peso price of their imports and a more than 50 percent rise in the cost of repaying short-term foreign loans.[34] As Filipino businessmen teetered on the brink or fell into the abyss of bankruptcy, the World Bank congratulated Marcos for his "commendable display of political courage."[35]

The *quid pro quo* for the IMF loan, however, went beyond devaluation. A Consultative Group of "interested nations and agencies" was created, ostensibly to monitor the external position of the economy as well as coordinate aid programs for the Philippines. The actual function of this body, however, went beyond mere monitoring and aid coordination according to a U.S. Treasury Department report: ". . . the [World] Bank has sought to influence borrowers' policies indirectly through the mechanism of intergovernmental Consultative Groups on particular borrowing countries. Through these groups, the Bank attempts to rally other donors around its recommendations."[36]

The events of 1970, however, proved to be but a prelude to an even more dramatic clash between U.S.-backed technocrats and the nationalists. For the savage punch failed to knock down the protectionist system and ideology. Indeed, the World Bank complained that in the early 70's, the economy continued to be marked by "heavily protected and inefficient manufacturing industries, controlled by politically well-connected Filipinos, which were gradually increasing in importance despite their inefficiency and the existing [sic] of some foreign competition."[37] But concern for inefficiency was but a cloak for a more profound fear which was expressed by a panel of high U.S. government and business officials assembled by Georgetown University's Center for Strategic and International Studies (CSIS) in 1971:

> As Filipino enterprises have grown and moved into new activities, Filipinos and American businessmen have become competitive and the former have coalesced into interest groups—importers, manufacturers, exporters, bankers and so forth—and have taken political action to minimize the threat of American competition. As the most influential political group motivated to limit access to Philippine resources and markets, they have provided a respectable nucleus around which diverse nationalist elements have coalesced to maintain pressures on Philippine policy in the [U.S.-R.P.] special relationship.[38]

Continued protectionism thus went hand in hand with what the World Bank saw as a "growing nationalist movement, articulated in Congress and the universities . . . focused on the issue of special rights of U.S.-owned property and business in the Laurel-Langley Agreement due to expire in mid-1974."[39] Alarmed, the World Bank advised Marcos to stiffen up and warned him against "legislative or administrative action which would unduly restrict the scope for foreign investment in the country."[40]

The Constitutional Convention called in 1970 to rewrite the basic law of the land provided a new forum for voices advocating nationalist development. Alarm spread in foreign business and technocrat circles that nationalists, relying on constitutional democratic processes, were getting the upper hand. The Georgetown roundtable of high government and business personalities warned: ". . .

the nationalist measures approved [by the Constitutional Convention] almost certainly will constrict the formal conditions of access by Americans and their enterprises to Philippine resources and markets."[41] Board of Investment (BOI) Chairman Vicente Paterno, a close associate of the World Bank, concurred:

> Although in the past there have been expressions of the desire to attract foreign investments into the Philippine economy, they were negated by other statements in Congress and in the Constitutional Convention proposing to make changes in the law of the land to impose further restrictions on foreign investment.[42]

Reading the signs of the times, foreign investors began taking their capital out of the country; capital inflow into the country between 1970 and 1973 was negative to the tune of $55 million.[43]

Dissent by representatives of the national industrialists within the formal institutions of the state was paralleled by a confrontation in the streets led by the nationalist left. A dangerous political convergence was occurring warned the high-level Georgetown panel in 1971:

> . . . the fundamental divergence between the interests of entrepreneurial elements seeking to reserve economic functions and resources to Filipinos recruited from the traditional elites, and the objectives of the ideological nationalists and their leftist fellow travelers, have been bridged by their shared interest in reducing the American economic presence in the Philippines."[44]

Demonstrations by peasants, students, and workers were escalating toward what Philippine and World Bank authorities considered dangerous levels. The stress felt by the World Bank was later expressed in its description of the period as "a time of deteriorating law and order, increasing polarization between opposing political tendencies, and an increasingly violent confrontation between the Government and its massed opponents in the streets."[45]

This dual pressure from national entrepreneurs in Congress and the Constitutional Convention on the one hand, and from the nationalist left in the streets on the other, forced the normally conservative Supreme Court to issue a number of controversial and far-reaching rulings in 1972. One, the "Quasha Decision," decreed that lands acquired by Americans since 1946 had been acquired illegally and were subject to forced sale or confiscation on or before 1974 when parity rights would come to an end. Another Supreme Court ruling banned foreigners from holding executive jobs in industries reserved for Filipinos.

It was in such a climate of sharpening struggle between the nationalist left and the U.S. and World Bank-backed Marcos regime that martial law was declared on September 22, 1972.

Erecting the Export Platform

Martial law provided the political framework necessary for the consolidation of export-oriented industrialization as the strategy for Philippine industrial development. This was asserted bluntly by Board of Investments Chairman Vicente Paterno: "The logic of foreign investment to participate in the generation of labor-manufactured exports is clear and incontrovertible, but the country needed martial law to attract such investment."[46]

The Bank, for its part, welcomed the fact that "the abolition of Congress provided the government with almost absolute power in the field of economic development."[47] In its first official statement after the declaration of martial law, the World Bank-led Consultative Group asserted: "The Group welcomed the measures taken by the Philippine government to improve the climate for foreign private investment. These measures are expected to enlarge the contribution of private capital to Philippine development."[48]

Export-led industrialization under the aegis of foreign capital, the World Bank told the government, was "a fundamental change seen as necessary during the next decade. . . ."[49] Consolidating the strategy required two sweeping alterations. The first was the complete dismantling of the ISI structure. As the World Bank bluntly told the government, "for the future, it should be the government's policy to gradually remove the quantitative restrictions [on imports], to restructure and lower tariff levels, and to delete the protective element from other fiscal and other monetary policies."[50] The second key thrust of the strategy was the establishment of a set of incentives that would lure foreign investors and local capitalists to export manufacture. Assessing the situation a decade later, the World Bank would grade the Marcos government as falling far short in the task of dismantling protectionism but quite successful in building the "export platform."

The Incentives System. Under World Bank guidance, the martial law regime proceeded to implement the provisions of the Export Incentives Act of 1970. Under the Act, export manufacturers could deduct a portion of labor costs and the cost of "indigenous raw material" from their taxable incomes. Furthermore, tariff exemptions were given through tax credits on products used in export production. This was implemented through a "drawback" scheme refunding tariffs paid and permission for certain firms to operate tax-exempt, bonded, manufacturing warehouses.

The impact of these incentives on the promotion of export manufacturing was significant. According to the World Bank, the total subsidies and rebates received under the Export Incentives Act by all recipient firms came to nine percent of their export sales in 1977.[51]

Foreign investors, however, were still not satisfied. As the Vice President of the Philippine-American Chamber of Commerce asserted, "While the Export Incentives Act adopted by the Philippines represents significant progress in limited respects, there are still built into the Philippine legislative and tax structures a number of penalties, disincentives, and blocks in the way of increased and profitable export production."[52] The World Bank concurred. "Ideally," it told the government, "all manufactured export industries should be on a free trade regime to the maximum extent feasible. This involves (a) duty-free importation of raw materials and components; and (b) provision of additional assistance where necessary."[53]

An important step toward the total free-trade regime prescribed by the World Bank was the establishment of Export Processing Zones (EPZ's). Two months after martial law, Marcos' Presidential Decree 66 (PD66) created the first EPZ in Bataan which provided a model for the rest of the country. Legislation to establish the EPZ had been passed in 1969, but little was achieved until PD66 provided the incentives necessary to attract foreign investors. Firms which exported 70 percent of their products were rewarded for locating in the 345-hectare Bataan EPZ with the following benefits:

- permission for 100 percent foreign ownership;
- permission to impose a minimum wage lower than in Manila;
- tax-exemption privileges, including tax credits on domestic capital equipment, tax exemptions on imported raw materials and equipment, exemption from the export tax and from municipal and provincial taxes;

- priority to Central Bank foreign exchange allocations for imports;
- low rents for land and water;
- government financing of infrastructure and factory buildings, which could then be rented out or purchased by companies at a low price; and
- accelerated depreciation of fixed assets.

By 1980, the Bataan EPZ had attracted 57 enterprises, the great majority foreign-owned, employing some 28,000 workers, Foreign garment manufacturers, in particular, took advantage of the opportunities offered by the Bataan EPZ, with 17 of them locating there. Many of these firms were "runaways" from increasing labor costs in South Korea, Hong Kong, and Taiwan and from quota restrictions placed by the United States on garment exports from these other areas. To support the operations of firms locating in the Bataan EPZ, the World Bank helped finance the establishment of a big training center just outside the zone, offering general and specially tailored schooling for zone workers.[54]

By the late 70's, additional EPZ's had been established in Mactan and Baguio. Big-name electronics firms, such as Texas Instruments, Fairchild, Motorola, and Mitsumi, soon flocked to the EPZ's, attracted by incentives which were virtual giveaways, such as the 26 cents (P2.00) per square meter rent being charged for land at the Baguio EPZ.

The creation of new EPZ's outside Metro Manila followed the Bank policy of "regional dispersal" of industry. "The system of industrial incentives must also encourage industrial decentralization," the Bank informed the government. "Because of the critical need to encourage rapid export growth, export incentives should be uniform throughout the country."[55]

Complying with the Bank's wishes, the government informed the Consultative Group in late 1979:

> [W]e are accelerating the dispersal of industries . . . by encouraging the private sector to locate outside the Metropolitan Manila area. We have just passed legislation which provides added incentives to industries that will establish their operations in less developed areas of the country. Likewise . . . we are expanding our export and industrial zones all over the country, and hope to have about twelve export and industrial processing zones all over the country, in addition to the three that currently exist.[56]

In addition, the regime announced plans to create 100 "bonded villages" or small village havens throughout the country, where multinationals could bring in all kinds of raw materials duty free and process these materials purely for reexport.

Labor Repression. Cheap, repressed labor was the key incentive promoted by the World Bank and the regime for foreign manufacturers to relocate in the Philippines. As the World Bank admitted in a confidential report, "The basic objective of the government's wage-price policy has been to promote the growth of employment and investment through, among other things, wage restraint."[57] Another key Bank document affirmed, "In addition to its strong resource base, the comparative advantage of the Philippines lies in the utilization of skilled, low-wage labor."[58]

Wage restraint came mainly in the form of Presidential Decree 823 which banned strikes in "vital industries." In theory, "vital industries" included only export-oriented manufacturing concerns, public utilities, transport and communication firms, hospitals, schools and colleges, food processors and distributors, and banks. In practice, it encompassed practically all industries.

The strike ban was complemented by tight restrictions on labor organizing. In 1976, under the guise of " nationalizing" labor-capital relations, the government unveiled its plan to create one giant labor federation per industry. As part of this effort, the government sponsored the formation of the Trade Union Congress of the Philippines (TUCP) to assist the Ministry of Labor in efforts to control the labor force and purge labor of militant unions. The TUCP-Ministry of Labor combine refused recognition to 5,640 out of 7,000 registered unions and labor federations, resulting in the dissolution of many and the harassment of others by the government.[59] In one of the most cynical assessments the Bank has made of this labor policy, it noted:

> . . . Marcos has kept tight control over the labor unions, which were restructured under martial law such that national-level, governmentally controlled organs in turn control the local unions in each industry. The emasculated unions deal primarily with minor issues, and martial law prohibits strikes in "vital industries" and politically motivated strikes in any industry.[60]

In addition to banning strikes and promoting yellow unions, the regime instituted a Labor Code that was extremely biased toward employers. Among the most controversial provisions of this code was the "preventive suspension" of any worker who "poses a serious danger to the life or property of his employer." Not surprisingly, the clause has been extensively invoked; in 1977 alone, for instance, 6,000 trade unionists were placed on the "preventive" blacklist. Management could afford to be arbitrary in employing this weapon, for out of every 1,000 cases of preventive suspension, the Ministry of Labor decided only 13 in favor of workers."[61]

Another provision of the Labor Code allowed employers to pay new employees only 75 percent of the basic minimum wage during a six-month probation period. After this probation period, workers were supposed to graduate to full pay. It was common practice, however, for employers to fire workers just prior to the close of the six-month probation, then rehire them on a probationary basis to get around paying the full wage. Many workers became so used to this practice that they jokingly referred to themselves as "permanent casuals."[62]

Workers, however, not only had to contend with labor-specific repressive laws and administrative acts. They were also exposed to the general repression of the martial law regime. The military, for example, was used extensively to break strikes, with Constabulary units even assigned on a protracted basis to certain firms to keep "order." "Preventive detention" of labor leaders became a common occurrence, especially prior to planned mass actions and demonstrations. And, according to the Catholic Church-linked Task Force on Detainees, "at least 37 labor activists have been 'salvaged' or unofficially executed since the imposition of martial law."[63]

Pampered by the martial law state, employers have had no reason to take seriously those decrees of the government that nominally protect labor. Thus even the Employers' Confederation of the Philippines admitted that only 30 percent of employers paid the minimum wage; the Ministry of Labor asserted that the real figure was closer to 10 percent.[64] One study examining the "rate of exploitation" of industrial workers found that the ratio of "surplus" going to the capitalist and the wage going to labor increased by 180 percent between 1971 and 1975.[65] In a confidential memo, the World Bank was forced to admit that between 1972 and 1978 real wages of skilled workers dropped by over 25 percent and those of unskilled workers declined by over 30 percent.[66]

The Physiognomy of Export Labor. Under EOI, the new labor force that arose to service the export industries acquired a physiognomy quite distinct from the older "home market" industrial labor force. The vast majority of the new workers were young women. For instance, 90 percent of workers in the electronics industry—one of the two prongs of EOI—were women.[67] A vast majority in the other leading export industry, the garment sector, were also young women. In the Bataan EPZ, 80 percent of the 28,000 workers were women aged 15 to 24.[68]

Employers rationalized their preference for women workers in terms of women's superior dexterity and patience. The real reason, according to one study, is management's belief that they can keep women's wages low or lay off women workers with relatively few repercussions because they are not supporting families.[69] Employers also consider young women more tractable than older women or men.

Such "tractability" has been reinforced by sexual division of labor within the enterprise, where supervisors are usually male and operators are generally female.[70] The government has encouraged the companies' preference for female workers. For instance, Presidential Decree No. 148, issued shortly after martial law, reduced maternity benefits from 60 percent of pay for 14 weeks to 100 percent of pay for 6 weeks.[71]

Because of the traditional cultural oppression of women, the predominantly female character of the labor force has also made union organizing—already difficult under martial law conditions—even more difficult. As one experienced labor organizer stated, "at this time it is very difficult to organize workers in the garment industry because most of the workers are women or housewives."[72] But if unions are weak in the garment industry, they are even weaker in the electronics sector. Most of the American-owned electronics establishments, for instance, have either managed to keep out unions or maintain company unions.[73]

The absence of genuine, representative unions has permitted labor conditions to be more oppressive in the labor-intensive export sector than in many "home-market" industries. Testimony prepared by Filipino labor organizers for the respected Permanent Tribunal on the Rights of Peoples in Antwerp, Belgium in October 1980 provides a glimpse of these conditions:

> In labor-intensive companies, the conditions are worse. Most garment workers complain of heat exhaustion. Fainting and dizziness are common among workers in Triumph International, a foreign-owned firm making brassieres. At Gelmart, a dress and glove firm owned by an American, a worker said: "The factory is very hot. Because of the sudden change in temperature when we go out, our bodies are prone to sickness." It was also in this factory that fire broke out and killed 11 workers with 53 others injured. . . .

Workers in the electronics industry tend to suffer from eye defects after three years of employment. Others complain of acid burns, skin rashes from epoxy resins and other allergy reactions due to solvents like trichloroethylene. Even if they are given gloves and masks, they do not use them because these could slow them down and they would fail to reach their quota. Besides this, they are not required by the company to use them and, in fact, are not taught about the need for protective devices.[74]

Labor conditions in the EOI showcase, the Bataan EPZ, were described by an investigator for the American Friends Service Committee as "reminiscent of the early days of the Industrial Revolution in England."

> Overcrowded living conditions in workers' dormitories are common, as are bad working conditions, overwork and overtime work. These conditions led to cases of over-exhaustion, fatigue and collapse. According to one dormitory supervisor, "textile workers at Intercon (a Taiwanese-Filipino outfit) were worked overtime so much that a lot of them simply collapsed. Some of them also vomited so they had to go to the clinic. This is partly because they were not getting enough sleep, they had to work overtime."[75]

These abysmal conditions for workers in the export industries have accomplished what the World Bank can only regard as positive results. As the Bank approvingly noted in 1979, while labor productivity in the export sector rose by 13 percent and kept pace with growth in productivity in South Korea, Japan, the U.S. and West Germany, wages in the Philippines declined steeply relative to these countries—by 50 percent relative to real wages in Japan and South Korea, 46 percent relative to those in Germany, and 17 percent relative to those in the U.S.[76] Wage repression led to highly attractive rates of return on investment in the Philippines. One electronics firm was reported to draw as much as $.54 for every dollar invested[77]—a figure which, while quite high, was probably a conservative estimate of profitability.

By the end of the 70's, Filipino labor, according to the widely consulted *Business International*, "remains one of the cheapest (employers prefer to call it competitive) in the world."[78] The result of seven years of faithfully following the World Bank prescription was proudly announced by Minister of Industry Roberto Ongpin to the Consultative Group at its annual meeting in Washington, D. C. in December 1979:

> The effective cost of labor in the Philippines, including fringe benefits in addition to the basic wage, is 49 U.S. cents per hour. In Singapore, it is 95 U.S. cents per hour; in Taiwan 85 U.S. cents per hour; and in Hong Kong, about three times as much as in the Philippines, $1.41 U.S. cents per hour.[79]

The competitive edge in labor costs began to attract export manufacturers from the first export-industrialization model, South Korea.[80] The move of Mattel Industries, a toy manufacturer, from South Korea to the Philippines was illustrative. Electronics companies, like Fairchild Semiconductor, one of the pioneers of the multinationals' thrust toward export processing in East Asia, chose to expand their operations in the Philippines instead of South Korea.[81] Japanese garment enterprises were also attracted to the Philippines by cheap labor as well as by the attempt to get away from the quotas imposed on U.S. garment imports from South Korea, Taiwan, and Hong Kong.[82]

By the end of the decade, "nontraditional manufacturing exports"—mainly electronics and garments—were growing at a sensational rate of over 33 percent per year.[83] By 1980, they were responsible for more than 32 percent of total export earnings—up from 16 percent in 1973. The World Bank had great reason to be satisfied, and so did foreign investors, but the price of this achievement was a brutal reduction in the real income of Filipino workers—a development that a 1979 World Bank Poverty Mission itself termed "startling."

Dismantling ISI: Round Three

Though the World Bank was satisfied with the Marcos regime's record in setting up the export-incentives system, it was frustrated with the government's vacillation in dismantling the protectionist system.

By the late 70's, the Bank arrived at the conclusion that some arm twisting was necessary. "Tariff reform is becoming increasingly urgent," warned the World Bank's East Asia Division in 1977, "since high effective production rates appear to be sheltering various inefficient industries."[84] One study concluded that protectionist mechanisms raised the cost of competitive manufactured imports by an average of 125 percent across all categories of goods.[85]

The source of the Marcos regime's vacillation in lowering or eliminating tariffs was the strong political clout of the national producers of consumer goods—a group that the World Bank described as continuing to be "a large and influential group of businesses."[86] Admitted the Bank: "Protectionism, one of the few bulwarks of the precarious local private entrepreneurial sector, is the major target of the liberalization program."[87] Though their future status was precarious, this sector nevertheless maintained enough political clout to force the technocrats to keep their distance, despite prodding from the IMF and the World Bank. Indeed, the national industrialists (as well as the foreign investors) benefited from government's policy of repressing labor. It was, for instance, against the workers of a home-market firm, La Tondeña Distillery, that the regime decided to test its hard no-strike policy in 1975 by arresting 500 striking workers.

The other source of hesitation was a muffled dispute between Marcos technocrats and the World Bank on the issue of whether or not import substitution was to be completely abandoned as a strategy. While the technocrats agreed with the Bank that the home market for consumer goods should be deprotectionized, some of them still argued strongly for encouraging import substitution in intermediate and capital goods industries. They argued that the bulk of foreign exchange went to pay for imports of intermediate goods and capital equipment. Apparently, there were some sympathetic voices within the Bank. The 1976 Country Program Paper draft, for instance, stated:

> A large group of intermediate goods industries also offers room for accelerated growth and significant

> foreign exchange savings in the decade ahead. . . . Investment plans for the coming years include import-replacing projects for intermediate and capital goods, including steel, fertilizers, other petrochemicals, pulp and paper, and shipbuilding.[88]

In another memorandum, a key World Bank officer wrote: ". . . in a fiercely competitive and fickle international market, Philippine handicrafts will be in fashion today, and tomorrow [*sic*]. The bread and butter and the basis of a modern manufacturing sector will always be at home."[89]

By 1978, however, the debate within the World Bank had apparently been won by technocrats demanding a total focus on export-manufacturing. The final Bank position was presented to the Philippine government at the 1978 Consultative Group meeting by Vice President Shahid Husain:

> The possibilities for efficient import-substitution in capital and intermediate goods industries are limited by constraints of market size, the need for advancing technology in a large number of areas simultaneously, and the capital intensity of the processes involved.[90]

Tightening the Screws. In 1979, the Bank began to tighten the screws. At the Consultative Group meeting late that year, Husain was blunt:

> The past decade has witnessed the emergence of a degree of dualism between labor-intensive export-oriented industries operated under free trade arrangements, and the remainder of the sector which is oriented to the protected domestic market. Given the level of skills in the Philippines, and the sophistication of the financial markets, the growth of the industrial sector has not kept up with the promise of the Philippine economy.[91]

Husain then called for the "restructuring of the economy itself and restructuring productive sectors of the economy."[92]

The Marcos regime got the message. Industry Minister Roberto Ongpin, in the face of an implicit World Bank and IMF threat to reexamine their loan programs, tendered the capitulation of the Marcos government:

> We are in agreement with the findings of the Bank that Philippine industry has suffered because of an over-protected system. We are determined to take the difficult and often painful decisions to dismantle some of the protective devices and thus to promote a free and competitive system.[93]

Among the immediate measures promised by the government was a reduction of the number of "overcrowded industries" (those with the highest level of protection) from 33 to 10 and lowering 100 and 70 percent tariff rates to 50 percent.[94] The IMF was pleased: "Further steps will be taken to reduce the level of protection in order to open import-substitution industries to the test of external competition."[95]

But while the regime's technocrats were willing to junk the national capitalists in the consumer goods sectors, they were not so acquiescent to the Bank's order that they forget about import substitution in the intermediate and capital goods sectors. By the end of the decade, in light of the international recession and the sharp rise of protectionism in the advanced capitalist countries, some technocrats were no longer very sanguine about the results of the complete free trade regime proposed by the World Bank. Moreover, the regime was becoming quite sensitive to the criticism leveled by economic nationalists that no viable industrial economy could be consolidated without the development of intermediate and capital goods industries. These doubts were reinforced by the material interests of the "bureaucrat capitalists," those Filipino businessmen whose success came courtesy of their close relationship to Marcos. They stood to benefit from multimillion dollar contracts to build industrial projects through joint ventures with selected foreign firms.

Thus, amidst much fanfare and in contradiction to the World Bank, in late 1979 the regime unveiled its plan to undertake 11 big industrial projects. These were: a copper smelter, an aluminum smelter, a phosphate fertilizer plant, diesel-engine manufacturing, cement industry expansion, coconut industry nationalization, an integrated pulp and paper mill, petrochemical complex, a heavy engineering industry, an integrated steel project, and alcogas (fuel made from sugar cane) production.

In an attempt to secure the Bank's approval, or at least acquiescence, the regime resorted to two arguments: first, it claimed that all the projects were "export-oriented." As Industry Minister Ongpin put it before the Consultative

Group, "The fertilizer project, the pulp and paper project, the aluminum smelter and the cement industry expansion projects are all designed to have a large portion of their outputs for export markets."[96] The other tactic that Ongpin employed to disarm the Bank was to purge the big industrial program of any hint of nationalism by claiming that foreign investors would be key participants in its execution.

> . . . a key element in our strategy to get these major projects implemented is to bring in a maximum of foreign investment, an objective, incidentally, in which we are meeting with very encouraging success. For example, the diesel engine manufacturing project . . . will be 100% foreign owned; as will the downstream petrochemical project . . . many of the other major industrial projects will be joint ventures, including the copper smelter, the aluminum smelter, the fertilizer project, the cement industry expansion project, the pulp and paper project and other projects.[97]

The Bank, however, was not persuaded. In its highly confidential 1980 Country Program Paper, it politely rejected Marcos' big-industry program: "Our view is that while some of these capital-intensive projects are economically well justified (such as the export-oriented copper smelter), others may not be, and do not harmonize well with the policy reforms."[98] Another report was less polite, deriding the program as a product of desperation economics, which could bring about highly destabilizing effects:

> . . . the Government's preference for a massive industrial program reflects an attempt (which many consider to be desperate) to use an administratively controllable program to avoid the (income distribution) tradeoff by triggering a much higher growth rate that could permit the "boom" atmosphere to overshadow the distribution question. If the industrial promotion does not yield a boom that benefits all sectors, the highly visible advantages going to the urban industrial sector will exacerbate the resentments and conflicts over income distribution.[99]

The government was forced to promise the World Bank that "the projects would be implemented only if found viable by rigorous economic analysis."[100] Nonetheless, it actively sought to solicit capital backing for the program—

an effort which did not get very far once foreign investors learned of the World Bank's veto. By the end of 1981, only five of the eleven projects had received some foreign backing. Of these five, three—the petrochemical, aluminum smelter, and diesel engine manufacturing projects—ran into trouble when foreign backers later cooled to their initial commitments.[101]

THE CRISIS OF EOI

The regime's technocrats had good reason to begin to doubt the EOI strategy. By the late seventies the Bank-promoted strategy was clearly in trouble. The crisis stemmed mainly from three sources: contradictions inherent in the strategy; increasing resistance from labor; and the disappearance of the necessary external conditions—continued expansion of export markets and a global non-protectionist climate—to sustain it.

The Inherent Contradictions of EOI

The Foreign Exchange Mirage. Export-oriented industrialization had been promoted as an expeditious way to acquire substantial foreign exchange for internal development. But by the late 70's, EOI was earning many fewer dollars than originally promised. The problem lay in the fact that, like the old import-substitution strategy, EOI was also burdened with high import requirements. In 1970 the Philippine import bill for raw materials and intermediate goods (excluding oil) was $432.1 million. By 1979, this bill had grown to $2.5 billion or 40.5 percent of all of the country's imports. Adding to this figure the 30.8 percent of Philippine imports devoted to capital goods, a significant portion of which went to export-oriented manufacturing industries, the total bill came to over 70 percent of all Philippine imports.[102] This import-dependent condition of EOI led to the paradoxical result that while export earnings were rising, import payments were rising even faster—leading to a steadily widening balance-of-trade deficit.

A substantial portion of "export earnings" was in fact illusory. About 56 percent of the value of garment exports, according to a recent study, was actually imported raw material and only 44 percent was value added by Filipino garment workers.[103] In other words, for every dollar's worth of garment exports, the Philippines' net foreign exchange earning came to only 44 cents. The situation was even worse in the electronics industry, where net foreign exchange earnings for every dollar's worth of exports came to only 13 cents.[104] As the Bank itself was forced to admit, ". . . due to the high cost and low quality of domestic inputs, nontraditional exports are largely dependent on imports and, as a result, have remained enclaves with only few backward linkages with the domestic manufacturing sector. *Consequently value added is only 25 percent of output.*"[105] That is, only a quarter of the export value of labor-intensive Philippine manufactures represented actual foreign exchange earnings for the country. When repatriated profits (amounting to 30 percent of value added in garment exports) are deducted from these small net earnings, the foreign exchange gained by the country from nontraditional exports is minimal at best.[106]

The Enclave Economy. The World Bank blamed the failure of EOI to earn more foreign exchange on the inability of the domestic manufacturing sector to provide "backward linkages" to the export sector.[107] Yet the World Bank had only itself to blame for fostering the development of an "enclave economy." Its policy had been to *discourage* the growth of the intermediate and capital goods sectors that could have provided the inputs. This policy was justified by the Bank's conviction that "efficient import substitution in capital and intermediate goods industries are limited by constraints of market size, the need for advancing technology in a large number of areas simultaneously, and the capital intensity of many of the processes involved."[108]

Moreover, the Bank failed to grasp—or chose not to grasp—the fact that the foreign manufacturers being attracted to participate in the export strategy were *not interested in establishing backward linkages.* There were several reasons for this.

In the first place, foreign export manufacturers operate with a very limited time horizon in a country like the Philippines. To most, five years is already the "long run." Enjoying annual rates of return on investment surpassing 15 percent and often close to 20 percent, these investors can normally expect to recover their initial investment within that short a time span, especially since the capital invested to start up an export manufacturing business tends to be relatively small. According to Bank estimates, the average capital investment per worker in export processing firms is only $2,800, compared to $10,000 in the manufacturing sector as a whole and $22,000 in domestic market firms.[109]

Export-oriented manufacturers also prefer to spread their production processes around the globe in accordance with the international division of labor, farming out the simplest, most labor-intensive jobs to countries like the Philippines. With few exceptions, the more highly skilled, capital- and technology-intensive work, on the other hand, remains within the advanced capitalist countries. The Philippines was assigned a very modest place in this system—and the Marcos government had reconciled itself to this. As Industry Minister Ongpin told the Consultative Group in 1979:

> We are paying special attention to . . . international subcontracting, where we provide facilities for large multinationals to come in and do the more labor-intensive aspects of their operations in this country. We know that we have a substantial labor cost advantage in the Philippines and we would like to capitalize on this by making an arrangement with the large multinationals whereby they would, in effect, subcontract the more labor-intensive aspects of their operations to us in the Philippines.[110]

In the case of semiconductor manufacturing, for instance, Filipino workers perform only one of roughly ten operations involved in the production process. That one operation—encapsulation or assembly—requires the least sophisticated technology, a combination microscope and soldering iron process. Similarly, in the garment industry, fabrics are woven on the latest vintage looms in the highly automated textile mills of the United States, Europe, and Japan—then sent to the Philippines for assembly and embroidery on a Singer sewing machine.

The global division of labor, limited time horizon of foreign investors, and limited investment characteristic of the export manufacturers' operations in the Third World serve to minimize the risk of financial loss. Equally important, they minimize the disruption of global operations in the event that an upstart nationalist government should decide to nationalize foreign firms. These factors also ensure that such a government would stand to gain little from that course of action, since it still could not gain access to the more sophisticated technology required to put together an integrated industrial production process. By the same token, the existing arrangement makes it relatively painless for foreign investors to pack their bags and leave at a moment's notice should the going get rough or labor costs rise, as the case of South Korea illustrates.

The Employment Question. World Bank proponents of export-led industrialization claim that "with the growth of labor-intensive, nontraditional manufactured exports after 1970 . . . labor absorption of Philippines manufacturing has improved . . . exports of nontraditional manufactures probably accounted for more than 30 percent of manufacturing employment created during the period 1970-77 while accounting for less than 8% of manufacturing investment."[111]

This was, however, a very narrow vision of EOI's impact on employment. For EOI's dependence on cheap, repressed labor was in fact aggravating the employment problem for the urban working class as a whole. As the Bank's *Poverty Report* itself pointed out: "In recent years, rapidly declining real family incomes among a large segment of the urban population, containing both current residents and nonmigrating people, has caused poorer families to offer an increasing supply of labor services and goods in the market . . . ."[112] In other words, as the head of the family could no longer make ends meet, other members were forced to seek employment, thus swelling the numbers of the unemployed and underemployed.

EOI-based employment, moreover, was even more unstable than traditional manufacturing employment, dependent as it was on the upturns and downturns of the international market. In 1979, as stagflation choked off growth in the export markets of advanced industrial countries, close to 340,000 Filipino workers were laid off; the layoffs increased by 100,000 in 1980 and by 300,000 in 1981, according to one estimate.[113] A significant number of those laid off were in garment and electronics manufacturing—the backbone of the EOI drive.[114]

The Foreign Investment Illusion. One of the key "virtues" of export-led industrialization, according to the World Bank, was its promise to bring in more foreign capital than the system of import substitution. Between 1973 and 1980, however, only $839 million entered the Philippines, a much smaller figure than the capital flowing to neighboring areas such as Singapore, Hong Kong, or South Korea.[115]

Even more disturbing was the pronounced downward trend of investment toward the end of the decade: from a peak of $216 million in 1977, net foreign investment inflow dropped to $171 million in 1978 and $99 million in

1979.[116] As investment inflow declined, the repatriation of profits and other forms of "direct investment income" still showed a consistent upward movement from $60 million in 1975 to $147 million in 1978.[117] Indeed, the "net flow of foreign investor capital" (net foreign investment inflow minus the outflow of investment income) came to only $87 million between 1973 and 1979, according to Bank figures.[118]

This did not mean, however, that foreigners were investing less. Indeed, the Bank asserted that in 1980, investment by foreign firms came to 500 percent more than the annual average for the 1970's.[119] These new investments by foreign firms, however, were being financed mainly from local profits or borrowings from domestic capital sources. Thus, while the foreign capital inflow slowed to a trickle, foreign concerns raised their cumulative borrowing from local sources from $1.9 billion in 1973 to about $3 billion in 1977, according to one estimate.[120]

The full-scale adoption of EOI promises to aggravate these tendencies. Because of the relatively small outlay needed to start a labor-intensive manufacturing operation, the capital brought in by foreign export producers tends to be quite low compared to other foreign investments. As noted earlier, the average capital investment per worker in export-processing firms is only $2,800, while in the manufacturing sector as a whole it comes to $10,000. Thus, according to Bank projections, the nontraditional export industries would make up less than 10 percent of the total manufacturing investments of $12.5 billion projected for the period 1977-1985.[121]

Already skewed toward low levels of investment, foreign export manufacturers are encouraged to bring in even less capital by the rules on local borrowing set by the Marcos regime. While foreign nonmanufacturing firms can borrow up to no more than 100 percent of their equity investment and nonexport firms can draw up to 122 percent, export manufacturers can borrow up to 150 percent. That is, for every dollar a foreign export industry invests in the country, only 40 cents need come in from outside.

The Fiscal Crisis of EOI. To attract export manufacturers, the government has had to spend billions of dollars to meet their energy, transportation, communications, water, and construction needs. For the model Bataan Export Processing Zone alone, for instance, government expenditure for development of physical and social infrastructure including a dam and water treatment plant, came to $150 million.[122]

Somebody has to pay for the infrastructure. The problem for the Philippine government was that in its effort to attract foreign investors away from alternative sites in Asia, it had, on advice from the Bank, eliminated a whole range of tariffs and other fiscal impositions on foreign capital and commodities which could otherwise have gone to help defray infrastructure costs. Taxes on international trade were brought down from 40 percent of national government revenues in 1976 to 34 percent in 1979.[123] The corporate income tax was also made more favorable to foreign investors: various deductions, exemptions and exclusions allowed export manufacturers to claim total deductions amounting to 70 percent of gross income reported.[124]

Because it reduced financial impositions on the foreign corporate beneficiaries of EOI, the regime increasingly had to resort to two alternative sources to fund the EOI infrastructure: foreign borrowing and local taxation.

Thus, a significant portion of the $15.2 billion foreign debt owed by the Philippines as of late 1981 was made up of loans for infrastructure projects, such as hydroelectric dams and the $1.2 billion nuclear power plant in Morong, Bataan, meant to provide electricity to export industries in the Bataan EPZ a few miles away and in Manila. For energy development alone, the regime plans expenditures of $9.5 billion in the period 1980-85, the bulk of which will come from foreign loans.[125] Total projected infrastructure outlays will amount to $27 billion between 1981 and 1987.[126]

This fiscal solution to EOI's infrastructure needs strongly undermines one of the primary goals of the strategy: relieving the country's critical balance-of-payments situation. Thus, while net earnings from nontraditional manufactured exports came to $375 million in 1979, a hemorrhage took place in debt-service payments, which totaled $1 billion.

The shortfall in infrastructure expenditures that the government cannot cover from foreign loans has to be filled from domestic sources. Indeed, the difficult external position of the economy, says the U.S. State Department, makes more intensive taxation the only option at this point:

> The cost of developing domestic energy resources, modernizing industry, building infrastructure, etc., is high and current Philippine debt puts limits on future external borrowing. Consequently, the development institutions are pressing for a higher level of savings to be generated at home. . . .[127]

Thus, the Bank's 1980 Country Program Paper happily notes: "The Government has introduced a large number of well-designed revenue-generating resources related to domestic taxation."[128] Most of these "well-designed" resources, such as a special tax on petroleum and petroleum products, a levy on the consumption of electric power, and a "value-added tax on the sale of secondhand articles," fall disproportionately on the middle and lower classes. This is not surprising given the government's reluctance to squeeze its upper-class social base.[129]

Yet even these new measures failed to satisfy the Bank's sister agency, the IMF. Expressing displeasure at the fact that the $3.8 billion in tax revenues for 1981 fell short of the $4.3 billion that it had expected the government to collect, the Fund told the regime to squeeze the population even more: "[T]here is need to improve the structure and administration of taxation. . . . Thus, the objectives of increasing government savings should be met in part through increased revenue mobilization."[130]

In sum, the expensive infrastructure needs of the beneficiaries of EOI—the multinational corporations—are being palmed off on the Filipino masses, who not only are taxed to finance current infrastructure expenditures but also shoulder the burden of repaying the massive foreign loans that the regime has incurred for infrastructure purposes.

Labor Resistance. There were further pitfalls to EOI in addition to the economic contradictions outlined above. EOI's most tempting bait for foreign investors was the offer of one of the lowest wage rates in Asia. By the late 1970's, labor in the Philippines was still cheap, but trouble was looming in the distance. The American Chamber of Commerce, the World Bank and the IMF began to worry about the increasingly militant labor movement.

Contained by repressive decrees and military force during the first three years of martial law, in October 1975 the labor movement burst onto the scene with a protracted but successful strike by over 500 workers at the La Tondeña Distillery in Manila. In the years after the 1975 La Tondeña strike, workers staged some 400 strikes—90 percent of them "illegal" or in violation of the ban on strikes in "vital industries."[131] Many of the firms struck were U.S.-owned, such as Gelmart, a garment manufacturer, and Mead Johnson, a drug corporation.

Especially worrisome to the government was the fact that many of the strikes were not spontaneous but organized by the underground opposition, the National Democratic Front (NDF). In 1975, NDF forces helped form *Bukluran,* an alliance of militant unions, and in 1977 they helped establish an even larger progressive alliance, *Kapatiran*. Through such organizations, labor linked up with opposition forces to challenge the regime in political confrontations, such as the exposure of the rigged Interim National Assembly elections of April 1978. On May 1, 1980 the Kilusang Mayo Uno (KMU, or May 1st Movement) was launched with a rally of 10,000 workers in Manila. KMU, which claimed the allegiance of 150,000 members, aggressively attacked the U.S., the IMF, and the World Bank, called for the restoration of civil liberties, and demanded the nationalization of foreign businesses. Alarmed by the new labor militancy, the regime responded by arresting several key leaders, including KMU General Secretary Ernesto Arellano, in September 1980.

When repression failed to hold the line, the government attempted to contain the workers' movement by establishing periodic "tripartite" negotiations among labor, business, and government representatives to fix the minimum wage, cost-of-living allowances, and prices. However, rank-and-file militance created severe pressures on Marcos' hand-picked labor bureaucrats, forcing many of them to adopt ambivalent positions. Thus, the acting head of the government-favored Trade Union Congress of the Philippines (TUCP) warned employers and the government of "symptoms of restrained discontent among the working masses" which could lead to "the dismantling of the existing political system."[132]

The IMF, however, exerted pressure on Marcos from the other direction: ". . . there is concern as to the extent to which recent adjustments in wages and related supplements have contributed to cost-push pressures in the economy."[133] It asserted that "the high rate of inflation has arisen primarily from cost-push pressures, associated, in turn, with the substantial increase in energy prices and wage costs. These have given rise to a profits squeeze."[134] The IMF thus instructed the government to firmly hold the line on labor: "The staff believes that in view of the weakening in economic activiey, the implications for employment should be given due consideration in the upcoming national wage negotiations.¾[135]

But labor would not be held back. In early 1979, shock waves were triggered by the invasion of the "export sanctuary" by militant unionism. Defying the presidential decree banning strikes in export industries, seven hundred workers at the Ford Body Stamping Plant launched the first strike in the history of the Bataan Export Processing

Zone. Furious, the government arrested 400 strikers. The wholesale arrests were to drive home the point that while strikes might be tolerated elsewhere, they would not be allowed in the sacrosanct export industrial sector.

To meet this alarming development, the government, supported by the IMF and the Bank, supplemented the iron fist with divide-and-rule tactics. Workers in the "home," import-substitution industries were granted agreed upon raises in the minimum wage and in cost-of-living allowances, but "certain labor-intensive, export-oriented industries, e.g. the cottage and handicrafts industry, and firms in the electronics industry were exempted from granting part of these pay awards."[136] The export sanctuary, in other words, was to be preserved at all costs.

Worker agitation was one of the key domestic factors that pushed Marcos to his cosmetic lifting of martial law on January 17, 1981. The lifting was to include an easing of the country's restrictive labor laws. To test this "normalization," workers held over 200 strikes in the first half of the year. Marcos responded by promising to lift P.D. 823, the notorious ban on strikes. This move was sharply attacked by George Suter, Jr., executive director of the American Chamber of Commerce in Manila, who called instead for "a law with strict enforcement that would only allow strikes as an outcome of a deadlock in collective bargaining issues." The behavior of the government in the face of the militant labor movement, Suter warned Marcos, "discourages badly needed foreign and local investment."[137] The World Bank, for its part, commented stoically that "thus far no viable approach has been found to surmount the difficulty of improving real wages for urban workers, maintaining profits for their employers, and keeping up the incomes of rural food producers."[138]

Faced with an impossible task, the regime resorted once again to cosmetic solutions. In August 1981, amidst great fanfare, the right to strike was "restored" to workers. However, the fine print gave the president "the authority to intervene at any time and exercise jurisdiction over any labor dispute adversely affecting the national interest," and empowered the Ministry of Labor "to forestall a strike or lockout" in companies engaged in the generation or distribution of energy, public utilities, banks, hospitals, and those in the export processing zone."[139]

But the lesson was obvious to foreign investors: Filipino workers, including those in the export industries, were no longer docile—and soon, they would no longer be cheap.

The External Threat. If the internal necessity of export-led industrialization was cheap labor, its external necessity was an expanding global economy. The export-oriented industrial strategy, the Bank told the Consultative Group, "is critically dependent on the willingness of the international community to support a reasonable climate of free trade."[140] But by the late 1970's, the favorable external conditions which had encouraged many Third World countries to adopt the strategy in the late sixties and early seventies had disappeared. "Stagflation" was choking off substantial growth in the key markets of nontraditional export manufacturers: Europe, the United States, and Japan.

With economic stagnation, pressures for protectionist trade policies arose in the industrialized nations, pressures so strong that McNamara was compelled to devote his speech to the issue at the 1979 Conference of the United Nations Conference on Trade and Development (UNCTAD):

> Since 1976 there has been a marked increase in protectionism in the industrialized nations . . . and the pressures for even further restrictive devices are strong . . . the devices utilized to provide such protection have multiplied. In addition to the traditional tariff measures, they now include cartel-like sharing agreements; voluntary export restraints; countervailing duties; subsidies and other assistance to domestic industries to sustain levels of protection; and a whole spectrum of administrative, nontariff barriers.[141]

EOI as a strategy for the Third World was directly threatened by this protectionist wave, said McNamara, since "the fear of future imposition of protectionist measures discourages governments in the developing world from adopting trade-oriented, outward-looking policies."[142]

In the case of the Philippines, nontraditional manufactured exports had sharply risen in value from $359 million in 1975 to $1.4 billion in 1979, and from 16 to 32 percent of the value of all exports.[143] *This impressive performance, however, proved to be their undoing.* In two years alone, 1978-80, the IMF identified at least 33 barriers erected against Philippine imports, mainly textiles and garments, by the United States, Australia, Canada, the Common Market, Japan, and five other advanced countries.[144]

To no avail the Philippines implored the United States, its largest market, on the basis of historic "special relations" between the two countries, to raise the quota constraining the import of Philippine-made garments.[145] This frustration and others led Industry Minister Roberto Ongpin to complain to the Consultative Group in December 1979 that, "quotas are now developing into a major problem for us in meeting our export targets. . . ."[146] Both the Bank and the IMF confirmed his fears. In a July 1980 report, the IMF concluded bleakly: "The staff shares the view of the authorities that export promotion has become more difficult in the present climate of uncertainty of the international economy as well as the trade restrictions faced by Philippine exports."[147] And in October 1981 a Bank study asserted that manufacturers in the Philippines and other developing countries:

> should expect high barriers to be maintained against the importation of traditionally protected labor-intensive manufacturers in industrial democracies. Moreover, they should anticipate that a rapid rise in an industry's level of import penetration, coupled with a poor performance in output or employment terms, could trigger import protection in the industrial countries for the industry. . . .[148]

But the Bank still sought to salvage its strategy, despite clear signs that it had been rendered obsolete by international developments. However, its prescription for the Philippine garment industry was clearly laced with desperation:

> To minimize the effects of quotas, the industry must be able to diversify and upgrade its product lines, so as to have the flexibility to shift production to lines unaffected by quotas. The industry needs to know the fashion and market situation in other countries, and facilities should be provided . . . to provide feedback on the latest trends in clothing markets and fashions.[149]

In short, in pursuit of a discredited doctrine, the World Bank had no qualms in saddling the country with industries doomed to permanent instability. With shrinking markets and rising protectionism, exports from one country could only grow if another's declined. This led competing countries to greater efforts to reduce the cost of the key factor of production, labor. In 1978 and 1979, for instance, South Korea, the "pioneer" of EOI, reported no growth in exports and lost international market shares to

Taiwan, Singapore, and Hong Kong.[150] The culprit, according to the Bank, was increased labor costs in South Korea, which made it lose "its 'competitive advantage' in the labor and resource intensive industries."[151]

But the position of the Philippines and other newcomers was itself unstable. A major reason for this instability was the World Bank's continuing aggressive promotion of the strategy of EOI to still other countries where the costs of labor might even be lower. Thus, in a controversial 1980 report, the Bank advised Indonesia to shift its industrial strategy from ISI to EOI and recommended that "the incentives for firms to locate there rather than in some other Southeast Asian country . . . must be provided."[152] Similarly, the Bank was successfully persuading one of its newest clients, the People's Republic of China, to make EOI the centerpiece of its development strategy. To this end, the Bank advanced the rationale that with "export successes . . . pushing up wage levels in such economies as Hong Kong and the Republic of South Korea,"[153] it had become attractive for China to engage in EOI, "given the abundance of skilled low-wage labor and the enormous potential for economies of scale."[154]

These moves revealed, with crystal clarity, that the World Bank's primary intention in pushing EOI in the Philippines and the Third World was not to promote industrial growth. It was to satisfy the multinational firms' need for cheap labor and the advanced metropolitan economies' craving for cheap light manufactured goods by pitting one Third World country's working class against the others in a race toward the bottom line of survival. By the early eighties, the Bank could no longer avoid acknowledging this. Thus, in prescribing EOI to China, the Bank inadvertently commented that export-oriented development is "a path that is not only new for China, but has been successfully trodden by few, if any, other countries."[155]

Conclusion

The World Bank's rural and urban development programs had a primarily political objective. That is, although they were framed partly with a view toward "enhancing the productivity of the poor," they were principally intended to defuse rural and urban unrest. The Bank's program in the industrial sector was guided with no such political purpose; "liberalization" was dictated solely by the objective of destroying the barriers to the inflow of foreign commodities and forestalling the imposition of nationalist controls on foreign investment.

The process of liberalization began in the early 60's, well before the declaration of martial law, its two milestones being the IMF-World Bank-imposed devaluations of the peso in 1962 and 1970. What was new in the martial-law period was not only a more intensified effort to destroy protectionist barriers, but also the attachment of a strategy of export-oriented industrialization to the liberalization program.

The theory of EOI represented a modification of the old Ricardian doctrine of comparative advantage, enshrined in neoclassical economic theory. According to this doctrine, the economic welfare of countries which are richly endowed with agricultural and raw material resources is best served if they specialize in producing these commodities. Seen in its historical context, the theory of comparative advantage became the main ideological buttress of the attempt to prevent Third World countries from pursuing significant industrialization efforts in the colonial and postcolonial international economic order.

The theorists of EOI simply substituted "labor" for agricultural and raw material resources as the commodity in abundance. This made it possible for established economies to accommodate some form of Third World industrialization, provided it was industrialization that focused on the production of *labor-intensive light manufactures*. This theoretical reformulation of the theory of comparative advantage did not, however, take place in a vacuum. It was an ideological response to a development which became especially pronounced in the 1960's—the outward thrust of U.S. corporations seeking low-cost Third World labor to offset the high wages which the trade union movement had won for workers in the advanced capitalist countries. The effort to limit Third World industrialization to labor-intensive production also responded to the effort of the advanced economies to monopolize skill-intensive and technology-intensive production processes.

Erected as World Bank doctrine in the early 1970's, EOI became an attractive ideological weapon to disarm Third World elites as the multilateral agencies and multinational corporations went about the task of battering down tariff walls and aborting incipient nationalist restrictions on foreign investment in countries like the Philippines.

EOI, however, was a panacea that lost its promise very soon after it began to be applied in the Philippines. Expected to bring in significant foreign exchange earnings, EOI actually encouraged a hemorrhage of foreign exchange for the expensive infrastructure needs and raw-material, intermediate-goods and capital-goods inputs of the labor-intensive export industries. Expected to foster rapid industrialization, EOI actually created enclaves of foreign-owned export industries that had no interest in stimulating "backward linkages." Expected to bring in huge doses of foreign capital, EOI attracted relatively little.

Yet the major factor that torpedoed EOI was the disappearance of the two key assumptions on which the strategy had been founded: cheap labor and expanding western markets. While still cheap in the late 1970's, Philippine labor, organized by militant underground unions, was no longer docile. It was only a matter of time before wage levels would rise to the point where the fly-by-night foreign investors would feel tempted to leave for better climes. The World Bank was, in fact, in the process of creating new low-wage nirvanas in places such as the People's Republic of China and Indonesia. More devastating, however, were the deepening stagnation of the advanced capitalist markets and the rising protectionism against light manufactured imports from the Third World in these economies.

With the prerequisite conditions for EOI vanishing, the World Bank and the IMF were left with an industrial strategy that was purely negative, purely repressive: the dismantling of protectionism, the destruction of the national capitalist class, and the total denationalization of Philippine industry.

CHAPTER SIX

Structural and Other Adjustments

By the beginning of the 1980's, the World Bank could no longer ignore the massive failure of its development program in the Philippines. The signs were everywhere: in the $2.7 billion current account deficit; the $15.2 billion external debt; and the increasing protectionist measures against Philippine exports on the world market. The GNP growth rate had declined to 2.5 percent a year; the real income of the masses in both the cities and the countryside had sharply dropped and income was more highly concentrated than ever in what the Bank itself described as the "new ruling coalition consisting of the Marcos family and personal associates, high-level technocrats, key bureaucrats and military officers and some wealthy businessmen."[1]

The plunge in living standards inevitably eroded the political stability of the regime. The principal rationale articulated by the regime—and reiterated by the Bank—for the imposition of martial law in 1972 had been that the "democratic stalemate"in the post-war Philippine Republic had prevented economic development and prosperity. By the end of the decade, however, the Bank conceded that this justification for the dictatorship had been effectively undermined:

> While poverty is generally a politically sensitive subject, it is even more sensitive in the Philippines than in most of our borrowing countries. First, the skewedness of income distribution is worse in the Philippines than elsewhere in the region, and is exceeded only in Latin America. Secondly, whereas military-dominated government in, for example, Thailand or Korea, has been justified on the basis of credible external threat, martial law in the Philippines has been justified considerably on the basis of its benefits for the poor.[2]

As a consequence, the Bank warned, the regime was marked by "increasing precariousness"—a condition "which could result in the lifting of martial law under a parliamentary system in which President Marcos, even if initially situated as Prime Minister, would have serious difficulty remaining in power; or a military government."[3]

It was in this atmosphere of impending crisis that the World Bank and the IMF formulated a last-ditch program of economic stabilization. It turned out, however, to be more of the same medicine of liberalization—a "cure" that consisted of administering more doses of the disease. The new cure was a formidably named program of "structural adjustment," financial reform, and devaluation.

In this chapter we examine the Bank's final assault on the Philippine economy through a program of structural adjustment meant to destroy all remaining protectionist barriers. The Bank's massive Structural Adjustment Loan was sorely needed by the debt-ridden and politically precarious regime, but, not surprisingly, it came with strings attached. Once the Marcos regime accepted those strings, the Bank imposed a series of financial "reforms," to allow foreign corporations easier access to local savings. These measures included the concentration of capital through new banking laws, the channeling of capital to the export sector (leading to financial loss, plant closings and bankruptcy for many local businessmen), and, once again, devaluation.

Structural Adjustment

A New Kind of Loan. At the IMF-World Bank annual meeting in Belgrade in September 1979, the Bank unveiled the "structural adjustment loan" (SAL). This new credit program was supposed to respond to the economic crises of Third World countries brought about by mounting levels of external debt and international recession.

In contrast to the traditional *project* loan issued by the Bank, SAL was a *program* loan—that is, it was meant to cover a whole economic sector, such as agriculture, industry, or energy. It was the World Bank bureaucrat's dream, for it formalized World Bank surveillance and control over a wide swathe of the economy. As such, it is not surprising that SAL's were viewed with such suspicion by so many borrowing governments that, as of mid-1980, only four countries, Kenya, Turkey, Bolivia, and the Philippines, were willing to accept the conditions that came with the loan.

The SAL was approved a few months after the IMF gave the regime two loans totaling $654 million to tide it through its external-debt problems. The conjunction of the three loans was not accidental. As a U.S. Treasury Department report explained, gaining leverage was the key consideration:

> . . . the collaboration of other donors and the IMF is particularly important when it comes to influencing macro-level policy. Thus, structural adjustment loans are usually approved only when the borrower has negotiated an Extended Fund Facility agreement with the IMF, a factor which is producing increasingly close Bank/Fund collaboration. Without the added weight and broader focus achieved through collaboration . . . the Bank's leverage over macro-level policy is limited.[4]

Preserving the Myth of Sovereignty. The Philippine SAL was designed to include "the liberalization of commodity import procedures, tariff reform, an appropriate exchange rate policy, strengthening of fiscal incentives for exporters, and administrative actions to promote and facilitate exports. . . ."[5] In short, SAL was a final offensive against protectionism and an effort to fully consolidate export-led industrialization.

That the measures proposed by SAL were the subject of heated debate within the Marcos ruling elite is suggested by the 1980 Country Program Paper:

> Although the Minister of Economic Planning had long advocated industrial policy reform, a cabinet consensus in favor of fundamental reform emerged only in 1979, following a major Philippine study of the incentives system and a Bank sector report that built on it.[6]

World Bank pressure, in other words, was decisive in resolving the conflict. The Bank sector report that forged the consensus was produced by a mission that visited the Philippines in February 1979. The mission's report formed the basis of negotiations for the SAL loan which took place between the Philippine government and World Bank representatives in Manila in August 1979. A restricted and confidential *aide* memoire by a Bank official reported the results of those discussions: "The Government of the Philippines broadly agrees with the general analysis and policy recommendations contained in the World Bank's report. . . . The World Bank is prepared to consider an Industrial

Program . . . lending support to the implementation of these policies."[7]

The myth of national sovereignty, however, had to be preserved. Publicly, the Philippine Government was projected as having initiated the reforms demanded by the Bank. Thus, in August 1980, Minister of Finance Cesar Virata, in "requesting" SAL, wrote to World Bank President McNamara outlining the "initiatives" the government had already taken or was prepared to take to "restructure" the industrial sector. *These were precisely the measures that had been "recommended" by the Bank industrial mission a year and a half earlier.* Indeed, as McNamara's confidential final report and recommendation on the loan commented: "[T]he Philippine government has implemented nearly all the recommendations on export promotion made in the Bank's industrial sector report."[8]

The Measures Taken. Among the measures taken by the regime to demonstrate its good faith was an October 1979 decree liberalizing requirements for bonded manufacturing warehouses, thus permitting "export industries to operate on a truly free-trade basis without being physically located in an export-processing zone."[9] Around the same time, the government reorganized the Export Processing Authority to facilitate the development of a dozen Export Processing Zones (EPZ's) in addition to the three already in operation in Bataan, Baguio, and Mactan. Next, Marcos offered a package of incentives for export-trading companies to set up overseas trade offices, operate bonded manufacturing warehouses, and utilize preferential export financing facilities.

SAL, approved almost a year later, was intended partly to finance these presidential decisions consolidating export-oriented industrialization, as well as other initiatives which took place after the signing of the loan, such as the construction of about 100 "bonded manufacturing villages," or mini-EPZ's throughout the archipelago.

The regime's measures against protectionism, however, constituted the real acid test for the Bank. Thus, prior to the granting of SAL, the regime demonstrated its newfound determination to adhere to World Bank directives by removing 95 items from the restricted import categories ("nonessential consumer goods" and "unclassified consumer goods") and making them freely importable. An official of the Ministry of Industry close to the SAL negotiations explained why this sign of good faith was necessary: "The World Bank wanted some sort of a commitment that we were serious about our future policy changes, rather than a verbal pledge . . . [the Bank] wanted policy announcements before the loan was finalized."[10]

The tariff reform was to go through four phases. Phase I would reduce peak tariff rates (ranging from 70 percent to 100 percent) to 50 percent in two stages, on January 1, 1981 and January 2, 1982. Phase II and III called for the "realignment" of tariff rates for 14 major industries over a period of five years beginning January 1, 1981. Finally, Phase IV would revise tariffs on industries and items not covered in the first three phases.[11]

To ensure that the regime's "political will" would not falter, the Bank divided the loan into two tranches, or installments; the first tranche of $100 million was released in September 1980 when Phases I - III were in the pipeline. The release of the second tranche of $95 million was made contingent on satisfactory performance in the first three phases.

This setup provided the World Bank with a noose it could tighten around Marcos' neck should the promised policy changes not materialize. The wisdom of this arrangement for World Bank interests became clear when Phase I, which involved drastic tariff reductions on 590 commodities,[12] got underway in January 1981. Marcos, afraid of the growing antigovernment stance of some of his one-time supporters among the national capitalists threatened by the reforms, "succumbed to direct pressure [by certain members] of the business sector," according to a government official involved with the tariff legislation. The president's capitulation took the form of an executive order decelerating the pace of tariff reductions. Marcos, confessed a Ministry of Industry liaison with the World Bank, "felt that the private sector was really up in arms against us," and was considering reneging on the promised Phase IV.[13]

Playing its trump card, the World Bank review mission in January 1981 promptly refused to release SAL's $95 million second tranche "until specific actions are completed to extend the liberalizing of import licensing and a realignment of tariffs."[14] It was not until some months later that the government finally satisfied the Bank that it was back on schedule in its final offensive against protectionism. As one Ministry of Industry official later put it, the installment plan gave "us [the technocrats] a weapon against political pressures" from the local entrepreneurial private sector. "I wouldn't fight these people without the World Bank loan," he added.[15]

Bitter Medicine. This form of structural adjustment, one Bank report noted, could bring about "a few highly visible plant closings . . ."[16] due to the inability of domestic firms to compete against the now more freely importable foreign commodities. One of the key subsectors "in need of rationalization," according to the Bank, was the textile industry.[17] Of the 32 member mills of the Textile Mills Association of the Philippines (TMAP), only a handful were large enough to survive restructuring, according to informed observers.

"Rationalization," industry sources agreed, would result in buttressing the half a dozen or so big, somewhat modernized textile mills. According to TMAP President Ramon Siy (himself most likely in the winners' circle as head of the highly mechanized Solid Mills), the smaller mills had to merge with the larger ones or "die a natural death . . . the weaker ones will have to close down."[18] Another executive, this one a likely loser, complained: "We've been making cloth that Filipinos have their tailors make into clothes. Now the government lets in similar cloth cheaper and, as if that weren't enough, it tells us we've got to specialize, we've got to export . . . or produce cloth for exporters [of garments]. Then, if we can prove we can cut production costs by 40 percent, and pay for a good chunk of the machines ourselves, we can get a loan for the rest. . . . We can't. So most of the companies like ours will die."[19]

By the Bank's own estimates, roughly 100,000 workers in "inefficient" garment and textile firms would lose their jobs.[20] This amounted to about 46 percent of the work force in the garment and textile sectors and about five percent of total employment in manufacturing. It was, however, a prospect that seemed scarcely to trouble the Bank. It simply rationalized the dreary fate to which its reforms condemned these workers by resorting to one of those notorious "long run" arguments ridiculed by Keynes: "Reabsorbing those who may be displaced in the process—and who would be best placed and qualified to compete for new jobs—is a minor task in comparison to solving the fundamental employment problem."[21]

Disarming the National Capitalists. If the fate of the workers did not worry the Bank, the reactions of the national industrialists did. These reactions varied. One, and a fairly spectacular one, was that of Dewey Dee, a major force within the textile and garment industry. In January 1981, Dee skipped the country, leaving about $100 million worth of bad debts and several ailing garment and textile firms, including Continental Manufacturing Corporation and Redson Textile Manufacturing Corporation.

No doubt Dee saw his firms doomed by the World Bank restructuring program and decided to get out while the getting was good. But in the process, he provoked a financial panic; frantic private bankers suspended their short-term loan operations or demanded immediate payment on current loans. Despite the bankruptcies or near bankruptcies that ensued, some technocrats saw a silver lining: "Actually," one senior government official admitted, "Dewey Dee has made it easier for us to weed out the firms that we'll help modernize . . . from those we can't. . . . Reducing means that we'll see firms collapsing, merging and modernizing as they're forced to export . . . the 'Dewey Dee affair' only got this off to a head start."[22]

Dee's Houdini-like disappearance was less disturbing to the Bank than the overt opposition of some national businessmen. The Ascher Memorandum, for instance, warned:

> In comparable situations (e.g. Brazil in the mid-1970's to the present) the domestic manufacturer or investor has reacted to the threat of being squeezed between powerful multinational corporations and highly capitalized state enterprises by withdrawing his support from the government. In other cases (e.g., Argentina currently) the elimination of protective tariffs and special subsidies has led to great dissatisfaction within the industries targeted for "streamlining." Therefore, in the Philippines, where the additional element of strongly perceived favoritism to Marcos' personal friends has created considerable resentment, the local business community has several mutually reinforcing reasons to try to undermine the policy directives of the current government.[23]

Especially worrisome to the Bank was the fact that Filipino industrialists were "now using the nationalist argument to criticize the government's policy, thereby finding common ground with the more ideologically oriented opposition centered at the universities."[24] And equally disturbing was the possible resort to violence—a fear underlined by the alleged participation of businessmen in a wave of bombings that hit Marcos-linked business establishments in the summer of 1980:

> In addition to trying to influence policymaking, the business sector can join in the political activities designed

> to remove Marcos along with his economic approach. Business sector support for the opposition press (albeit subdued), opposition movements in exile, and . . . even the recent bombings have been attributed to elements of the local business sector. The apparent aim is to provoke enough disruption to force Marcos into holding elections.[25]

To disarm the grumbling national industrialists, the Bank and the regime resorted to a number of exercises in persuasion, such as government-business seminars. At the "Policy Conference on Tariff Reform" held in Manila on April 22 and 23, 1981, for example, government technocrats cleverly steered the discussion away from the explosive political implications of tariff reform to the domain of academic economics where they, of course, reigned supreme. For example, in response to questions concerning the accelerating bankruptcies, unemployment, and inflation which followed the tariff changes, a progovernment technocrat filled blackboard after blackboard with confusing mathematical symbols accompanied by a narrative which, for most of the entrepreneurs in the audience, represented an equally foreign language. In the end, when the left side of the technocrat's equation equalled the right, she congratulated her audience on "sacrificing in the short run for promised returns in the long run." There was little response from those who were likely, in the "long run," to be financially dead as they sat like schoolchildren copying down the blackboard's wisdom. As several admitted in private later, they found it unfathomable, but impressive nonetheless.

After softening up the manufacturers with mathematical economics, the government then subjected them to the harsh language of "real life,"—delivered by then Minister of Planning Gerardo Sicat. If you're sick, Sicat's message went, you don't postpone going to the doctor when the weather is bad or you will be sicker when the weather is fair.

Such iron-hand-in-velvet-glove tactics elicited the following reaction from one industrialist: "The technocrats are clever. They know when individual businessmen get hurt, they become antigovernment, even nationalistic. But we are not united. . . . [Our] good is our own profit. . . . If the tariff rates that affect me are lowered . . . well, then I care about them, but not [about] the tariff changes that hurt you."[26] To bring off the structural adjustment, Marcos and the Bank worked hard to keep those outlooks individualistic.

The Financial Reforms

In addition to sending an industrial mission to the Philippines in 1979, the Bank and the IMF commissioned a team of experts to come up with proposals to "streamline" the financial sector so that it could better serve the objectives of export-led industrialization. As a result of the mission, the Bank promised a special "APEX" financial sector loan totaling $150 million. As in the case of SAL, however, this was contingent on concrete moves by the regime to show that it really deserved the loans.

Channeling Capital to EOI. Soon after the IMF-Bank mission, the government removed almost all interest rate ceilings on both deposit and lending rates, with the exception of short-term lending, as recommended by the mission. Then, in April 1979, the Central Bank, again on World Bank prodding, introduced a short-term rediscount facility for export financing. (Rediscounting involves the Central Bank lending to banks using the loan papers of a bank's clients as collateral.) Later it raised the rediscount rate for traditional exports such as sugar and coconut while reducing the rate for nontraditional manufactured exports in an effort to channel credit to the latter. All these changes were part of the World Bank and IMF plans for gearing the Philippine economy more totally on EOI; all were likewise part of the preconditions that had to be met before the Bank's APEX money would flow. The general thrust of the new interest rate policy was to economize on capital by penalizing its "inefficient" use while preferentially allocating loan capital to the "more efficient" export manufacturing sector. In other words, the Bank was seeing to it that investment money was not channeled into the more capital-intensive home market firms of the national entrepreneurs. As the Bank noted, "The interest rate is probably the single most influential determinant of the cost of using capital in projects."[27]

Concentrating Capital. Most important among the "signs of good faith" displayed by the regime in return for the APEX loan was the National Assembly's rubber-stamping of laws promoting universal banking or "unibanking" in April 1980. The World Bank's concealed but decisive role in this process was laid out in the 1980 Country Program Paper:

> The [Bank and Fund's] financial sector report made a number of recommendations. . . . In March 1980, the Government passed legislation, derived considerably from the report, to move commercial banks toward multipurpose banking by permitting them to invest in equities.[28]

The unibanking laws permitted commercial banks with a minimum capitalization of P500 million (about $66 million) to engage in activities previously reserved for investment banks. For example, they could acquire up to 100 percent equity ownership in most "allied" businesses (banks and associated activities) and up to 35 percent in "nonallied" ventures (manufacturing, agriculture, and mining). They were also allowed to carry a lower capital-to-risk ratio than the 10 percent prescribed for ordinary commercial banks. In other words, they could lend out more than ten times their combined capital accounts.[29] For the largest, most powerful financial institutions, whose directors were already serving as board directors on the entire range of Philippine companies, unibanking offered unprecedented opportunities for expansion and control.

Filtering reality, as always, through the lens of "efficiency," the IMF and the World Bank saw unibanking as a way to "rationalize" the banking sector to better serve the needs of export-oriented growth. "Rationalization" in this case meant pooling finance capital in fewer larger institutions, supposedly to achieve "economies of scale," and channeling this capital through medium or long-term loans to or equity investments in export-oriented manufacturing industries.

At the time the unibanking legislation took effect, only the government-owned Philippine National Bank (PNB), which held 26 percent of the total resources of the commercial banking system, was big enough to qualify for unibank status. PNB was soon joined by Defense Minister Juan Ponce Enrile's United Coconut Planter's Bank, whose control of coconut exports provided it with enough capital to become the first private bank to receive unibanking status. Beginning in March 1981, the unibanking laws precipitated a flurry of mergers in the financial sector, generally between a commercial bank and an investment bank, as the banks sought to reach the P500 million minimum capital base requirement. Far Eastern Bank and Trust Company (whose largest shareholders are the Japanese Mitsui Bank Ltd. and the American Chemical International Finance Ltd., each with 12.5 percent[30]) linked up with the Private Development Corporation of the Philippines (PDCP), an investment house founded in 1963 at the instigation of the World Bank and owned by a group of about 30 international institutions.[31] Not to be outdone, the wealthy Ayala family's Bank of the Philippine Islands (in which both the Philippine Catholic Church and J. P. Morgan have substantial shares) and Commercial Bank and Trust Company of the Philippines (Comtrust, whose largest stockholder is Chase Manhattan with 30 percent[32]) underwent what they termed an "amicable union." American Express' Bancom Development Corporation merged with the partner of its choice, the Philippine government's Land Bank of the Philippines.

This flurry of activity, however, took place only among a favored few. Of the 28 domestically-owned commercial banks, only a handful were capable of reaching the P500 million lower limit that would give them access to unibanking privileges. The World Bank-instigated financial reforms offered the smaller financiers the same fate that the Bank-supported industrial reforms held out to the small, "inefficient" national industrialists: bankruptcy.

The Muffled Debate. Unibanking did not come about without resistance. Indeed, when the joint IMF-World Bank mission first proposed the plan, Central Bank Governor Gregorio Licaros headed up a faction of officials within the Central Bank that opposed it. Their reasons were laid out in an internal Central Bank memo:

> When a bank acquires equity in a private corporation, the probability of abuse in the extension of credit to that corporation will be increased . . . the history of banking in the Philippines shows that the management of banks have not always exercised objectivity in processing loan applications of firms with special relations with the bank. We feel that if banks are allowed to acquire equities of private corporations, it would give rise to similar and perhaps more difficult problems.
>
> If banks are allowed to acquire equities in private corporations, this might result in concentration of too much power in the hands of a few individuals . . . unfortunately, [a] majority of the banks in the Philippines are owned or controlled by a group of people who are related to each other. . . . [T]he ability of an individual or a group of individuals to dominate the operations of a bank with very little opposition from other stockholders who, per records, hold substantial stocks of the

> bank, is a very clear manifestation of this reality [of dummy stockholders]. . . .
>
> If the banking institutions, through merger and integration with related financial intermediaries, become larger, it may be even more difficult [than it is now] for the smaller borrowers to obtain financing since it has been observed that the larger institutions have shown preference for servicing loan requirements of larger and well established firms.[33]

Behind the closed doors of the Central Bank, transnational banks and corporations were the major targets of criticism. A knowledgeable source close to the bastions of power in Manila explained, "It was felt that, following the precedent of the 1972 World Bank-IMF financial reform which led to the merger and consolidation [of Philippine commercial banks] with foreign banks, the foreign presence in banks will only increase with universal banking . . . . And big commercial banks favor big companies, like multinational corporations."[34] In short, a tight community would become even tighter. Many of the bigger Filipino bankers, wearing another of their numerous hats, were the local partners of multinational firms which borrowed substantial amounts domestically. Universal banking, reasoned some Central Bank officials, might well lead to the hoped-for greater mobilization of local savings for long-term lending, but much of the new savings would find its way into the hands of the foreign investors leading the push to EOI. "Why should we follow an IMF directive if we know better?" one of the deputy governors reportedly demanded of colleagues at a Central Bank committee meeting.[35]

But by April 1980, just one year after the World Bank/IMF financial mission set the process in motion, seven unibanking laws were already in the statute books. President Marcos, in a well-publicized order, gave the rubber-stamp Interim National Assembly exactly two weeks to pass the laws. Otherwise, he vowed, he would push them through himself with presidential decrees.

Naturally the technocrats were pleased. One of the most satisfied was Armand Fabella, a former government technocrat who had served as the Filipino co-chairman of the joint IMF-Central Bank panel which formulated an earlier set of reforms to enlarge the capitalization of banks in 1972. "Expanded commercial banking," he expounded, "is a technique for separating the men from the boys . . . . the philosophy behind expanded commercial banking is how much competition to [allow] .... Because competition can be very expensive. And some bigness can be very useful."[36]

But the World Bank was not so cavalier in its internal assessments. It was coldbloodedly conscious of what was in store for the Philippines.

> Concentration in the financial sector tends to create excessive market power for a few institutions. If the banks were free to invest in equities and hold them in their own account, there would clearly be a danger of them obtaining a controlling interest in other corporations.[37]

ADFU: The World Bank in the Central Bank. With the financial reforms in motion, the Bank agreed to grant the Philippines an "APEX" loan. This was to be channeled to financial institutions that would, in turn, relend to medium and large-scale industries that were "labor intensive" and "export oriented."

The World Bank, however, demanded one more key condition, one which elicited even more controversy within the Central Bank: that a special unit, the APEX Development Finance Unit (ADFU), be created to administer the loan.

Central Bank officials were at first quite concerned about ADFU's proposed autonomy. As the head of the special unit later explained, "The ADFU was spun off by itself . . . to be rather autonomous . . . because of the unusual character the World Bank wanted it to have . . . an institution-building character."[38] The Central Bank officials eventually capitulated as a result of strong World Bank pressure. "You have to see this in its proper perspective," one of them explained. "It is a matter of our own involvement with the World Bank. . . . Ours is a good relationship, with lots of loans."[39]

Nonetheless, some Central Bank officials outside the ADFU continued to fear that ADFU would serve as a beachhead from which the World Bank could expand to directly control most of the government's external-borrowing policies. As former Governor Licaros later disclosed,

> The World Bank wanted part, if not all, of our current loan borrowing to be channeled through ADFU. . . . I did not agree to this, because the ADFU will be controlled by World Bank policies and reviewed by the World Bank. . . . My thinking is that the more money the World

> Bank channels to the Philippines through ADFU, the better. And if those World Bank loans involve cofinancing [with private international commercial banks], that too can go through ADFU. But no more. . . . Having all our commercial [international] borrowing go through ADFU as a general rule would subvert approval of all our borrowing to World Bank conditions and evaluations.[40]

Licaros' fears of a greatly expanded role for the World Bank in determining the Philippine external financial dealings were confirmed when Jaime Laya, a World Bank favorite, took over as Central Bank Governor. An April 1981 World Bank staff report on developments related to ADFU asserted:

> The guidelines approved [by the government] were generally satisfactory but some modifications were necessary to bring them in line with the basic philosophy of the proposed Bank financing, as are some additions to make them more comprehensive. First, instead of being restricted to administering foreign exchange funds obtained from the Bank and ADB [Asian Development Bank], ADFU should have the capability of mobilizing and administering funds raised from other sources, including foreign commercial banks. . . . The Central Bank agreed to incorporate the necessary amendments in the operating policy guidelines and has since obtained approval for the revised guidelines.[41]

The reason for these modifications became apparent in light of the reactions of foreign business to the economic crisis that had begun in 1979. U.S. commercial banks, to which the Philippines owed an astounding $4.2 billion by late 1980, had always regarded the IMF-World Bank seal of approval as a decisive factor on keeping their lines of credit open to Marcos. As the World Bank 1980 Country Program Paper acknowledged, "The Government regards the IMF's role as essential not only for the large volume of resources provided, but also for the reassurance on economic management provided to private sources of finance."[42] By 1981, however, with export growth dwindling, external debt growing, and bankruptcies shaking the industrial sector, the foreign financiers wanted even more solid reassurance. They were only too happy, therefore, to accept a new structure, ADFU, which assured that the majority of their loans could be channeled to "viable" (i.e., World Bank-approved) industrial projects. In the eyes of international financiers, the new setup enhanced the chances of repayment. In the World Bank's eyes, the arrangement would ensure that most foreign borrowings would go to export-oriented projects.

The Standard Tonic

The stepped-up liberalization program would have been incomplete without that standard IMF tonic, devaluation. Under the flexible exchange rate system imposed by the IMF and the Bank after the devastating devaluation of 1970, the peso depreciated from P6.43 to the dollar in 1970 to P6.78 in 1973 to P7.50 in 1975. By 1979, IMF and World Bank complaints about the "overvalued" peso began to be heard again. For the IMF, devaluation represented a "quick fix" to the Philippines' worsening external payments position; it would supposedly "cheapen" Philippine exports, resulting in a much greater volume of goods sold and more foreign exchange earnings.

But as usual, the two agencies had another, more strategic objective in pushing devaluation; by raising the peso prices of raw material, intermediate goods, and machinery imports, monetary depreciation would help squeeze out the remaining "inefficient" Filipino producers in the import substitution sector of industry.

The IMF plan, however, encountered opposition from several Filipino officials. Prominent among them was Central Bank Governor Licaros, who argued that the relief would at best be temporary and superficial while the consequence—recession—would be severe.

Formerly quite receptive to IMF-World Bank advice, the aging Licaros began to have second thoughts by the late 1970's. After his forced resignation in 1981, Licaros explained his opposition to devaluation: "When IMF people look at the exchange rate, they are easily disturbed. They look at figures, formulas, especially the 'purchasing power parity [formula]' which I personally don't understand."[43] He was referring to that elegant formula that textbooks warn is valid only for a country beginning from an "equilibrium position" and no longer suffering from inflation. And even in the best conditions, "equilibrium position" is a far cry from reality. But IMF staffers use the formula anyway, and World Bank bureaucrats copy the IMF.

The growing gulf between the IMF and Licaros is captured in a number of secret IMF documents. An IMF mission in May 1980 recommended that to achieve “external competitiveness” and “promote greater balance of payments adjustment . . . the authorities permit greater flexibility in the exchange rate. . . .”[44] The response of Licaros and his Central Bank team, however, was disconcerting to the mission: “The Philippine representatives regarded the current level of the exchange rate as broadly appropriate. They pointed to the high growth of export and stressed that there was no evidence as yet that domestic producers were becoming uncompetitive.”[45]

In August 1980, the World Bank added its voice to the IMF’s call for devaluation, informing the Philippine government that ‘the foreign exchange account could be balanced by a moderate devaluation.‘[46] The process of depreciating the peso began that month—but Licaros was still putting up some resistance.

With this stance, Licaros placed himself out on a limb. Not only did he oppose devaluation, he positioned himself against the World Bank assault on protectionism. As one Ministry of Industry employee directly involved in negotiations with the Bank explained scornfully, “Licaros just wasn’t open on [lowering existing] protectionism.” Moreover, the “old man,” as the younger technocrats disdainfully referred to him, had expressed major reservations about the role of the ADFU special unit.

An opportunity for the bank and the technocrats to get rid of Licaros emerged in early 1981, in the aftermath of the “Dewey Dee affair.” After Dee fled the country leaving $100 million in bad debts, it was discovered that Licaros had been receiving kickbacks from Chinese-Filipino friends like Dee whenever the Central Bank approved their foreign exchange deals. The Licaros affair was hushed up by the government for fear of the impact on the Philippines’ credit rating should it become widely known that the Central Bank Governor was not, after all, a model of bourgeois propriety. Yet when Marcos subsequently dismissed Licaros, the technocrats, the World Bank, and the IMF were not displeased.

With Licaros out of the way, the “moderate devaluation” demanded by the IMF and the Bank took off. By June 1981, the exchange rate had deteriorated from P7.4 to the dollar to P7.9. By early 1982, it stood at P8.3 to the dollar.

The IMF was pleased, but it also made it clear to the new authorities that the currency had to be debauched even more to make up for Licaros’ earlier “stubbornness”:

> There had been a marked loss in the competitiveness of Philippine tradables during 1979-80 when exchange rate policy had not adequately compensated for adverse relative price movements. Only in the last six months has policy bcome sufficiently flexible to enable a part of the loss in competitiveness which occurred earlier in 1981 to be recouped. The staff would encourage the authorities to continue with their recent policies until the competitiveness lost during the past few years has been restored.[47]

The new Central Bank governor, Jaime Laya, informed the IMF that he would certainly be more pliable than Licaros: "The authorities replied that they would, indeed, maintain the recent flexible exchange rate policy."[48]

Conclusion

By the end of the 1970's, technocrats from the World Bank, IMF, and the government all agreed that the economy was afflicted by a "fundamental disequilibrium." What most refused to acknowledge, however, was that this condition had resulted to a great extent from the steps that the multilateral agencies had imposed in order to open up the economy to "the winds of international competition," as one bureaucrat put it. Given this position, it was not surprising that the cure proposed by the technocrats consisted of heavier doses of the disease of liberalization, structural adjustment, and devaluation.

With the failure of the antipoverty containment programs in the city and the countryside, the stern visage of the Bank as a determined servitor of foreign interests was fully revealed to most Filipinos. Indeed, the Bank dropped its antipoverty rhetoric and advanced the disciplinarian's dictum in justifying the structural adjustment program: "Pain in the short term, relief in the long term." But this sham logic, clothed in stoic economese, could no longer convince even long-time friends of the Bank like Central Bank Governor Licaros. The agency therefore increasingly felt the necessity of deploying its trusted technocrat cadres more strategically within the state apparatus in order to more completely control economic policy making. This process, which resulted in a "World Bank" Cabinet, is the subject of the following and last chapter.

CHAPTER SEVEN

Technocrats Versus Cronies

The World Bank Cabinet

In the first six months of 1981, the Marcos regime carried out a number of highly publicized moves to show the world that it was "democratizing" the political system. On January 17, Marcos lifted martial law but only after issuing a number of presidential decrees that assured him of dictatorial powers. In April, the regime declared that the results of a national referendum approved Marcos' initiative to institute a six-year presidential term. And on June 16, Marcos proclaimed himself the victor in elections boycotted by 40 percent of the electorate and in which many others participated only because a presidential decree penalized nonvoting by imprisonment.

But while these cosmetic moves caught the attention of the international press, more significant moves were afoot. In June, Marcos appointed the World Bank's most trusted agent in the Philippines, Finance Minister Cesar Virata, to the post of prime minister. By August 1981, a presidential cabinet dominated by Bank-sponsored technocrats was in place. In addition to Virata, the cabinet included the following World Bank favorites: Industry Minister Roberto Ongpin; Central Bank Governor Jaime Laya; Minister of Planning Placido Mapa, Jr., who had previously served as executive secretary for the Philippines at the World Bank; and, to everyone's surprise, Alejandro Melchor, Jr., an old friend of the Bank and board member of the Asian Development Bank, who was restored to grace as a cabinet-rank presidential adviser after years in the doghouse for opposing the First Lady's extravagant projects.

Less visible but equally significant were Bank-backed appointees who were named to second-level positions. For example, Roy Zosa, investment officer for East Asia of the World Bank's private investment affiliate, the International Finance Corporation (IFC), was tapped to serve as one of the governors overseeing the reorganization of the corruption-wracked Development Bank of Philippines (DBP).

The cosmetic lifting of martial law and the creation of a cabinet dominated by technocrats were the results of intense behind-the-scenes pressure exerted on Marcos by the Bank and the U.S. government. The Ascher Memorandum, dated November 6, 1980, warned Marcos that "martial law had increasingly become a liability."[1] To show that it meant business, in 1981 the Bank followed up this warning with a refusal to grant the $600 million in development aid requested by the regime, reducing its commitment to only $475 million.[2] As a further warning, the Bank made a move which stunned the regime: it vetoed the government's repeated requests for an energy sector loan. This denial was particularly harsh and unexpected since the Bank had previously encouraged the regime to prepare an energy development program. The Bank had, in fact, already tentatively budgeted $330 million for such a program in the 1982-85 period.[3]

The World Bank's tightening of the screws was a response to four concerns. The first was the agency's fear that its multibillion-dollar investment in the Philippines was going down the drain. With 63 percent of all its projects classified as "problem projects" by 1979, the Bank told the government that "a larger program would not be justified until the deteriorating trend of project implementation is reversed."[4] Placing the technocrats at the helm of government, the Bank felt, would increase the chances of salvaging the program.

The second key reason for creating the technocrat cabinet was to assure the international banks that the regime continued to be a good credit risk, that the necessary measures would be taken to repay the country's $15 billion debt to them. The choice of Virata as Prime Minister was partly symbolic, for he was virtually the only Filipino high official trusted by the bankers.

A third reason for forcing the creation of a cabinet to its liking was the Bank's fear that the regime might lose its political nerve in pursuing the final offensive against protectionism. Signs of flabbiness on the part of Marcos in 1980 prompted the Bank to warn the regime in its August 1980 Country Program Paper that "the proposed volume of lending is predicated on the assumption that the Government will remain willing to undertake policy reform related to structural adjustment . . . unsatisfactory Government performance in any of these areas could lead to a shortfall in the overall volume of lending."[5] When Marcos, in fact, attempted to decelerate the pace of tariff reduction in January 1981, the Bank, alarmed, felt that stronger measures were needed.

The fourth motive behind the World Bank's installation of the technocrat cabinet is the subject of this final chapter: the Bank's desire to discipline Marcos' cronies.

All the President's Men

Marcos' cronies had a unique role in Philippine society, particularly in the martial law economy. This circle of friends and relatives of the president were called "bureaucrat capitalists" by the left because of the way they exploited their ties with Marcos and public agencies to build private empires. The cronies constituted one of the three pillars of the regime, the other two being the technocrats and the military. The relations between the technocrats and the cronies had always been uneasy, but by the late seventies the cronies were making a mockery of the technocrats' attempts to project neutrality in economic policy-making. "Local firms with particularly good connections with the Marcos administration are consolidating their advantages," the Bank complained.[6] Thus, selling the structural adjustment program to the national capitalists was made difficult by the "element of strongly perceived favoritism to Marcos' personal friends."[7]

The cronies were, in Imelda Marcos' tolerant description, the equivalent of America's late nineteenth-century "robber barons." Their elite ranks included, for example, Roberto Benedicto, former Philippine ambassador to Japan and a sugar and shipping magnate. Benedicto, taking advantage of the great sugar market bust of the late 70's which had depressed sugar exports by over 70 percent between 1974 and 1978, was able to achieve overwhelming dominance in the industry. As head of the government Philippine Sugar Commission (PHILSUCOM), Benedicto gained monopoly control over the export marketing of sugar and was able to buy up plantations by using the agency's mandate to "assume control over any sugar mill or refinery which fails to meet its formal and other contractual obligations for two years or has become inefficient in its operations."[8] Benedicto also set up the Republic Planters' Bank in 1978 to control crop loans—with the result that all phases of the industry came under his direction.[9]

In the vastly important coconut industry, two friends of Marcos worked as a team—Defense Minister Juan Ponce Enrile and "Coconut King" Eduardo Cojuangco. Enrile was chairman of the board of Cojuangco's United Coconut Mills, or UNICOM. Enrile was also honorary chairman of COCOFED, the association of big coconut planters, while Cojuangco served as a director of the government regulatory board, the Philippine Coconut Authority (PCA). In the fall of 1979, Marcos stunned Manila business circles with a presidential decree ordering all coconut processing companies to sell out to or affiliate with UNICOM. This was the first phase of what the Enrile-Conjuangco conglomerate candidly and cynically described as "vertical integration" of the industry. Vertical integration was being financed by an onerous levy imposed on millions of smallholders of about $10 for every 100 kilograms of copra they produced.[10]

While Benedicto and the Enrile-Cojuangco team built their empire by monopolizing agribusiness, Rodolfo Cuenca made his from government-initiated construction contracts. Cuenca's construction conglomerate, the Construction and Development Corporation of the Philippines (CDCP), was, by 1980, one of the country's top ten companies in terms of assets and one of the top 15 in net sales.[11] Eighty percent of CDCP's construction work was done on government contract—among them, the "Marcos Bridge" connecting the islands of Leyte and Samar, the Manila International Airport, the Manila North Expressway, and the Manila Bay Reclamation Project.[12] From construction, CDCP branched out to real estate, mining, and resort hotels, borrowing heavily from both local and international banks to finance its expansion.

The Herdis and Silverio empires were built in essentially the same fashion. Like Cuenca, neither Herminio Disini, head of the Herdis group, nor Ricardo Silverio had notable success in their early business careers. Disini's passport to riches was his family relationship to the First Lady. He was awarded a virtual monopoly of the cigarette-filter business by a presidential decree which imposed a 100 percent tariff on the imported raw materials of Disini's competitor while keeping the usual ten percent tariff on those used by Disini's company.[13]

In less than eight years, Disini built up a conglomerate of more than 30 companies, dealing in such diverse activities as construction, logging, insurance, and petrochemicals.

His most spectacular coup was the estimated $5 million to $35 million "commission" he received from Westinghouse for securing the government contract to build a $1.1 billion nuclear reactor in Bataan. Westinghouse's competitor, General Electric, had offered to construct *two* reactors for $700 million, but GE did not have such strong government connections. Herdis companies then proceeded to secure the subcontracts for engineering, construction management, and insurance for the nuclear reactor project.

Like Disini, Silverio started out as a small businessman and used his relationship to Marcos as the highway to economic power. His Delta Motors Corporation acquired the exclusive right to assemble and distribute Toyota automotive parts in the Philippines. From this base, Silverio built an empire of some 30 companies engaged in everything from auto assembly to electronics, from air and sea transport to insurance and banking.[14]

Subsidizing the Cronies

The Bank, despite its attempt to distance itself from the cronies, was not an innocent bystander in the latter's meteoric rise to economic dominance. In many of their profit-making ventures, the Marcos cronies received valuable assistance from the World Bank. The building of Metro Manila's North Expressway by Cuenca's CDCP, for instance, was partly financed by the Bank. Disini's Cellophil, a giant private logging venture, was assisted by World Bank funds in a project to develop a "pine plantation" in northern Luzon.[15]

The International Finance Corporation (IFC), the World Bank affiliate that provides equity as well as loan capital to corporations operating in the Third World, developed tie-ups with a number of corporations that were partly owned by the cronies. These included Mariwasa Manufacturing, a joint venture in which Japanese capital and the Silverio group had significant shares; Philippine Polyamide Industrial Corporation, owned jointly by Japanese capital and the Marcos-linked Tan-Lee family group.

Recently, the IFC has decided to invest $5 million in the much ballyhooed copper smelter project,[16] financed by Marubeni, which has significant links to sugar magnate Benedicto.

Foreign Capital and the Cronies

Why, then, did the Bank make its dramatic move against the cronies and their previously invulnerable bastions of economic power? The reason lay primarily in the increasing alarm felt by foreign capital over competition from the cronies. At first glance, the foreign investors' negative attitudes toward the cronies might seem surprising since Marcos' friends were closely tied to influential foreign capitalist groups. Benedicto, for instance, was so closely associated with the Japanese giant Zaibatsu Marubeni that other Japanese firms, jealous of Marubeni's ties with Benedicto, took to calling him "Maru-benedicto."[17] Disini not only served as the well-paid Philippine agent for Westinghouse, he also had joint ventures with diverse foreign firms, including Hooker Chemicals, the Occidental Petroleum subsidiary involved in the Love Canal chemical dumping scandal.[18] CDCP's Cuenca had developed ties with a number of Japanese corporations, like Izusu Motors, while Silverio was associated with the German Maschinen Fabriken Augsburg (MAN) and the Japanese Mariwasa Corporation as well as Toyota.[19]

But while individual foreign investors certainly benefited from their ties with the cronies, foreign capital as a whole, especially U.S. capital, was frustrated by the favoritism that began to pervade economic decision making. As *Fortune* put it, "Of all the country's problems, the one that most seriously undermines the confidence of international bankers and investors is the high-level corruption that pervades Philippine life like jungle rot."[20] Alarm really set in, however, when Marcos' friends began to use their influence in government to move against foreign competitors.

It was, for instance, a British-American owned filter company that Disini put out of business by securing government imposition of a 100 percent tariff on the former's imported materials.[21] The American-owned Granexport Corporation, the largest exporter of copra, was also brought to heel. When firms like Granexport refused to sell out voluntarily to the Conjuangco-Enrile combine, Marcos issued the 1979 executive order decreeing that all coconut-processing companies sell out to or affililate with the Cojuangco-Enrile controlled UNICOM.[22] Viewing these moves, foreign investors could not but be reminded of the piratical tactics that Marcos used to expropriate the vast holdings of his main economic rival, the Lopez family, in 1973.

These moves were resented by the international finance community, but sparks really began to fly when the bureaucrat capitalists got in the way of the U.S. giants. General Electric, whose nuclear reactor bid was rejected in favor of a higher bid by Westinghouse, made its dissatisfaction well known in international business circles. Ford and General Motors were equally upset. The auto giants had been told by the Marcos government that if they made components that could be exported from the Philippines, this would offset the requirement that the cars they assembled in the country should contain a substantial amount of locally made parts. As a result, GM invested $17 million in a transmission plant, and Ford set up a $36 million factory at the Bataan Export Processing Zone (BEPZ) stamping out body parts. The rules, however, changed in midstream. After the factories were already in production, the government decreed that component exports would offset only 15 percent of local content. What angered the two automobile giants even more than the rule change was the fact that Silverio's Delta Motors, the Toyota assembler, was exempted from the new decree.[23]

Taming the Cronies

The long-awaited opportunity for foreign capital to put the bureaucrat capitalists in their place emerged in early 1981. A major financial crisis swept the country in the wake of the flight of Dewey Dee, who left behind an estimated $100 million in bad debts. In panic, local and international bankers stopped short-term lending and recalled their loans. The cronies were caught in the crunch. The total outstanding debt of Cuenca's CDCP and its numerous subsidiaries, for instance, stood at P5 billion, or about $633 million.[24] A number of Herdis companies, such as Cellophil Resources Corporation, Asia Industries, Atrium Capital Corporation, and Asia-Pacific Finance were hit by cash-flow problems.[25] The flagship of the Silverio group, Delta Motors, was bankrupted by a loss of over $2.5 million in 1980—a conglomerate bust exacerbated by a massive fraud that brought down Silverio's Philippine Underwriters Finance Corporation (Philfinance).[26] Marcos' cronies, in short, were trapped in a classic overexpansion motivated by greed and financed by debt.

The crisis of the cronies triggered an acrimonious debate in finance and government circles over what to do with the victims' bankrupt businesses. A key figure linked to foreign capital, Jaime Ongpin, head of the Benguet Consolidated mining firm whose Engineering Equipment subsidiary is CDCP's main competitor for government contracts, argued for letting nature take its brutal course:

> Considering that many, though not all, of the victims are in deep trouble despite their gross exploitation of political connections and unbridled access to government financial institutions in the past, what reasonable basis can there be for concluding that massive additional funding in the future will not simply result in 'throwing good money after bad'?[27]

Ongpin then warned that "The Philippines will never solve its economic problems unless it can convince capital not only to remain in the country but also to come in from abroad. That day will never come unless the administration demonstrates in unequivocal terms that it is prepared to abandon its failed policy of favoritism and to start dealing a fresh deck and an even hand."[28]

Casting the cronies adrift, however, posed a major economic problem; their businesses and financial institutions had become so central in the postmartial law economic order that allowing them to collapse risked bringing the whole structure down. As Jaime Ongpin's brother, Industry Minister Roberto Ongpin, put it, "the collective liabilities of these companies total many billions of pesos and their wholesale liquidation would have a domino effect on the entire financial system damaging even innocent bystanders including the 'legitimate segments of Philippine business.' "[29]

But it was not only the possibility of economic collapse that stayed the Bank's and technocrats' hand. An even more important factor was political. The cronies constituted one of the three pillars of the regime—and, from Marcos' view, the most reliable pillar, given the fact that he had to compete with the Americans for influence over the technocrats and the military. Marcos had created his cronies, and they were totally dependent upon and utterly loyal to him. The cronies, then, could not be eliminated, but they had to be disciplined and put in their place as junior partners of U.S. capital.

The terms of the compromise were worked out by mid-1981, with the World Bank in command. The first key point was the establishment of the World Bank cabinet, with Finance Minister Virata assuming the premiership. Second was the creation of a $630 million "rescue-of-troubled-companies fund" from local and foreign capital, aimed primarily at resuscitating the cronies' conglomerates. This was closely linked with the third point—the administration of the rescue fund by the Apex Development Finance Unit (ADFU) of the Central Bank, the establishment of which had been ordered by the World Bank in 1980 in connection with the financial sector reforms.[30] In short, the World Bank would supervise the rescue operation. Third, access to rescue funds was "premised on [the cronies'] subsidiaries to be sold," as Prime Minister Virata put it. "They have to get back to their basic business . . . and concentrate on that."

The salvaging plan triggered a round of strong criticism from the business community, especially from smaller firms, which, lacking the cronies' ties to the government inner circles, were not targeted for financial assistance. This anger forced the Central Bank, now under Laya's technocratic hand, to respond defensively:

> The Central Bank is sensitive to misunderstanding on the part of the business community . . . that the initally listed companies are favored by the government. Criticism notwithstanding, the bigger companies, because of their bigger financial needs, will have to be attended to first since placing their financial structure on a sounder footing would benefit not only them but the rest of the system as well.[31]

The conditions of the rescue effort revealed the stern visage of the Bank. As the ADFU put it, "the fund is aimed to be used to provide basic structural changes in the financial makeup of a qualified company accompanied by required changes in the management, ownership and organizational structures of the enterprise."[32]

The ailing corporations were, for one thing, required to accept government-appointed technocrats as financial controllers and board members. This often went hand-in-hand with the government's acquisition of controlling shares in the company. Industry Minister Ongpin, for example, was appointed CDCP's new chairman, although Rodolfo Cuenca was allowed to remain president.[33] At the same time, the government's Development Bank of the Philippines (DBP), after being cleaned up of crony-linked bureaucrats, acquired majority ownership of CDCP's Resort Hotels and moved to divest the conglomerate of its Galleon Shipping Corporation.[34] Two financial institutions belonging to the Silverio group, the scandal-wracked Philfinance and Pilipinas Bank, were taken over by the government's Philippine National Bank.[35] And three troubled finance corporations of the Herdis Group—Atrium Capital Corporation, Asia Pacific Finance Corporation, and Interbank—were forced into a merger with the DBP, with the latter assuming a 70 percent equity in the new superbank.[36]

As the World Bank came down on Disini, Cuenca, and Silverio with its double-edged rescue plan, it teamed up with the U.S. Department of Justice to whip the Enrile-Cojuangco faction into line. In February 1981, the U.S. government filed a lawsuit against the coconut conglomerate, UNICOM, and three U.S.-based companies it either controlled or cooperated with—Granex, Crown Oil Corporation, and Pan Pacific Commodities—for conspiring to create a shortage of coconut oil to drive up its price. This bid to create a "COCOPEC" had failed, since U.S. and world consumers merely switched to other substitutes.[37] As a glut developed and prices fell, the coconut monopoly became suddenly vulnerable. Taking advantage of UNICOM's weakened position, the World Bank supplemented the Justice Department attack by pressuring Marcos (through the technocrats) to abolish the onerous levy on coconut producers that had been used to further Enrile and Cojuangco's grip on the industry.

The ensuing "battle over the levy" in the coconut industry exposed the antagonisms that had been provoked by the World Bank's drive to more directly control the economy as a whole. At first, Marcos succumbed to Bank pressure and canceled the levy in September 1981. By the next month, with counterpressure exerted by Enrile and Cojuangco, he restored the levy while Prime Minister Virata was out of the country.

The struggle over the levy was, however, only the most visible conflict between the technocrats and the cronies. Pressure from Marcos' cronies forced the technocrats to depart from the ceiling agreed upon by the IMF and the government for bailing out the cronies' troubled companies. The unilateral government move, raising the rescue financing from $193 to almost $400 million in 1981, provoked the IMF to veto the regime's request for a standby credit agreement for 1982.[38] Agents of both camps locked horns in corporate board rooms and all the way down the line. And the fight sometimes got rough; one former Bank official now serving as a governor of the Development Bank of the Philippines was trailed to the rest room of a Manila hotel by thugs, roughed up, and warned to stop scrutinizing the books of the company of one of Marcos' cronies or risk bodily harm to both himself and his family. Another former Bank technocrat who joined the Ministry of Human Settlements was framed by business associates of the deputy minister (Joly Benitez, Imelda's *eminence grise*), accused of salting away thousands of pesos, and stripped of his position. "It's rough," remarked one Bank technocrat. "You risk losing not only your reputation but also your life."

In short, the cronies might have seen the handwriting on the wall, but they served notice that they were going to kick and scratch each step of the way back to junior status.

Equilibrium and Disequilibrium

The installation of the World Bank Cabinet and institution of technocrat control of key financial and industrial firms marked a significant shift in the correlation of forces among the groups supporting the regime. A new equilibrium was achieved; the technocrats were now in command.

This political equilibrium, however, was precarious. Although the technocrats enjoyed the decisive support of the World Bank and the IMF, they were totally bereft of an indigenous base. This fact worried their key sponsor, the Bank, which noted:

> The technocrats . . . in theory could comprise a political force, but they never had to demonstrate or cultivate a base of support. There is no evidence that the economic expansion of the first five years of martial law has created a favorable image of the technocrats that could offset the blame they have incurred for the sluggish growth, higher inflation, and unemployment of the last few years.[39]

For the moment, however, the technocrats were ascendant. Their position was reinforced by serious splits within the cronies' ranks, as the Romualdez faction headed by the First Lady found itself locked in bitter struggle with the Enrile-Cojuangco conglomerate in a war of position for the succession to Marcos.

The grip of the technocrats was further consolidated when the U.S. State Department gave them its formal blessings. In Congressional hearings in November 1981, Daniel O'Donohue, Acting Deputy Assistant Secretary of State, asserted that in contrast to the Carter policy of abstaining on multilateral bank loans to the Philippines, the Reagan "administration changed the U.S. vote in the multilateral development banks to 'yes' on Philippine loans in recognition of the improvements [in political and human rights] that have occurred, and in expectation that these positive trends will continue."[40]

O'Donohue also awarded the U.S. government's seal of approval to the SAL and APEX programs, stating that "the political dislocations created by the several economic reforms pressed on the Philippine Government will not seriously test their ability to manage them."[41] In conclusion, he asserted:

> the planned gradual application of all [the key reforms], as proposed, will create some political difficulties that are transitory, manageable and worth the pain. The most serious political effect would be created by failure to pursue the reforms—which would affect confidence in the future. But the economy's management team is held in high regard and we don't see that happening now.[42]

By the end of 1981, then, the World Bank—an agency, it must always be remembered, controlled by the U.S. government—had achieved a position of undisputed dominance over economic policy making in the Philippines. It was, however, a Pyrrhic victory, for the Bank no longer framed its role in terms of "development" but of containing the rapid unwinding of its decade-old strategy of export-oriented development. As one disillusioned Bank technocrat put it, "It is no longer a question of development, but of keeping the patient alive."[43]

But while the cronies might have been whipped into line, the people of the Philippines could not be. Economic stagnation, increasing absolute poverty, and tightening foreign control fueled discontent. This discontent was manifested in the citizenry's increasingly defiant moves, such as the widespread boycott of the 1981 presidential elections, and in the growing strength of the revolutionary nationalist underground opposition, the National Democratic Front.

The Bank realized that time was running out on the regime . . . and on itself. If the technocrats failed in their attempt to stabilize the economy, then the prospect was *le déluge*: nationalistic political scenarios, including one, warned the Ascher Memorandum, dominated by the Communist Party's New People's Army, which "could appear as the main armed opponent of the Government if things fall apart dramatically after Marcos."[44] The society was, in other words, afflicted with a "strategic disequilibrium" that first aid treatments by the World Bank could no longer cure.

CONCLUSION

Development Debacle

On June 30, 1981, Robert McNamara resigned from the World Bank. The atmosphere surrounding his departure was reminiscent of that which prevailed thirteen years earlier when he left the Pentagon at the height of the Vietnam War.

There was however, one difference: this time the fusillade was coming from the right, which had just won the American presidency. The *Wall Street Journal* accused McNamara of having created a highly paid, 6,000-person-strong bureaucracy doling out $12 billion worth of welfare checks annually to the Third World. Other critics, such as the Heritage Foundation, went further: the Bank, they said, was encouraging socialism in the Third World because its lending policies were biased toward state enterprises rather than private businesses. The institution even had its resident "Maoist," they claimed, in the person of Mahbub Ul-Haq, the director of McNamara's elite corps, the Policy Planning and Program Review Department. An international civil servant in the British mold, Haq had come to be known as the "brains" behind McNamara's antipoverty, "basic needs" approach.

But not all criticism came from the outside. Within the Bank's beleaguered headquarters in Washington, D.C., bureaucrats joked cynically about McNamara's obsession with statistics and the game of generating meaningless numbers that this had produced. Others grumbled about the overcentralization and authoritarianism which put a premium on loyalty rather than creativity or objectivity. And almost everyone concurred that staff morale had degenerated significantly in the four years leading up to McNamara's departure.

In the midst of this crisis of confidence, the Bank was subjected to fire from snipers on the left. In late 1980 and throughout 1981, the Congress Task Force, *Counterspy* magazine, the Institute for Food and Development Policy, and the Southeast Asia Resource Center fed the international press with a steady stream of confidential documents on Bank programs in the Philippines, Indonesia, South Korea, and China.[1] The leaked reports dramatically shattered the myth of a prosocialist Bank advanced by the right. They showed, especially in the case of the Philippines, the instrumental role that the Bank played in refashioning Third World political and economic structures to better serve the needs of U.S. multinational corporations and the U.S. government. The reports revived the memory of McNamara's cynical manipulation of World Bank policy to serve U.S. foreign policy in 1971, when he cut off assistance to the Allende administration in Chile as part of the Nixon-Kissinger strategy to destabilize that government.

The debate between left and right about the role of the Bank was "settled" in February 1982—in favor of the left. The umpire was an unlikely one, the U.S. Treasury Department, which arrived at its conclusions with the help of some of the documents which we had earlier leaked to the international press.[2] In the landmark report, *U.S. Participation in the Multilateral Development Banks*, the Treasury Department dismissed the right's allegations about the prosocialist bias of Bank policies and painted a picture of an institution solidly dominated by the United States and faithfully promoting not only strategic U.S. economic goals but short-term political objectives as well.

Failure of an Experiment

The internal World Bank documents on the Philippines, however, did not only illustrate the essential character of the Bank as a valuable instrument of U.S. foreign policy. They also were a testament to the failure of a key model for Third World economic development.

As we have seen, the Bank set in motion in the Philippines a development program with two key objectives: "pacification" and "liberalization." The pacification component consisted of rural and urban development programs aimed at defusing rural and urban unrest. Liberalization referred to the drastic restructuring of Philippine industry and external trade strategy to open up the country more completely to the flow of U.S. capital and commodities. To implement this strategy of "technocratic modernization," the Bank encouraged the formation of an authoritarian government and carefully cultivated a technocratic elite.

The strategy failed, largely because of its internal contradictions. Rural development was undone by the overwhelming focus on productivity combined with the absence of any serious effort to alter the relations of political and economic inequality that were themselves thwarting productivity. Urban development fell apart because of the Bank's insistence on applying the criteria of cost recovery and other principles of capitalist finance to its urban housing and development projects for the poor and its refusal to grant "beneficiaries" any meaningful role in making decisions on issues that affected their lives. Thus, instead of social peace, these programs spawned popular resistance.

With the failure of the pacification program, the legitimacy of the Bank's overwhelming presence in the Philippines came to rest mainly on its strategy of export-led industrialization—a program that would allow the country a modicum of "industrialization" while at the same time integrate it more fully into a global economic system dominated by multinational corporations. But EOI was a short-lived panacea, undone by its internal contradictions and the disappearance of the two pillars on which the model rested: docile cheap labor and an expanding international market.

With the collapse of rural development, urban development, and export-oriented industrialization, the Bank and its sister agency, the IMF, were left with a purely repressive program of liberalization. The main tenets of this strategy were battering down tariff walls, destroying the national capitalist class, transforming the financial structure to better serve the needs of U.S. corporations and banks, and debauching the currency. This course was suicidal for the Philippines since it was being made more completely dependent on the world market at a time when the market was being savaged by an international recession that threatened to turn into an international depression. The World Bank's and the IMF's institution of direct rule in the form of a technocrat cabinet that could only justify the imposition of the repressive strategy with the metaphor of "bitter medicine," was a confession that a debacle of major proportions had overtaken the Philippine development effort.

The Philippine debacle, however, was not just the failure of a program in one country. With its westernized elite and neocolonial ties to the United States, the Philippines had opened itself up in the 1960's and 1970's to the influence of U.S. and U.S.-dominated agencies to a greater degree than any other Third World country. By the time the World Bank entered in force in 1972, the country had a reputation as one of the most "exciting places" for experiments in development. Over the decade the Philippines became the testing ground for many World Bank projects in rural development. It was also the site for the Bank's first urban-upgrading project. Together with Kenya, Bolivia, and Turkey, it served as the guinea pig for the new structural adjustment loan. Most important, the World Bank effort in the Philippines was the first coordinated, broad-front experiment in technocratic, authoritarian modernization. Thus, what went down the drain in the Philippines was not just a country program but a larger model for Third World development.

Politics, Ideology, and the Bank

This conclusion still leaves many apparent questions. Why did the Bank continue to plug away in the face of evidence of repeated failures? Or, more fundamentally, how could an agency supposedly devoted to development contribute instead to underdevelopment, to the creation of an economic disaster?

Bureaucratic inertia is part of the answer, but only a small part. A more popular explanation resorts to conspiracy theory. McNamara's rhetoric about the Bank's meeting basic needs and alleviating poverty is, in this view, nothing more than a smokescreen for diametrically opposite motives. While it is easy to see why many in progressive circles might subscribe to this Machiavellian image of the Bank, reality in this instance is much more complex.

Many World Bank bureaucrats, especially those at the middle and lower levels who are directly involved in operations in Third World countries, are well-intentioned indivduals. Many are, in fact, likeable Benthamites who believe that what they are doing will bring about the "greatest good for the greatest number." Indeed, some are people with considerable sensitivity—the very sensitivity that turns into cynicism after years of serving the Bank and realizing that their work has reaped more bad than good.

Where then should we locate the problem?

The explanation, we think, can be arrived at by examining three areas: the position of the Bank in the international economic and political power structure; the influence of the ideological assumptions that Bank technocrats bring to their work from their academic training; and the role of ideological predispositions that spring from the Bank's character as an authoritarian and technocratic organization.

It is only by addressing these theoretical underpinnings which define the efforts of the Bank that we can really understand why the Bank does what it does despite resistance from the people it claims to serve and the subsequent failure of its programs. In the following pages, therefore, we become more theoretical than usual, but hopefully, not hopelessly so.

Politics and Planning. The World Bank is a pillar of the current international structure of wealth and power. Development within this system is the mandate implicitly entrusted to technocrats by the Western governments that dominate the institution, in particular the U.S. government. This task is problematic, since maintaining the current structure and providing development that benefits the majority of Third World countries are essentially contradictory goals.

If U.S. multinational corporations—and American conservatives—had their way, they would assign just one role to the Bank: that of directly supporting private financial and investment efforts in the Third World. They would have the World Bank perform nothing more than the "accumulation function," (i.e., directly support profit-making enterprises) to use James O'Connor's term.[3] But the World Bank has gone far beyond this basic function to become a highly active political and ideological institution; its role is also to *legitimize* the international structure of power among those countries that objectively suffer, or draw only marginal benefits, from the current system. Thus, promoting "development" is a necessary task for the Bank, in the same manner that some agencies of the liberal capitalist state must specialize in co-opting low-income, structurally disadvantaged classes. The conservative view of the Bank as the equivalent of the Welfare Department within a liberal international order is, in many ways, correct. Where the conservatives are wrong is in their corollary opinion that neither the Welfare Department nor the World Bank is necessary for the maintenance of the established order.

The tension between the accumulation and legitimation functions of the Bank appears in the form of "negative" and "positive" guidelines that frame the work of the World Bank technocrat. The key negative guideline is that development plans must never infringe on the interests and operations of the multinational corporations and banks of the Western industrialized countries. The main positive guideline is that, whenever possible, development planning must incorporate benefits for the corporations and banks. If the interests of the poor can be somehow fitted into the framework, all the better. Indeed, a basic principle which guides the Bank's rural development programs actually applies to its whole approach to planning development within an international system dominated by a few rich countries: "It may frequently be desirable to design a project so that all sections of the community benefit to some degree . . . avoiding opposition from the powerful and influential sectors of the community is essential if the program is not to be subverted from within."[4]

These very powerful political constraints on the conceptualization and application of policy prescriptions explain the emergence and evanescent popularity of "export-oriented industrialization" growth as a strategy for development. For this strategy appeared to offer a way of responding to Third World demand for indigenous industrialization without disturbing—and, in fact, reinforcing—the prevailing international structure and distribution of economic power. It offered, it seemed, the best of all possible worlds: Third World countries would be placated with the prospect of industrial development, multinational firms would get their cut-price labor, and the advanced capitalist countries would be assured of a flow of cheap, labor-intensive commodities.

As we have seen, export-oriented industrialization was an ill-conceived strategy that papered over the very real contradictions that eventually torpedoed it as a model for Third World development. But it was the best that the Bank could offer the Third World. Its swift collapse revealed how very little, indeed, the Bank—biased and hemmed in by the constraints of the prevailing economic power structure—could offer its clients in the way of meaningful development. That is, the Bank was unable to support strategies of growth that would enable the poor countries to leave the subordinate and passive roles to which the current system assigned them.

Ideology and Development. The work of the Bank technocrat must not, however, be vulgarized as merely a series of negotiated attempts to iron out unstable compromises between opposing interests to the advantage of the dominant economies. What makes the process complex is that the crude realities of power, inequality, and poverty that confront the technocrat are filtered through the lens of ideology—a set of deeply held assumptions and propositions that reorganize reality, as it were, in order to make it "manageable."

Most World Bank technocrats, particularly the economists, are recruited from the cream of the American academic establishment. Trained at such prestigious institutions as Harvard, Berkeley, Stanford, Princeton, and Yale, their intellectual formation takes place in the context of the all-pervasive neo-Keynesianism that is sacrosanct doctrine in these places.

In the neo-Keynesian world view, the relations of conflict and exploitation that govern economic life disappear. The actors in the economic drama are depoliticized and transformed into the functionally complementary categories of consumers, savers, and investors. Economic development becomes, first and foremost, a technical problem that involves raising the rate of savings in an economy, channeling a substantial portion of savings into productive investment, and filling the gap between domestic and planned investment with external capital. Translated into public policy, this theory involves removing obstacles to entrepreneurial activity, increasing the rate of taxation to provide the government with funds to finance new infrastructure projects that spark economic activity, and facilitating the inflow of foreign investment and loans.

With development viewed as a "technical question," the power and control that accompany substantial foreign investment hardly figure as a problem. When technocrat Gerardo Sicat expressed the view that at this stage in Philippine history, it does not matter who controls the economy, he was exposing the bias and the blindspot of established economic ideology.

Instead of power and control, "efficiency" is the *problematique* of the dominant paradigm. Labor unions, as well as protective barriers to imports and nationalist checks on foreign investment, are viewed primarily as obstacles to efficient production. In the rarefied world of the neo-Keynesian technocrat, the real interest of the Filipino people and that of foreign investors coincide in the commodities which the latter can allegedly produce more efficiently and cheaply than can national producers. The classic formulation is found in the U.S. State Department's justification of the Bank's Structural Adjustment Program: "Lowering of tariffs and easing of import restraints . . . is . . . directed at creating competition for consumption goods that should lower household costs generally. . . ."[5] "Consumer sovereignty" thus becomes the ideological buttress for a pervasive foreign economic presence. It is not, however, simply made up out of nowhere. Rather, it flows "logically" from the ideological assumptions of the neo-Keynesian perspective.

Like foreign capital, poverty is abstracted from the context of the unequal relationships of power that create and perpetuate it. The problem of poverty is transformed principally into a problem of scarcity. The solution to scarcity is economic growth. And the key to economic growth is efficient production. Redistribution of wealth is a secondary issue in the neo-Keynesian paradigm—and one which establishment economists expect will become less important with growth since the resulting larger income pie, though still distributed unequally, will provide larger absolute slices for all. Moreover, redistribution is conceptualized in a very superficial way; it is viewed as a modification in the sharing of national income, rather than a manifestation of a deeper problem—control over the means of production by those who have no interest in the needs of the majority.

In spite of the disclaimers of McNamara, Mahbub Ul-Haq, Vice President Hollis Chenery, and other theoreticians of the basic needs approach, the World Bank never really abandoned the "trickle down" theory. The sidestepping of the structural causes of poverty in rural development programs was motivated not only by conscious political decision. *It was also a reflection of the secondary and minor status of the distribution question in established economic ideology.*

The "antipoverty" strategy of McNamara thus came to resemble his friend Lyndon Johnson's Great Society effort to promote Black enterprises in the ghettoes in the 1960's. Rural development aimed to make a limited number of peasants "more efficient producers." This was like throwing a life preserver to a swimmer caught in a typhoon. For the real dynamics of the system were such that "cost effectiveness" went to those with bigger landholdings, bigger blocks of capital, more political influence, and more access to advanced mechanical and biochemical technology.

The result was growth in production going hand in hand with an increase in absolute poverty. This could not, however, go on indefinitely since the "minor" issue of distribution created new limitations, this time in the form of a limited domestic market which restricted further growth. Faced with this contradiction but still unwilling to tackle the redistribution question, Bank bureaucrats saw a solution in "export-led growth"—that is, in hitching industrial growth to foreign rather than domestic markets. But no sooner had one obstacle emerged than another took its place: once growth became dependent on achieving cost competitiveness in the ruthless international market, *growth became dependent on constricting and depressing wages, that is, on increasing poverty and repression.*

And when international recession and the rising protectionist wave in export markets banished the vision of limitless growth offered by export-oriented development, the last emergency exit was slammed shut in the neo-Keynesian ideological trap. There was no more escaping the specter of radical redistribution of wealth and power—the social necessity which the whole elaborate edifice of neoclassical economic ideology had been erected to counter. In the Philippines, this specter took the form of a spreading revolutionary movement. By the late 1970's, reality was breaking through the ideological defenses of many Bank bureaucrats, who began to shed the bankrupt economic ideology. Afraid for their positions, however, they did not oppose the dominant current and the structure of power it represented. Instead they sank into a corrosive cynicism.

The Technocratic Bias. The ideological assumptions that Bank bureaucrats bring to their work are not only those they carry over from their academic training. The Bank itself cultivates certain ideological predispositions. Bank technocrats are encouraged to look upon themselves as an elite corps of experts who have the last word in development planning.

In the bureaucratic mind, "politics" is counterposed to "expertise." "Politics" is the irrational variable that sabotages the smooth flow of the planning process, of economic development. "Politics" is associated first and foremost with the give and take of the democratic process. This distaste for democracy is captured in the authoritarian and hierarchical decision-making structure of the Bank—a structure which became even more centralized and hierarchical under McNamara, the technocrat *par excellence.* General policy is formulated at the presidential level (with crucial input from the U.S. government), rubber stamped at the Executive Board level, and adapted to each country at the program and project offices.

It is therefore hardly surprising that this elitist institution had no qualms in teaming up with the equally authoritarian Marcos regime to impose a program of development from above. For both administrative elites, *control* of the development process was a high priority. For both, democracy was something to pay lip service to but not to take seriously. Thus, when the slum dwellers of Tondo, the tribespeople of Chico, and the local government of Cagayan de Oro demanded a say in development projects that threatened their very existence, both World Bank and regime technocrats instinctively recoiled. The people demanded democracy—and this was something that challenged the unacknowledged but fundamental assumption of the technocratic approach: that policy making is best left in the hands of experts.

To conclude, the World Bank debacle in the Philippines was not just the failure of a country program. It was not merely a case of an experiment in Third World development that came apart. It was also the "Tet" of neo-Keynesian technocratic economics—a sobering lesson in how established ideology can be blasted by reality.

Table 1: World Bank and International Development Association (IDA) loans to the Republic of the Philippines (Up to May 1982)

Fiscal Year	Description	Amounts ($ Million)
Up to 1971	17 loans and 2 credits	290.5
1972	Rice processing and storage	14.3
1972	Power	22.0
1973	Education II (IDA)	12.7
1973	Ports	6.1
1973	Second highway	68.0
1974	Aurora Penaranda Irrigation	9.5
1974	DFC-DBP I	50.0
1974	Power	61.0
1974	Population	25.0
1974	Shipping	20.0
1974	DFC	30.0
1975	Tarlac Irrigation	17.0
1975	Rural development	25.0
1975	Small and medium industries	30.0
1976	Magat Irrigation	42.0
1976	DFC-DBP II	75.0
1976	Education III	25.0
1976	Livestock II	20.5
1976	Chico irrigation	50.0
1976	Manila urban	10.0
1976	Second Grain processing	11.5
1976	Manila urban	22.0
1976	Second fisheries	12.0
1977	Third highways	95.0
1977	Jalaur irrigation	15.0
1977	Fourth education	25.0
1977	Fourth rural credit	36.5
1977	National irrigation system impvmnt.	50.0
1977	Provincial cities water supply	23.0
1977	Second rural development	15.0
1977	Seventh power	58.0
1978	Smallholder tree-farming	8.0
1978	DFC (PDCP)	30.0
1978	Second national irrigation system improvement	65.0
1978	Rural infrastructure (IDA)	28.0
1978	Education V	2.0
1978	Rural electrification	60.0
1978	DFC-PISO	15.0
1978	Magat II	150.0
1978	Industrial Investment III	80.0
1978	Manila water supply II	88.0
1979	National extension	35.0
1979	Magat multipurpose	21.0
1979	Small farmer dev. land bank	16.5

Table 1: World Bank and International Development Association (IDA) loans to the Republic of the Philippines (Up to May 1982)

Fiscal Year	Description	Amounts ($ Million)
1979	Second urban development	32.0
1979	Highway IV	100.0
1979	Water supply II	16.0
1979	Water supply II (IDA)	22.0
1979	Small and medium industry	25.0
1979	Population II (IDA)	40.0
1980	Samar Island rural development	27.0
1980	Medium-scale irrigation	71.0
1980	Rainfed agricultural dev.	12.0
1980	Rural roads improvement	62.0
1980	Ports III	67.0
1980	Urban III	72.0
1981	Watershed management	38.0
1981	Livestock/fisheries II	45.0
1981	Apex I (Industrial finance)	150.0
1981	Structural adjustment	200.0
1981	Education VI	100.0
1982	Agricultural support services	45.0
1982	Urban engineering	8.0
1982	Textile/structural adjustment	58.0
1982	National fish development	22.4
1982	Communal irrigation	71.1
1982	Coal exploration	16.3
1982	Small-medium industry dev.	132.0
		Total 3389.9

Source: Various World Bank documents; 1982 figures from phone interview with World Bank public relations office, May 3, 1982

Table 2: Investments of the International Finance Corporations (IFC) in the Philippines, as of June 30, 1981

Name of business	Type of business	Fiscal years in which commitments were made	Investments held for the Corporation in thousands of U.S. dollars: Loans	Equity (at cost)	Total
Acoje Mining Company, Inc.	Mining	1977	1,415	1,221	2,636
Cebu Shipyard and Engineering Works, Inc.	Ship-repairing	1978	2,100	—	2,100
Davao Union Cement Corporation	Cement and construction material	1981	16,000	—	16,000
Filipinas Synthetic Fiber Corporation	Textiles and fibers	1974	631	—	631
General Milling Corporation	Food and food processing	1979	4,000	1,082	5,082
Manila Electric Company	Utilities	1967	261	—	261
Maria Cristina Chemical Industries, Inc.	Iron and steel	1974, 1979	638	640	1,278
Marinduque Mining and Industrial Corporation	Mining	1972	6,875	—	6,875
Mariwasa Manufacturing, Inc.	Cement and construction material	1970, 1972	—	98	98
Philagro Edible Oils, Inc.	Coconut oil and copra	1976, 1980	2,153	—	2,153
Philippine Associated Smelting and Refining Corporation	Mining	1981	—	5,000	5,000
Philippine Long Distance Telephone Company	Utilities	1970	1,432	—	1,432
Philippine Petroleum Corporation	Chemicals and petrochemicals	1971, 1977	2,170	872	3,042
Philippine Polyamide Industrial Corporation	Textiles and fibers	1975	5,250	—	5,250
Piso Leasing Corporation	Money and capital market	1980	2,000	152	2,152
Private Development Corporation of the Philippines	Development finance	1963, 1973, 1977	4,800	—	4,800
RFM Corporation	Food and food processing	1974	507	—	507
Sarmiento Industries, Inc.	Plywood	1977	2,800	—	2,800
Ventures in Industry and Business Enterprises, Inc.	Money and capital market	1980	—	269	269
Victorias Chemical Corporation	Chemicals and petrochemicals	1973	266	—	266
Loans to seven corporations for small and medium-scale enterprises	Money and capital market		18,500	735	19,235
			71,798	10,069	81,867
(Piso Leasing Corporation	Money and capital market	1982)			(50)
(Copper Smelter Project	Copper smelting	1982)			(5,000)

Source: International Finance Corporation, *IFC--25 Years: Annual Report* (Washington, D.C.: 1981), p. 48
Phone Interview with IFC Philippine desk, May 3, 1982

Table 3: Summary of World Bank-Philippine Govt. Financial Relations

IBRD/IDA lending operations:[1]	Disbursed IBRD	Disbursed IDA	Undisbursed
	(In millions of U.S. dollars)		
Structural adjustment lending:	195.66	—	4.34
Agricultural and rural development	472.44	15.96	493.39
Education	47.70	12.70	148.16
Power	331.91	12.21	245.68
Transportation	161.92	—	211.49
Industry	305.54	—	162.56
Population	16.88	0.54	47.58
Urban development	39.89	—	96.09
Total	1,571.94	41.41	1,409.29

Repayments[1]	$227.77 million
Debt outstanding:[1 2]	$2,869.91 million
Commitments, February 1981–January 1982:	$303.00 million
Disbursements, February 1981–January 1982:	$425.88 million
IFC investments:[1]	$78.80 million (investments held for the Corporation including undisbursed balances).
Projected commitments, FY 1982–86	$3270 million[3]

[1]As of January 31, 1982.
[2]Includes disbursed amounts, undisbursed amounts, loans approved but not signed, and loans signed but not effective.
[3]See World Bank, "Country Program Paper CPP," Washington, D.C., Aug. 29, 1980, Attachment 1a

Source: International Monetary Fund, "Philippines—Staff Report for the 1982 Article IV Consultation," Washington, D.C., March 24, 1982, p. 26
World Bank, "Country Program Paper CPP," Washington, D.C., Aug. 29, 1980, Attachment 1a

Table 4: Summary of IMF-Phil. Govt. financial relations, as of Feb. 28, 1982

Date of membership:	December 27, 1945
Quota:	SDR 315 million[1]
Use of Fund Resources:	Total outstanding purchases SDR 858.3 million, including SDR 137.5 million under Compensatory Financing Facility (CFF), SDR 35.4 million under 1975 Oil Facility, SDR 333.0 under Supplementary Financing Facility (SFF), SDR 168.3 million in the credit tranches, and SDR 145.4 million under the Extended Fund Facility.
Fund holdings of pesos:[2]	SDR 1,134.6 million or 360.2 percent of quota; of which holdings related to the credit tranches were SDR 168.3 million (53.4 percent of quota), under the CFF were SDR 137.5 million (43.7 percent of quota), under the Oil Facility were SDR 35.4 million (11.2 percent of quota).
Arrangements with the Fund:	Programs using Fund resources have been operative in each year since 1962. The last stand-by program covered the two years 1980-81 in the amount of SDR 410 million, of which SDR 333 million was provided under the Supplementary Financing Facility.
SDR position:	Net cumulative allocation amounts to SDR 116.6 million. Holdings amount to SDR 3.7 million or 3.1 percent of net cumulative allocation.
Gold distribution:	Received 132, 654 fine ounces of gold in the four phases. Received profits amounting to US$24.6 million in the three distributions.
Trust Fund:	Received loans totaling SDR 64.2 million in the first period, and disbursements of SDR 87.2 million in the second period.
Exchange rate system:	Formally an independent float since February 1970. The U.S. dollar is used as the intervention currency. From early 1977 through end-1979, the peso/dollar rate remained stable around P7.4 per U.S. dollar. The exchange rate was P8.33 per U.S. dollar as of March 12, 1982.

[1]1 SDR is equivalent roughly to $1.30.

[2]Level of indebtedness to IMF.

Source: International Monetary Fund, "Philippines—Staff Report for the 1982 Article IV Consultation," Washington, D.C., March 24, 1982, p. 24.

Table 5: Basic economic indicators

Population (1981)	49.5 million
Population growth per annum	2.5 percent
Real GNP growth per annum (1971–81)	5.9 percent
GNP per capita (1981)	US$ 783
GNP	US$39 billion

Aggregates as percent of GNP	**1978**	**1979**	**1980**	**1981**[1]
Gross domestic investment	28.9	29.9	30.5	30.1
Gross domestic savings	22.9	25.0	24.9	24.6
Agricultural production	26.4	25.4	23.3	22.5
Manufacturing production	25.4	25.1	25.8	26.4
National govt. revenue	13.5	13.5	13.1	11.7
National govt. expenditure	14.7	13.7	14.4	15.6
Overall budget deficit	-1.2	-0.1	-1.3	-3.9
Exports of goods and services	11.7	19.0	20.5	19.3
Imports of goods and services	23.2	24.3	26.0	24.8
Current account deficit	4.9	5.3	5.8	6.2
Total disbursement of external debt[2]	25.6	24.0	24.1	26.0
External debt service[3]	3.3	3.8	3.6	4.3
Annual percentage change in selected indicators				
Gross national product (1972 prices)	6.5	5.9	5.4	2.5
Consumer price index	7.6	18.8	17.8	11.8
National govt. revenue	20.0	22.9	17.6	2.9
National govt. expenditure	14.9	13.7	27.9	24.9
Merchandise exports, f.o.b.	8.7	34.3	25.8	2.1
Merchandise exports, f.o.b.	20.9	29.8	25.8	8.7
International reserves *(in millions of $)*				
Gross official reserves	1883	2423	3155	2697
(in months of imports)	4.8	4.7	4.9	3.9
Net international reserves of banking system	153	-426	-778	-1265

[1]Actual or latest estimate as of April 7, 1982
[2]Excludes loans of maturation of one year or less
[3]On debts with maturation of over one year, including IMF

Source: IMF, "Philippines: Recent Economic Developments," Washington, D.C. April 7, 1982

Table 6: Summary Balance of Payments, 1978–82

(In millions of U.S. dollars)

	1978	1979	1980	1981	1982		
			Original	Revised Estimate[1]	Preliminary Estimate[2]	Preliminary Actual	Official Projections
Merchandise trade	-1,307	-1,541	-1,939	-2,280	-2,290	-2,490	-2,450
Exports, f.o.b.	(3,425)	(4,601)	(5,788)	(7,080)	(6,520)	(5,910)	(6,550)
Imports, f.o.b.	(-4,732)	(-6,142)	(-7,727)	(-9,360)	(-8,810)	(-8,400)	(-9,000)
Investment income (net)	-406	-527	-732	-990	-1,000	-948	-1,332
Other services (net)	228	137	186	180	300	556	596
Transfers (net)	313	355	434	450	500	470	526
Current account balance	-1,172	-1,576	-2,051	-2,640	-2,490	-2,412	-2,660
Medium- and long-term capital (net)[3]	908	1,061	1,044	1,785	1,460	1,392	1,911
Short-term capital (net)	263	80	765	225	390	202	118
Exceptional financing (net)[4]	59	88	81	130	227	227	125
Monetization of gold	32	41	128	125	130	400	132
Errors and omissions[5]	-180	-273	-319	—	-92	-295	—
Overall balance	-90	-579	-352	-375	-375	-486	-500

[1]As per EBS/80/270.
[2]As modified in EBS/81/160.
[3]Includes all transactions relating to the nuclear power project.
[4]Includes the Trust Fund, SDR allocations, and the IBRD Structural Adjustments Loans.
[5]Includes valuation adjustments.

Source: International Monetary Fund, "Philippines—Staff Report for the 1982 Article IV Consultation," Washington, D.C., March 24, 1982, p. 12.

Table 7: Debt service statistics, actual and projected, 1977–1987 (in millions of U.S. $)

	1977	1978	1979	1980	1981	1982[1]	1983[1]	1984[1]	1985[1]	1986[1]	1987[1]
External debt outstanding	5004	6200	7137	8554	10,054	11,422	12,716	13,997	15,172	16,323	17,738
Debt service	762	910	1082	1259	1652	2313	2709	3100	3430	3458	3954
Exports of goods and non-factor services	3151	3425	4601	6927	7301	8144	9121	10,216	11,442	12,815	14,353
Debt service/exports of goods and services (Debt-service ratio)	[illegible]3.4	17.0	18.7	18.2	22.6	28.4	29.7	30.3	30.0	30.1	27.5

[1]IMF projections

Sources: IMF, "Philippines—Staff Report for the 1982 Article IV Consultation," Washington, D.C., March 24, 1982
IMF, "Philippines—Recent Recent Economic Developments," Washington, D.C., April 7, 1982

Table 8: Foreign investment account (in U.S. $ million)

	1972	1973	1974	1975	1976	1977	1979	1979	1980	1981
Direct Investment inflow (net)	-22	64	28	125	144	216	171	99	45	392[1]
Direct investment income[2]	33	60	80	73	135	158	147	NA	NA	NA

[1]This figure does not accurately capture trends and is irregular since much of it, according to the IMF, was "foreign equity participation in certain specific projects" pushed aggressively by the government, like the copper smelter.

[2]Does not include income outflow through such mechanisms as transfer pricing and other "hidden" corporate mechanisms.

Source: World Bank, *The Philippines: Domestic and External Resources for Development* (Washington, D.C.: Nov. 12, 1979), p. 57
IMF, "Philippines: Recent Economic Developments," Washington, D.C., April 7, 1982, p. 79

Table 9: Exchange Rate Movements, 1975–81[1]

	Peso/US$ rate	Peso/SDR rate[2]
1975	7.25	8.80
1976	7.44	8.59
1977	7.40	8.64
1978	7.37	9.22
1979	7.38	9.53
1980	7.51	9.78
1981	7.90	9.32
1978 I	7.37	9.00
II	7.36	9.03
III	7.36	9.31
IV	7.37	9.56
1979 I	7.38	9.51
II	7.38	9.41
III	7.37	9.60
IV	7.38	9.61
1980 I	7.42	9.67
II	7.49	9.72
III	7.55	9.97
IV	7.58	9.75
1981 I	7.68	9.54
II	7.86	9.29
III	7.96	9.03
IV	8.10	9.41
1981 June	7.95	9.18
July	7.95	9.03
August	7.96	8.93
September	7.99	9.14
October	8.06	9.31
November	8.11	9.46
December	8.20	9.54

[1]All data are period averages.
[2] 1 SDR = $1.30

Source: International Monetary Fund, "Philippines: Recent Economic Developments," Washington, D.C., April 7, 1982, p.85

Table 10: Time Trends in Poverty, 1957–75

	Consumer Price Index (1965 = 100.00)	Per capita poverty line (pesos/yr)	Percent families below per capita poverty line			Family poverty line (pesos/yr)	Percent families below family poverty line
			Total	Urban	Rural		
1957	72.0	225	Data N/A			1,348	72.1
1961	79.8	249	Data N/A			1,494	57.9
1965	100.0	312	37.2	20.3	44.4	1,873	43.3
1971	160.2	500	38.7	17.6	47.8	3,000	44.9
1975	292.1	912	46.5	27.6	54.8	5,470	53.2

Source: World Bank, "Poverty, Basic Needs and Employment," Confidential first draft, Washington, D.C., January 1980, p. 36

Table 11: Real Wage-Rate Index of Skilled and Unskilled Laborers in Manila and Suburbs: 1955–78

(Establishment Data) (1972 = 100)[1]

	Skilled laborers	Unskilled laborers	Salaried employees	Wage earners
1955	141.5	117.8	123.5	113.8
1960	133.4	107.9	133.5	119.3
1965	115.2	102.7	119.3	107.8
1970	114.4	111.6	109.7	105.9
1975	72.7	72.9	82.4	76.1
1976	71.2	72.3	86.7	82.3
1977	72.9	70.4	—	—
1978	76.1	68.4	—	—

[1]Real wage-rate index has been obtained by deflating money wage-rate index by the consumer price index (1972 = 100) in Manila.

Source: World Bank, "Poverty, Basic Needs and Employment," Confidential first draft, Washington, D.C., January 1980

Notes

INTRODUCTION

1. Jeane Kirkpatrick, "Dictatorships and Double Standards," *Commentary*, July 1979.
2. Robert Ayres, "Clausen and the Poor," (Op-ed), *New York Times*, July 1, 1981.
3. *Journal of Commerce*, May 15, 1981, cited in *Multinational Monitor*, Sept. 1981, p. 11.
4. Frances Moore Lappé, Joseph Collins, and David Kinley, *Aid as Obstacle* (San Francisco: Institute for Food and Development Policy, 1980), p. 11.
5. International Finance Corporation (IFC), *Annual Report 1981* (Washington, D.C.: 1981), p. 4.
6. Cheryl Payer, *The Debt Trap* (New York: Monthly Review Press, 1974).
7. *San Francisco Examiner*, April 2, 1982.

CHAPTER ONE

1. Teodoro Valencia, *Philippine Daily Express* (Manila), March 2, 1981, p. 4.
2. World Bank, "Political and Administrative Bases for Economic Policy in the Philippines," Memorandum from William Ascher to Larry Hinkle, Washington, D.C., Nov. 6, 1980, p. 2. Hereafter to be referred to as Ascher Memorandum.
3. *Ibid.*, p. 9.
4. *Ibid.*
5. Valencia, p. 4.
6. See World Bank, "The Philippines: Priorities and Prospects for Development," Vol. 1, Confidential draft, Washington, D.C., 1976, "Social Indicators" page.
7. World Bank, "Priorities and Prospects for Development," Vol. 1 (Confidential version), Washington, D.C., Statistical Appendix, Table A-5.
8. *Ibid.*
9. *Ibid.*, Table C.7.
10. See Joel Rocamora and David O'Connor, "The U.S., Land Reform, and Rural Development in the Philippines," in *Logistics of Repression* (Washington D.C.: Friends of the Filipino People, 1977), pp. 63-92.
11. Permanent Peoples' Tribunal, Session on the Philippines, *The Philippines: Repression and Resistance* (London: KSP, 1981), p. 267.
12. Cited in Renato Constantino, *The Nationalist Alternative* (Quezon City: Foundation for Nationalist Studies, 1979), p. 38.
13. See, among others, Manuel Castells, *The Economic Crisis and American Society* (Princeton: Princeton University Press, 1980).
14. Jeff Frieden, "Borrowing from Commercial Banks by the Less Developed Countries," *Appeal to Reason*, Vol. 6, No. 1, Summer 1980, p. 62.

15. *Ibid.*, p. 60.
16. Howard Wachtel, "A Decade of International Debt," *Theory and Society*, Vol. 9, No. 3, May 1980, pp. 505-506.
17. Ascher Memorandum, p. 3.
18. Vicente Paterno, "The BOI: Its Role in the Philippine Industrial Development," *Philippine Quarterly*, June 1973, p. 27.
19. *Ibid.*, p. 29.
20. See Major Boyd Bashore, U.S. Army, "Dual Strategy for Limited War," in Franklin Mark Osaka, ed., *Modern Guerrilla Warfare* (New York: Free Press, 1962); also Edward Landsdale, *In the Midst of Wars* (New York: Harper and Row, 1972).
21. For excellent analyses of the premartial law Philippine political system, see Amado Guerrero, *Philippine Society and Revolution* (Oakland: International Association of Filipino Patriots, 1979); Renato Constantino, *The Philippines: A Past Revisited* (Quezon City: Taal Publishing, 1975); and Steve Shalom, "U.S.-Philippine Relations: A Study of Neocolonialism," Ph.D. Dissertation, Boston University, n.d.
22. The "First Quarter Storm" of January 1970, which was triggered by police firing on unarmed student demonstrators, marked the start of the rapid growth of the National Democratic Movement led by Jose Maria Sison, whose ideas are contained in Jose Maria Sison, *Struggle for National Democracy* (Quezon City: Amado Hernandez Memorial Foundation, 1972).
23. Figures from World Bank, "Philippines: Priorities and Prospects. . . ," Table C.2. Actually, "Net direct private foreign investment was negative from 1965 up to 1972 mainly due to withdrawal of foreign investments from the Philippines and domestic capital flight for direct investments abroad." World Bank, "Philippines: Country Program Paper," Memo from Michael Gould, Washington, D.C., March 26, 1976, p. 6. Hereafter to be referred to as Gould Memorandum.
24. Quoted in Sam Bayani, "What's Happening in the Philippines," *Far Eastern Reporter*, Nov. 1976, p. 26.
25. Letter to the Editor in response to article of Richard Kessler, *Asia Wall Street Journal*, Dec. 13, 1980.
26. Cheryl Payer, *The Debt Trap* (New York: Monthly Review Press, 1974).
27. See also Alejandro Lichauco, *The Lichauco Paper* (New York: Monthly Review Press, 1973).
28. Figures from World Bank, "Priorities and Prospects . . . ," Table C.2, G.1.
29. Quoted in Robert Stauffer, "The Political Economy of Refeudalization," in A. Rosenberg, ed., *Marcos and Martial Law in the Philippines* (Ithaca, New York: Cornell University Press, 1979), p. 196.
30. World Bank, "Priorities and Prospects . . . ," p. 2.
31. Jim Browning, "Inside Story: The Philippines and the IMF," *Asia Wall Street Journal*, Aug. 15, 1979.
32. On the function of Consultative Groups, see U.S. Treasury Dept., "*Assessment of U.S. Participation in the Multilateral Banks in the 1980's*, "Washington, D.C., Septemberr 21, 1972, chapt. 1, p. 43.
33. Pacific Asia Resource Center, "Japanese Transnational Enterprises in Indonesia," *AMPO*, Vol. 12, No. 4, 1980, p. 4.
34. International Monetary Fund, "Fund-Bank Collaboration," Memo from Managing Director to Department Heads, Washington, D.C., Dec. 13, 1966, pp. 10-11.
35. *Ibid.*
36. *Ibid.*
37. Gould Memorandum, p. 6.
38. World Bank, "Priorities and Prospects . . . ," p. 6.
39. Stauffer, p. 196.

40. Ascher Memorandum, p. 3.
41. World Bank, *Sixth Power Project* (Washington, D.C.: 1974).
42. *Ibid.*
43. Gould Memorandum, p. 17, 2.
44. World Bank confidential statistics for 1976, 1979, 1980, and 1981. See especially, World Bank, "Working Level Draft CPP (Country Program Paper)," Washington, D.C., Aug. 29, 1980, Attachment 1a.
45. World Bank, *Annual Report 1980* (Washington, D.C.: 1980), pp. 182-184.
46. Gould Memorandum, p. 17.
47. World Bank, "Priorities and Prospects . . . ."
48. Robert Ayres, "Breaking the Bank," *Foreign Policy*, No. 43, Summer 1981, p. 111. Emphasis added.
49. World Bank, "Priorities and Prospects . . . ," p. 35.
50. David Steel, "Philippines: Random Thoughts on Rural Development," Memo from David Steel to Michael Gould and Larry Hinkle, Washington, D.C., September 1, 1977, p. 5.
51. Shahid Husain, "Concluding Statement" in World Bank, "Meeting of the Consultative Group for the Philippines: Report of Proceedings by the Chairman," Paris, Nov. 30—Dec. 1, 1978, p. 66.
52. Gould Memorandum, p. 11.
53. World Bank, "Priorities and Prospects . . . ," p. 11.
54. Paterno, p. 27.
55. Ascher Memorandum, p. 8.
56. World Bank, "Priorities and Prospects . . . ," p. 32.
57. *Ibid.*, p. 8.
58. Gould Memorandum, p. 7.
59. *Ibid.*, p. 8.
60. World Bank, "Government-IBRD Implementation Review," Washington, D.C., 1980, p. 8.
61. Gould Memorandum, p. 2.
62. Romeo Ocampo, "Technocrats and Planning: Sketch and Exploration," *Philippine Journal of Public Administration*, Vol. XV, No.1, Jan. 1971, pp. 42-43.
63. Samuel Huntington, *Political Order in Changing Societies* (New Haven: Yale University Press, 1968).
64. See O. D. Corpuz, *Liberty and Government in the New Society* (Manila: 1973).
65. Ferdinand Marcos, *The Third World Alternative* (Manila: Ministry of Public Information, 1980), pp. 23, 25.
66. Juan Gatbonton, *President Marcos: A Political Profile* (Manila: Ministry of Public Information, 1980), p. 1.
67. Ascher Memorandum, p. 3.
68. See the classic work on the rise of the absolutist monarchies by Perry Anderson, *Lineages of the Absolutist State* (London: New Left Books, 1974).
69. Paterno, pp. 29-30.
70. Ascher Memorandum, pp. 4, 5.
71. *Ibid.*, p. 6.
72. *Ibid.*
73. *Ibid.*
74. Home Defense, *Military Civic Action* (Manila: Armed Forces of the Philippines), p. 166, n.d.
75. *Ibid.*
76. *Ibid.*, p. 6.
77. U. S. Treasury Dept., chapt. 3, p. 1.
78. *Ibid.*

79. *Ibid.*, p. 2.
80. *Ibid.*, chapt. 2, p. 1.
81. *Ibid.*, chapt. 2, p. 18.
82. *Ibid.*, appendix V, p. 11.
83. Congressional Research Service, *The United States and the Multilateral Banks* (Washington: U.S. Gov't. Printing Office, 1974), p. 5.
84. U.S. Treasury Dept., chapt. 2, p. 2.
85. *Ibid.*, chapt. 3.
86. Congressional Research Service, p. 5.
87. Frances Fitzgerald, *Fire in the Lake* (New York: Random House, 1973), pp. 116-117.
88. This analysis receives fuller discussion in Walden Bello and Elaine Elinson, *Elite Democracy and Authoritarian Rule: The Crisis of the Political Regime of U.S. Domination in the Philippines and the Third World from the Kennedy Years to the Reagan Era* (San Francisco: Philippine Solidarity Network, 1981).
89. Severina Rivera and Walden Bello, "The Anti-Aid Campaign after Four Years," in *Logistics of Repression* (Washington, D.C.: Friends of the Filipino People, 1977), p. 4.
90. Section 502-B of the Foreign Assistance Act. This was followed by another amendment tying the granting of economic aid, through both bilateral and multilateral channels, to this aid benefiting "needy people."
91. Gould Memorandum, p. 16.
92. House Appropriations Committee, Subcommittee on Foreign Operations, "Hearings on Foreign Assistance," 95th Congress, First Session, March 2, 1977, p. 48.
93. Phone interview with Steve Cohen, former Human Rights Officer for East Asia, State Department, in the Carter administration, Jan. 26, 1982. Confirmed by office of Daniel O'Donohue, Acting Deputy Assistant Secretary of State, U.S. State Department, Jan. 27, 1982.
94. U. S. Treasury Dept., Appendix V, p. 50.
95. With the U.S.-Philippine Bases Agreement concluded in 1979, however, Carter ended his vacillation with regard to Marcos. The regime was promised $500 million in military and military-related assistance over five years.

CHAPTER TWO

1. World Bank, *Sixth Power Project* (Washington, D.C.: 1974).
2. *Ibid.*
3. World Bank, "Philippines: Country Constraints in Project Implementation," Washington, D.C., 1979, p. 6.
4. *Ibid.*
5. "McNamara's World Bank Leans Toward Economic Program Aid," *Washington Post* (Washington Business Supplement), Sept. 29, 1980, p. 15.
6. World Bank, *Sixth Power Project.*
7. World Bank, "Working Level Draft CPP [Country Program Paper]," Memorandum from Bruce Jones, Washington, D.C., Aug. 29, 1980, p. 19.
8. World Bank, "Issues Paper: Government-IBRD Implementation Review," Washington, D.C., 1980, p. 1, Annex table.
9. *Ibid.*, Annex table.
10. World Bank, "Working Level Draft CPP," p. 15.
11. World Bank, "Issues Paper: Government-IBRD Implementation Review," p. 1.
12. World Bank, "Energy Sector Survey," Washington, D.C., Nov. 1980.
13. World Bank, "Political and Administrative Bases for Economic Policy in the Philippines," Memo from William Ascher, Washington,

D.C., Nov. 18, 1980, p. 7. Hereafter to be referred to as Ascher Memorandum.

14. This will be analyzed in greater detail in the next chapter.

15. World Bank, *Rural Development: Sector Working Paper* (Washington, D.C.: 1975), p. 40.

16. See next chapter, especially section "Undermining the Smallholder: Three Case Studies."

17. See next chapter, section "Undermining the Smallholder . . . ."

18. See next chapter, section "*Masagana 99* and the High Technology Treadmill."

19. Blondie Po, *Policies and Implementation of Land Reform in the Philippines: A Documentary Study* (Quezon City: Institute of Philippine Culture, 1981), pp. 52-53. See also Joel Rocamora and David O'Connor, "The U.S., Land Reform, and Rural Development in the Philippines," in *Logistics of Repression* (Washington, D.C.: Friends of the Filipino People, 1977), pp. 72-74.

20. World Bank, "Philippines—Land Reform," Memo from A. J. Blackwood to Owen Price, Washington, D.C., May 25, 1977, p. 1.

21. Ascher Memorandum, p. 2.

22. World Bank, "Consultative Group for the Philippines: Chairman's Report of Proceedings," Washington, D.C., March 20, 1980, p. 18.

23. *Ibid.*, p. 71.

24. Robert McNamara, *1974 Address to Board of Governors* (Washington, D.C.: World Bank, 1974), p. 12.

25. World Bank, *The Philippines: Country Economic Memorandum*, Report No. 1765-PH (Washington, D.C.: 1977), Annex B, p. 15.

26. World Bank, *The Philippines: Domestic and External Resources for Development*, Report No. 2674-PH (Washington, D.C.: 1979), Table 3.3, p. 59.

27. *Ibid.*, Table 3.7, p. 63.

28. *Ibid.*

29. *Ibid.*, Table 3.1, p. 56.

30. International Monetary Fund, "Philippines—Request for Stand-by Arrangement with Supplementary Financing," Memo from Secretary to Members of Executive Board, Washington, D.C., Feb. 6, 1980, Table 12, p. 46.

31. World Bank, *Industrial Development Strategy and Policies in the Philippines*, Vol. 1 (Washington, D.C.: Oct. 29, 1979).

32. World Bank, "Consultative Group for the Philippines," p. 17.

33. See World Bank, "Working Level Draft CPP," Attachment 3C.

34. *Ibid.*

35. World Bank, "Consultative Group for the Philippines," p. 48.

36. World Bank, "The Philippines: Priorities and Prospects for Development," Vol. 1, Confidential draft, Washington, D.C., 1976, p. 16.

37. World Bank, "Working Level Draft CPP," Attachment 3C.

38. Interview with officer of East Asia Division, anonymity requested, Dec. 15, 1980, by Walden Bello.

39. Jim Browning, "Inside Story: The Philippines and the IMF," *Asian Wall Street Journal*, Aug. 15, 1979.

40. World Bank, "Working Level Draft—CPP," p. 13.

41. *Ibid.*, p. 14.

42. *Ibid.*, p. 14.

43. Lyn Adkins, "Recycling OPEC's Surplus," *Dun's Review*, May 1980.

44. U.S. Federal Reserve Board estimate cited in *Filipino Reporter*, April 24-30, 1981, p. 17.

45. World Bank, "Working Level Draft CPP," p. 14.

46. World Bank, "Consultative Group for the Philippines," p. 58.

47. *World Financial Markets,* Dec. 1979, p. 8. See also "Japanese Banks Are Restricting Lending to the Philippines . . . ," *Asia Wall Street Journal,* Sept. 22, 1981, p. 10.

48. *World Financial Markets,* Dec. 1979, p. 8.

49. World Bank, "Working Level Draft CPP," p. 14.

50. Ferdinand Marcos, Statement in *Journal of Commerce,* Supplement for New Jersey World Trade Conference, Nov. 18, 1981, p. 1C.

51. World Bank, *The Philippines: Domestic and External Resources for Development,* statistical appendix, pp. 56-57.

52. Ascher Memorandum, p. 7.

53. Edberto Villegas, "The Philippines and the IMF-World Bank Conglomerate," Quezon City, Third World Studies, Appendix II.

54. Business International, *Investing, Licensing and Trading Conditions Abroad: Philippines* (New York: Business International, April 1980), p. 1.

55. Minutes of "First International Political Risk Management Seminar," Washington, D.C., May 6-7, 1981.

56. Ascher Memorandum, p. 7.

57. Jaime Ongpin, Letter to the Editor, *Fortune,* Aug. 24, 1981.

58. World Bank, "Consultative Group for the Philippines," p. 36.

59. World Bank, *The Philippines: Domestic and External Resources for Development,* p. 112.

60. Enrico Paglaban, "Philippines: Workers in the Export Industry," *Pacific Research,* Vol. IX, Nos. 3 and 4, March-June 1978, pp. 26-28.

61. International Monetary Fund, "Philippines—Staff Report for the 1980 Article IV Consultation and Review of Stand-By Arrangement," EBS/80/159, Washington, July 17, 1980, p. 8.

62. Quoted in "Marcos Soft on Labor—Suter," *Ang Katipunan,* Aug. 1-15, 1981, p. 3.

63. See International Monetary Fund, "Philippines—Staff Report for the 1980 Article IV Consultation . . . ," p. 8.

64. World Bank, "Philippines—Manila Urban Development Issues Paper," Memo from Donald B. Cook and Anthony Pellegrini, Sept. 2, 1975.

65. The following complaint in a World Bank review of the project testified to the effectiveness of this network: "Misinformation about the nature of the Project and the attitude of residents toward the Project continues to persist mostly outside the Philippines." World Bank, "Manila Urban Development Project: Report on the Status of the Tondo Foreshore Development Project," Washington, D.C., Dec. 12, 1977, p. 14.

66. Dieter Oberndorfer (KFW), "Some Observations on the Low Cost Housing Projects in Tondo/Manila Financed by the World Bank," Freiburg, Germany, November 1979.

67. See Chapter Four, section "Confrontation in Cagayan de Oro."

68. World Bank, *Sixth Power Project.*

69. For a good account of the Chico project and the international support it generated, see Martha Winnacker, "The Battle to Stop the Chico Dams," *Southeast Asia Chronicle,* No. 67 (October 1979), pp. 22-29.

70. See, for instance, the list "Projects in Execution" attached to World Bank, "Samar Island Rural Development Project," Sec. M79-751, Washington, D.C., October 22, 1979. Virata concession is in Joan Orendain, "A Conversation with Philippine Prime Minister Cesar Virata," *Balikbayan,* October 1981.

71. Interview with Pantabangan residents by Robin Broad, May 1981.

72. World Bank, *Economic Development and Tribal Peoples: Human Ecologic Considerations* (Washington, D.C.: July 1981), p. 1.

73. World Bank, "Poverty, Basic Needs, and Employment: A Review and Assessment," Confidential first draft, Washington, D.C., January 1980. Hereafter to be referred to as *Poverty Report.*

74. *Ibid.*, p. 21.
75. World Bank, "Working Level Draft CPP," p. 17.
76. *Poverty Report*, p. 316.
77. *Poverty Report*, pp. 312-317.
78. Roberto Ongpin, "Statement" in World Bank, "Consultative Group for the Philippines . . . ," p. 33.
79. International Monetary Fund, Press release no. 80/20, Feb. 28, 1980.
80. "World Bank, in Shift, Lending for Trade Debts," *New York Times*, May 26, 1980.
81. World Bank, "Summaries of Discussions at the Meeting of the Executive Directors of the Bank and IDA, September 16, 1980," Washington, D.C., Nov. 20, 1980, p. 8.
82. World Bank, "Working Level Draft CPP," p. 7.
83. *Ibid.*
84. *Ibid.*, p. 14.
85. International Monetary Fund, "Philippines—Staff Report for the 1982 Article IV Consultation," SM/82/55, Washington, D.C., March 24, 1982, p. 21.
86. Interview with officer of East Asia Division, World Bank, anonymity requested, Dec. 15, 1980.
87. "Marcos' Power Waning, World Bank Study Warns," *Asian Wall Street Journal*, Dec. 8, 1980, pp. 1, 20.
88. Ascher Memorandum, p. 2.
89. *Ibid.*, p. 8.
90. *Ibid.*, p. 9.
91. *Ibid.*
92. *Ibid.*, p. 5.
93. *Ibid.* pp. 10, 13, 14.
94. *Ibid.*, p. 6.
95. Louis Kraar, "The Philippines Veers Toward Crisis," *Fortune*, July 27, 1981, p. 37.
96. Teodoro Valencia, "World Bank-IMF Formula Could Sink RP Economy," *Philippine Daily Express*, March 2, 1981.
97. U.S. State Department, Responses to "Questions for the Record Asked by the Committee" submitted to House Foreign Affairs Committee, Subcommittee on Asia-Pacific Affairs, Washington, D.C., Nov. 18, 1981, p. 2.
98. Jeane Kirkpatrick, "Dictatorships and Double Standards," *Commentary*, July 1979, p. 37.

CHAPTER THREE

1. Joel Rocamora and David O'Connor, "The U.S., Land Reform, and Rural Development in the Philippines," in *Logistics of Repression* (Washington, D.C.: Friends of the Filipino People, 1977), p. 64.
2. Joel Rocamora, "U.S. Imperialism and the Economic Crisis of the Marcos Dictatorship," in Permanent Tribunal for the Rights of Peoples, Session on the Philippines, *Philippines: Repression and Resistance* (London: KSP, 1981), p. 68. According to the World Bank, "in the 1970's . . . the export crops began once again to share in the increase in productivity and began dominating the increase in land area extension." World Bank, "Poverty, Basic Needs, and Employment," Confidential draft, Washington, D.C., January 1980, p. 125. Hereafter to be referred to as the *Poverty Report*.
3. Rocamora, p. 75.
4. Quoted in Investor Reponsibility Research Center, Inc., "Land Acquisition Practices in the Philippines," Washington, D.C., September 5, 1978, p. X-10.

5. See Joel Rocamora, "Imperialism, the Marcos Regime, and the Economic Plunder of the Moro People," in Permanent Tribunal for the Rights of Peoples, p. 243, Elinor McCallie and Frances Moore Lappé, "The Banana Industry in the Philippines," San Francisco, Institute for Food and Development Policy, 1978, pp. 2-4; Temario Rivera, "Will a Major Social Change be Far Behind?" *Diliman Review*, Vol. 28, No. 6 (Nov.-Dec. 1980), pp. 22-24.

6. *Ibid.*, Rivera.

7. World Bank, "Priorities and Prospects for Development," Confidential first draft, Washington, D.C., Statistical appendix, Table C.7.

8. Blondie Po, *Policies and Implementation of Land Reform in the Philippines: A Documentary Study (Quezon City: Institute of Philippine Culture, 1981), p. 29-30.*

9. Robert McNamara, *1973 Address to Board of Governors* (Washington, D.C.: World Bank, 1973), p. 19.

10. Robert Ayres, "Breaking the Bank," *Foreign Policy*, Summer 1981, No. 43, pp. 111-112.

11. Robert McNamara, *1974 Address to Board of Governors,* (Washington, D.C.: World Bank, 1974), pp. 2-3.

12. World Bank, *Rural Development: Sector Working Paper* (Washington, D.C.: 1975), p. 40.

13. World Bank, *Sixth Power Project* (Washington, D.C.: 1974).

14. Rocamora and O'Connor, pp. 72-73.

15. Po, pp. 52-53.

16. Figures from *Poverty Report*, p. 119.

17. *Ibid.*

18. Po, pp. 58-59.

19. World Bank, "Philippines—Agrarian Reform," Memo from A. J. Blackwood to Owen T. Price, Washington, D.C., May 25, 1977, p. 1.

20. World Bank, "Aide Memoire—Philippines Agrarian Reform," Washington, D.C., January 4, 1977, p. 4.

21. *Poverty Report*, p. 119.

22. World Bank, "Desk Review of Support Services for Food Production, Land Reform and Settlement," Washington, D.C., undated, p. 5.

23. Untitled study attributed to Dale Hill, agricultural loan officer for Philippines, undated, p. 159. Hereafter to be referred to as the *Hill Report.*

24. *Poverty Report*, p. 178.

25. *Ibid.*

26. Development Alternatives, Inc., "New Directions and the Rural Poor: The Role of Local Organization in Development," Vol. 1, First draft, Washington, D.C., Aug. 1979.

27. James Anderson, "Rural Organization in Law for Development: Prospects in Philippine Natural Resources Management," Paper read at Seventh Symposium on Law and Development, Windsor, Ontario, Canada, March 19-21, 1981, pp. 5-6.

28. World Bank, "Initial Project Brief: Support Services for Rural Development Project," Report prepared by Michael Gould and Dale Hill, Washington, D.C., undated, p. 9.

29. World Bank, "Summaries of Discussion and Meeting of the Executive Directors of the Bank and IDA," Washington, D.C., Dec. 4, 1979, p. 3.

30. World Bank, "Aide Memoire—Philippines Agrarian Reform," p. 6.

31. World Bank, "Initial Project Brief . . . ," p. 9.

32. World Bank, "Philippines Agrarian Reform," Memo from A. Golan to S. S. Kirmani, Washington, D.C., March 10, 1977.

33. *Poverty Report*, pp. 178, 214.

34. Ferdinand Marcos, quoted in *Hill Report*, p. 37.

35. *Hill Report*, pp. 31-32.

36. *Ibid.*, p. 84.

37. World Bank, "Report and Recommendation of the President of the IBRD to the Executive Directors on a Proposed Loan to the Republic of the Philippines for Chico River Irrigation Project, Stage I," Washington, D.C., March 11, 1976, p. 7. Hereafter to be referred to as *Chico River Irrigation Project.*

38. Quoted in *Hill Report*, p. 37.

39. *Ibid.*, pp. 148-149.

40. Emmanuel Esguerra, "Masagana 99," *Diliman Review,* Nov.-Dec. 1980, pp. 30-31.

41. World Bank, "Small Farms and Rainfed Agriculture in the Philippines," Confidential first draft, Washington, D.C., Dec. 4, 1979, p. 40. A government spokesman was less euphemistic: "We didn't give a damn about who was going to get the loans, we were worried about a critical rice shortage." Maximo Soliven, quoted in *Hill Report,* p. 47.

42. *Ibid.*, p. 36, 62.

43. Jessie Divinagracia and Kenneth Smith, "Palay Productivity and Profitability for Small Farmers," Quezon City, Department of Agriculture, 1975. Cited in *Hill Report*, pp. 169-170.

44. *Ibid.*

45. World Bank, "Desk Review of Support Services . . . ," p. 9.

46. World Bank, "Sector Survey of Agricultural Support Services," Washington, D.C., Jan. 23, 1980, p. 8.

47. *Ibid.*, p. 5. See also *Hill Report*: "Since [the country] had anauthoritarian government anyway, and it had already been demonstrated that PC [Philippine Constabulary] Commanders knew how to collect loans, things began to go differently. Two notices (that a loan was due) went out. The third came from the local PC Commander . . . . It worked." (Interview cited on p. 101.) Failure to comply with government regulations on M99 loan repayments provoked Presidential Letter of Instruction No. 372, which stated that "Prosecution of such offenses shall be by, under the direction of military officers and shall be turned before the appropriate military tribunals." (Cited on p. 105.)

48. World Bank, "Sector Survey of Agricultural Support Services," p. 8.

49. *Ibid.*, p. 7.

50. *Ibid.*, p. 8.

51. *Ibid.*, p. 5.

52. "To Keep Hunger at Bay, Rice Experts Turn to New Fertilizer Techniques," *Christian Science Monitor*, April 28, 1981, p. B11.

53. *Ibid.*

54. World Bank, "Sector Survey: Agricultural Support Services," Jan. 23, 1980, pp. 27-29.

55. *Ibid.*, p. 34; also World Bank, "Desk Review of Support Services, Input Supply, Retention, and Use," p. 15.

56. *Hill Report*, p. 88.

57. *Ibid.*

58. World Bank, *The Philippines: Domestic and External Resources for Development*, (Washington, D.C., 1979), Table 3.7, p. 63.

59. World Bank, "Sector Survey: Agricultural Support Services," p. 7, Fertilizer input, complained one Bank report, "has resulted in a large foreign exchange cost to Government . . . ." World Bank, "Desk Survey . . . Summary, Conclusions, and Recommendations," p. 5.

60. World Bank, "Sector Survey: Agricultural Support Services," p. 37.

61. *Ibid.*

62. See David Weir and Mark Schapiro, *Circle of Poison* (San Francisco: Institute for Food and Development Policy, 1981).

63. *Ibid.*, p. 50.
64. *Ibid.*, pp. 50-51.
65. *Ibid.*, p. 13.
66. *Ibid.*, p. 35.
67. *Ibid.*
68. World Bank, "Sector Survey: Agricultural Support Services," p. 37.
69. *Ibid.*
70. Weir and Schapiro, pp. 79-80.
71. World Bank, "Sector Survey: Agricultural Support Services," p. 37.
72. *Hill Report*, p. 62.
73. *Ibid.*, p. 169.
74. *Poverty Report*, p. 212.
75. "The Magat Multi-Purpose Project," *Philippine Development*, Vol.VI, No. 20 (March 15, 1979), p. 17.
76. *Chico River Irrigation Project*, p. 7.
77. World Bank, "Desk Review of Support Services for Food Production: Irrigation," pp. 4-5.
78. *Ibid.*
79. *Ibid.*, p. 6.
80. World Bank, "Random Thoughts on Rural Development," Memo from David Steel to Michael Gould, Washington, D.C., World Bank, Sept. 1, 1977.
81. World Bank, "Initial Project Brief: Support Services of Rural Development Project," p. 9.
82. *Chico River Irrigation Project*, p. 13.
83. From summary in "People's War in the Cagayan Valley Region," *Philippine Liberation Courier*, Nov. 17, 1978, pp. 4-5.
84. *Ibid.*
85. See Anti-Martial Law Coalition-Friends of the Filipino People Investigating Team, *Conditions of the Filipino People Under Martial Law* (Oakland: Anti-Martial Law Coalition:Friends of the Filipino People, 1979), pp. 14-15.
86. Interview with Filipino World Bank consultant, anonymity requested, July 15, 1980.
87. Gene Stoltzfus and Dorothy Friesen, "Pantabangan: Victim of Development," *MSPC Communications*, April 1978, p. 16.
88. "A Conversation with Philippine Prime Minister Cesar Virata," *Balikbayan*, Oct. 1981.
89. Carmen Flores and Dionisio Tan-Gatue, Jr., "Pantabangan Relocation," *Philippine Journal of Public Administration*, Vol. XIX, Nos. 1 and 2, Jan-April 1975, pp. 138, 142-143.
90. Stoltzfus and Friesen, p. 16.
91. *Ibid.*
92. As Prime Minister Cesar Virata put it, "We are taking corrective action and planting trees." "A Conversation with Prime Minister Virata," *Balikbayan*, Oct. 1981.
93. World Bank, "Rural Development II Project (Loan 1421-PH) Supervision Report," Washington, D.C., Feb. 4, 1980, Annex 5, p. 1.
94. *Ibid.*
95. *Ibid.*
96. World Bank, "Philippine Agrarian Reform," Memo from A. Golan to S. S. Kirmani, March 10, 1977, p. 1.
97. World Bank, "Smallholder Treefarming and Forestry Project (Loan No. 1506-PH) Supervision Report," Feb. 26, 1980, Supervision summary, p. 2.
98. *Ibid.*, Annex 6, p. 1.
99. *Ibid.*, Annex 6, p. 2.

100. *Ibid.*
101. *Ibid.*, Annex 6, Appendix 2, p. 1.
102. *Ibid.*, Annex 6, Appendix 2, p. 2.
103. *Ibid.*, Attachment 2, pp. 1 and 2.
104. See "Cellophil-Tinggian Controversy," *Tribal Forum,* Vol. 1, No. 1 (Nov.-Dec. 1979), pp. 12-18.
105. *Ibid.*
106. World Bank, "Third Rural Credit Project (Loan 1010-PH) Project Performance Audit Report," Washington, D.C., Jan. 9, 1980, p. iv.
107. *Ibid.*
108. *Ibid.*, p. 16.
109. *Ibid.*, p. iv.
110. *Ibid.*, p. v.
111. *Ibid.*, p. 13.
112. *Ibid.*, p. iv.
113. *Ibid.*, p. 38.
114. *Ibid.*
115. *Ibid.*
116. *Ibid.*, pp. 1-2.
117. *Ibid.*, p. 36.
118. *Ibid.*, p. 38.
119. See "Presentation of NDF (National Democratic Front) Spokesperson," in Permanent People's Tribunal," p. 203.
120. Development Alternatives, Inc., "New Directions and the Rural Poor," Vol. 1, Draft, Washington, D.C., Aug. 1979, p. 87.
121. Robert Whymant, *Manchester Guardian,* cited in BMP (News from the Free Philippines), March 3, 1974.
122. Juan Crisostomo, "Marcos and the Philippines: How Much Longer?" *AMPO*, Aug. 1976, p. 22.
123. Interview with Filipino World Bank consultant, anonymity requested, July 15, 1980.
124. Development Alternatives, Inc.
125. World Bank, *Appraisal of the Rural Development Project Philippines* (Washington, D.C.: March 14, 1975), p. 1.
126. *New Philippines*, Vol. XXVIII, No. 2, April 1975, p. 23.
127. World Bank, *Appraisal of the Rural Development Project*, p. 2.
128. *Ibid.*
129. Cited in Joel Rocamora, "The Political Uses of PANAMIN," *Southeast Asia Chronicle, no. 67 (Oct. 1979), pp. 11-21.*
130. *Ibid.*
131. PANAMIN, "Report and Recommendations on the Non-Muslim Minority Hill Tribes," Manila, undated, pp. 1 and 2.
132. PANAMIN, "Summary Report on PANAMIN Settlements," *PANAMIN Annual Report* (Manila: 1979).
133. Bernard Wideman, "NPA Gaining in Philippines Samar," *New Asia News* (NAN), 1979.
134. See, for instance, Task Force Detainees, *Pumipiglas: Political Detention: Political Detention and Military Atrocities in the Philippines* (Manila: Task Force Detainees, 1980), pp. 58-60.
135. "World Bank Approves $27 Million Loan to the Philippines for Rural Development," World Bank News release, No. 80/25, Dec. 6, 1979, p. 1.
136. World Bank, "Samar Island Rural Development Project: Staff Appraisal Report," Washington, D.C., Nov. 12, 1979, p. 4.
137. Australian Development Bureau, "Northern Samar Rural Development Program," undated, p. 17. Emphasis added.
138. World Bank, "Samar Island Rural Development Project. . . ," p. 15.

139. International Commission on the Militarization of Samar, *Militarization of Samar* (Hong Kong: Resource Center for Philippine Concerns, Oct. 1979), p. 11.

140. *Ibid.*, p. 9.

141. *Ang Bayan* (The People), March 15, 1981, p. 3. For an account of recent events, see Sheilah Ocampo, "An Island in Death's Shadow," *Far Eastern Economic Review*, March 27, 1981, pp. 30-32.

142. Interview with World Bank East Asia Division officer, anonymity requested, Feb. 13, 1981.

143. *Ibid.*

144. *Ibid.* The euphemistic official account reads: "A speaker wondered why the project did not include components for external services and agricultural credit facilities similar to other projects and what portion of the other projects actually benefitted the Island of Samar. Staff said . . . two most important needs of Samar were infrastructure development and extension services . . . . The infrastructure development would be provided by this project. . . . The same speaker pointed out that the progress of land reform had been slow and the Second Rural Development Project had encountered difficulty because of this. World Bank, "Summaries of Discussion and Meeting of the Executive Directors of the Bank and IDA," Washington, D.C., Dec. 4, 1979, pp. 2-3.

145. *Poverty Report*, p. 36.

146. Estimate of the Bureau of Agricultural Economics (BAECON), cited in *Philippine Liberation Courier*, May 1980, p. 2.

147. *Poverty Report*, p. 158.

148. Alain de Janvry, "The Strategy of Rural Development," Draft, Berkeley, p. 53.

149. Ascher Memorandum, p. 5.

150. *Ibid.*, p. 2.

151. James Anderson, p. 6.

CHAPTER FOUR

1. World Bank, "Third Urban Development Project: Staff Appraisal Report," Report No. 2703a-PH, Washington, D.C., Feb. 26, 1980, p. 1.

2. Calculated from statistics provided in *ibid.*.

3. World Bank, "Manila Urban Development Project: Staff Project Report," Washington, D.C., May 5, 1976, p. i.

4. World Bank, "Second Urban Development Project: Staff Appraisal Report," Report No. 2048a-PH, Washington, D.C., Dec. 1, 1978, p. 1.

5. World Bank, "Third Urban. . . ," p. 1.

6. World Bank, "Report and Recommendation of the President of the IBRD to the Executive Directors on a Proposed Loan to the Republic of the Philippines for a Third Urban Development Project," Washington, D.C., Feb. 1980, p. 9.

7. World Bank, "Third Urban. . . ," p. 2.

8. Dieter Oberndorfer (KFW), "Some Observations on the Low Cost Housing Projects in Tondo Foreshore/Manila Financed by the World Bank," Freiburg, Nov. 1979, p. 5.

9. World Bank, "Second Urban. . . ," p. 2.

10. *Ibid.*

11. Mary Racelis Hollnsteiner (and Peter Tacon), "Urban Migration in Developing Countries: Consequences for Families and Their Children," Paper read at American Association for the Advancement of Science Conference, January 1982, p. 18.

12. World Bank, "Third Urban. . . ," p. 3.

13. *Ibid.*

14. Robert McNamara, *Address to Board of Governors, 1975* (Washington, D.C.: World Bank, 1975), p. 20.

15. World Bank, "Political and Administrative Bases for Economic Policy," Memo from William Ascher, Nov. 6, 1980, p. 4. Hereafter to be referred to as Ascher Memorandum.
16. *Ibid.*
17. *Ibid.*
18. See Walden Bello and Severina Rivera, eds., *Logistics of Repression* (Washington, D.C.: Friends of the Filipino People, 1977), p. 29.
19. Antonio Pacho, "Variations on a Theme," *Philippine Journal of Public Administration*, Vol. 18, April 1974, p. 166.
20. *Ibid.*, p. 165.
21. *Ibid.*, p. 168.
22. World Bank, "Philippines—Manila Urban Development Project Issues Paper," Memo from Donald B. Cook and Anthony Pellegrini, Sept. 2, 1975, p. 7.
23. World Bank, "Third Urban. . . ," p. 12.
24. World Bank, "Briefing for Visit of Mrs. Imelda Marcos: The Urban Sector in the Philippines," Memo from Gregory Votaw to Robert McNamara, Washington, D.C., Nov. 10, 1975, p. 4.
25. World Bank, "Third Urban. . . ," p. 12.
26. *Ibid.*
27. World Bank, "Briefing for Visit of Mrs. Imelda Marcos. . . ," p. 2.
28. National Media Production Center, *Metropolitan Manila* (Manila: National Media Production Center, 1980), p. 18.
29. Quoted in *ibid.*
30. "Luxury Living in Manila Bay," *Far Eastern Economic Review*, Jan. 2, 1976.
31. Quoted in *Metropolitan Manila*, p. 24.
32. "Squatters: Imelda's Plans," *Far Eastern Economic Review*, Feb. 13, 1976.
33. Quoted in *Philippine Times*, Jan. 16-31, 1976. Also cited in *Far Eastern Economic Review*, Jan. 2, 1976, p. 30.
34. For a good account of these relocation measures, see Anti-Martial Law Coalition, *The Refugee Crisis in the Philippines* (Chicago: Anti-Martial Law Coalition, 1977), pp. 18-24.
35. *New York Times*, Oct. 7, 1976.
36. World Bank, "Briefing for Visit of Mrs. Imelda Marcos. . . ," p. 2.
37. *Asia Record*, Aug. 1980, pp. 8-9.
38. Interview with a former community organizer, anonymity requested, by Walden Bello, Washington, D.C., Jan. 3, 1982.
39. Coordinating Council of People's Organizations of Tondo Foreshore, Navotas, and Malabon, "Philippine Squatters and Martial Law Remedies," Statement prepared for the U.N. Human Settlements Conference, Vancouver, British Columbia, May-June 1976, p. 4.
40. *Ibid.*
41. World Bank, "Briefing for Visit of Mrs. Imelda Marcos. . . ," p. 3.
42. World Bank, "Third Urban. . . ," p. 4.
43. Edward Jaycox, "The Bank and Urban Poverty," *Finance and Development*, Vol. 15, No. 3, Sept. 1978, p. 13.
44. *Ibid.*
45. World Bank, "Briefing for Visit of Mrs. Imelda Marcos. . . ," p. 2.
46. Interview with former community organizer, anonymity requested, by Walden Bello, Washington, D.C., Jan. 3, 1982.
47. World Bank, "Briefing for Visit of Mrs. Imelda Marcos. . . ," p. 2.
48. World Bank, "Philippines—Manila Urban Development Project Issues Paper," p. 6.
49. World Bank, "Loan Agreement (Manila Urban Development Project) between Republic of the Philippines and International Bank for Reconstruction and Development," Washington, D.C., June 9, 1976, p. 10.

50. *Ibid.*, p. 11.
51. Jaycox, p. 13.
52. See World Bank, "Manila Urban Development Project: Staff Project Report," p. vii. The estimate of the number of squatter families or "structures" to be displaced is taken from World Bank, "Minutes of a Meeting between World Bank and KFW," Washington, D.C., March 6-7, 1980, p. 1.
53. World Bank, "Philippines: Manila Urban Project: Report on the Status of the Tondo Foreshore Development Project," Washington, D.C., Dec. 12, 1977, p. 7.
54. Interview of Tondo residents conducted by Lloyd Jansen, Manila, June 1981. Estimate of number facing displacement from World Bank, "Meeting between World Bank and KFW," p. 1.
55. World Bank, "Manila Urban Project: Report on the Status of the Tondo Foreshore Development Project," p. 7.
56. *Ibid.*
57. World Bank, "Philippines—Manila Urban Development Project Issues Paper," p. 9.
58. World Bank, "Manila Urban Project: Report on the Status of the Tondo Foreshore Development Project," p. 8.
59. Oberndorfer, p. 2.
60. *Ibid.*, p. 3.
61. World Bank, "Comments to the German Government Critique of Urban Development in the Philippines," Memo from Anthony Churchill to Erberhard Kurth," Washington, D.C., January 24, 1980, p. 3.
62. *Ibid.*, p. 4.
63. *Ibid.*
64. Interview with World Bank urban projects officer, anonymity requested, conducted by Arnaldo Ramos, Washington, D.C., Dec. 10, 1981.
65. *Ibid.*
66. Jaycox, p. 13.
67. Oberndorfer, p. 1.
68. World Bank, "Comments to the German Government Critique. . . ," p. 1.
69. Interview wit5h World Bank urban projects officer, anonymity requested, Washington, D.C., Dec. 10, 1981.
70. World Bank, "Manila Urban Project: Report on the Status of the Tondo Foreshore Development Project," p. 12.
71. National Resource Center on Political Prisoners in the Philippines (defunct), *Human Rights and Martial Law in the Philippines* (Oakland, CA.: NRCPP, 1977), p. 27.
72. *Ibid.*
73. *Ibid.*, p. 6.
74. World Bank, "Manila Urban Project: Report on the Status of the Tondo Foreshore Development Project," p. 11.
75. *Ibid.*
76. Interview with Herb White of the United Church of Christ, former Tondo organizer, Nov. 18, 1981.
77. World Bank, "Disbursement Status of the Manila Urban Development Loan No. 1272-PH; 1282-PH," Memo from Caroline Sewell to Inder Sud, Washington, D.C., Aug. 20, 1979, p. 1.
78. Oberndorfer, p. 1.
79. World Bank, "Manila Urban Development Project (Loan 1282-PH; Loan 1272-PH)," Memo from Caroline Sewell *et al* to Inder Sud, Oct. 25, 1979, Annex 4, p. 1.
80. *Ibid.*
81. World Bank, "Manila Urban Development Project (Loan 1282-PH; 1272-PH)," Memo from Caroline Sewell *et al* to D. Ahmad, Aug. 14, 1980.

82. Interview with World Bank urban projects officer, anonymity requested, by Arnaldo Ramos, Dec. 10, 1981.
83. *Ibid.*
84. *Ibid.*
85. Interview with Michael Bamberger, World Bank Urban and Regional Economics Dept., Manila, by Robin Broad, March 16, 1981.
86. *Ibid.*
87. Interview with American consultant attached to National Housing Authority, anonymity requested, by Lloyd Jansen, Manila, June 1981.
88. World Bank, "Second Urban. . . ," p. 7.
89. *Ibid.*, p. 43.
90. *Ibid.*
91. *Ibid.*
92. *Ibid.*, p. 39.
93. *Ibid.*, p. 40.
94. Oberndorfer, p. 4.
95. *Ibid.*, p. 5.
96. *Ibid.*
97. *Ibid.*
98. Interview with National Housing Authority financial officer, anonymity requested, by Lloyd Jansen, Manila, June 1981.
99. Oberndorfer, p. 6.
100. World Bank, "Second Urban. . . ," pp. 12, 29, 30.
101. Interview with Mayor Aquilino Pimentel by Robin Broad, Cagayan de Oro, June 2, 1981.
102. Congress Task Force, "Philippine Mayor Brings Fight Against World Bank to Washington, D.C.," Washington, D.C., Sept. 7, 1981.
103. *Ibid.*
104. Interview with Mayor Pimentel by Walden Bello, Washington, D.C., Sept. 2, 1981.
105. World Bank, "Second Urban. . . ," p. 30.
106. *Ibid.*
107. *Ibid.*, p. 44.
108. Interview with Pimentel by Robin Broad, Jan. 2, 1981.
109. *Ibid.*
110. World Bank, "Manila Urban Development (Loan 1282-PH; 1272-PH; Second Urban Development Project (Loan 1647-PH), Memo from Caroline Sewell *et al* to D. Ahmad, Annex 4, p. 4.
111. Interview with Pimentel by Walden Bello, Washington, D.C., Sept. 2, 1981.
112. See *Bulletin Today*, July 17, 1981, pp. 1, 13; also "Comelec Outvoted," *Far Eastern Economic Review*, July 24, 1981.
113. Transcripts of meeting between Pimentel and World Bank officials, Aug. 31, 1981. See also "World Bank Challenged by Small-Town Mayor from the Philippines," *Multinational Monitor*, Oct. 1981, p. 11.
114. Transcripts of meeting, Aug. 31, 1981.
115. *Ibid.*
116. *Ibid.*
117. *Ibid.*
118. Transcripts of press conference, Washington, D.C., Sept. 2, 1981.
119. World Bank, "Third Urban. . . ," pp. 14-15.

CHAPTER FIVE

1. World Bank, *Industrial Development Strategy and Policies in the Philippines*, Vol. II (Report No. 2513-PH) (Washington, D.C.: World Bank, Oct. 29, 1979), p. 2.

2. World Bank, "The Philippines: Priorities and Prospects for Development," Vol. 1, Confidential draft, Washington, D.C., 1976, Statistical appendix, Table B.3.
3. *Ibid.*, Table A-5.
4. William Pomeroy, *An American-Made Tragedy* (New York: International Publishers, 1974), pp. 58-59.
5. For figure, see World Bank, "The Philippines: Priorities and Prospects. . . ," Social indicators page. For assessment vis-a-vis other countries in region, see World Bank, "Philippines—Working Level Draft CPP [Country Program Paper]," Washington, D.C., Aug. 29, 1980, p. 17.
6. World Bank, "The Philippines: Priorities and Prospects. . . ," Social indicators page, Statistical appendix, Table C.7.
7. Amado Guerrero, *Philippine Society and Revolution* (Oakland, CA.: International Association of Filipino Patriots, 1979), Table, p. 171. Figures based on research by now defunct *Manila Chronicle.*
8. Permanent Tribunal for the Rights of Peoples, *The Philippines: Repression and Resistance* (London: KSP, 1980), p. 267.
9. Cited in Alejandro Lichauco, *The Lichauco Paper* (New York: Monthly Review Press, 1973), p. 28.
10. Amado Guerrero, p. 41.
11. Key works synthesizing the nationalist and left critique include Guerrero's pathbreaking *Philippine Society and Revolution*; Lichauco's *The Lichauco Paper*; and the preeminent historian Renato Constantino's various works, including *The Nationalist Alternative* (Quezon City: Foundation for Nationalist Studies, 1979).
12. Anthony Macleod, "Extension of Remarks," in Center for Strategic and International Studies, *U.S.-Philippine Economic Relations* (Washington, D.C.: Georgetown University, 1971), p. 150.
13. On effects of decontrol, see Robert Baldwin, *Foreign Trade Regimes and Economic Development: The Philippines* (New York: National Bureau of Economic Research, 1975), pp. 55-62.
14. Center for Strategic and International Studies, p. 24.
15. John Power and Gerardo Sicat, *The Philippines: Industrialization and Trade Policies* (New York: Oxford University Press, 1971), p. 38.
16. Cheryl Payer, *The Debt Trap* (New York: Monthly Review Press, 1974), p. 67.
17. Lichauco, p. 35.
18. Pomeroy, p. 58.
19. World Bank, *Transition Toward More Rapid and Labor Intensive Industrial Development: The Case of the Philippines*, World Bank Staff Working Paper, No. 424 (Washington, D.C.: World Bank, October 1980), p. 5.
20. World Bank, *Industrial Development Strategy and Policies in the Philippines*, Vol. II, p. 2.
21. Peter Evans, *Dependent Development* (Princeton: Princeton University Press, 1979), p. 320.
22. World Bank, "Korea During the Fifth Five-Year Plan Period: An Advisory Report Prepared for the Government of the Republic of Korea," Preliminary, Prepared by Bela Balassa, Washington, D.C., World Bank, July 31, 1980, p. 1.
23. Peter Evans, "Continuities and Contradictions in the Evolution of Brazilian Dependence," *Latin American Perspectives*, Vol. 3, No. 2, p. 50.
24. Robert McNamara, *1975 Address to Board of Governors* (Washington, D.C.: World Bank, 1975), pp. 28-29.
25. See James Shapiro, "Taiwan," *Multinational Monitor*, June 1981, pp. 11-13.
26. Gustav Ranis, cited in Shapiro, p. 11.
27. *Ibid.*
28. Cited in Pomeroy, p. 143.

29. Gerardo Sicat, *Economic Policy and Philippine Development* (Manila: NEDA, 1972), p. 10.
30. *Ibid.*
31. Quoted in Payer, p. 71.
32. World Bank, "Priorities and Prospects . . . ," p. 2.
33. World Bank, "Poverty, Basic Needs, and Employment: A Review and Assessment," Confidential first draft, Jan. 1980, p. 316.
34. Payer, p. 71.
35. World Bank memo cited in Robert Stauffer, "The Political Economy of Refeudalization," in David Rosenberg, ed., *Marcos and Martial Law in the Philippines* (Ithaca: Cornell University Press, 1979), p. 196.
36. U. S. Dept. of the Treasury, "Assessment of U.S. Participation in the Multilateral Development Banks in the 1980s," Consultation draft, Washington, D.C., Sept. 21, 1981, Chapt. 1, p. 43.
37. World Bank, "Political and Administrative Bases for Economic Policy in the Philippines," Memo from William Ascher, Washington, D.C., Nov. 6, 1980, p. 3. Hereafter to be referred to as the *Ascher Memorandum*
38. Center for Strategic and International Studies, p. 72.
39. Ascher Memorandum, pp. 2-3.
40. Quoted in Stauffer, p. 196.
41. Center for Strategic and International Studies, p. 128.
42. Vicente Paterno, "The BOI: Its Role in the Philippine Industrial Development," *Philippines Quarterly*, June 1973, p. 27.
43. World Bank, "Priorities and Prospects . . . ," Statistical Appendix, Table C.2.
44. Center for Strategic and International Studies, p. 72.
45. Ascher Memorandum, p. 3.
46. Paterno, p. 29.
47. World Bank, "Priorities and Prospects . . . ," p. 1.
48. World Bank, Press release, May 31, 1973.
49. World Bank, "Priorities and Prospects . . . ," p. 35.
50. *Ibid.*, p. 6.
51. World Bank, *Industrial Development. . .* , Vol. II, p. 31.
52. Henry Thompson, "Extension of Remarks," in Center for Strategic and International Studies, p. 152.
53. World Bank, *Industrial Development Strategy and Policies in the Philippines*, Vol. 1 (Washington, D.C.: Oct. 29, 1979), p. 9.
54. "Government Seeks Investors for Industrial Plants in New Trade Zones," *Journal of Commerce*, Supplement for New Jersey World Trade Conference, Nov. 18, 1981, p. 8c.
55. World Bank, "The Philippines: A Development Strategy and Investment Priorities for the Central Visayas (Region VII)," Vol. 1 (Main Report), Report No. 2264-PH, Washington, D.C., Jan. 4, 1979, pp. vi-vii.
56. Roberto Ongpin, "Statement," in World Bank, "Consultative Group for the Philippines: Chairman's Report of the Proceedings," Washington, D.C., March 20, 1979, Annex VI, page 6.
57. World Bank, "Priorities and Prospects . . . ," p. 32.
58. World Bank, "Transition Toward More Rapid and Labor Intensive Industrial Development: The Case of the Philippines", p. 5.
59. "Testimony of a Worker," in Permanent Tribunal for the Rights of Peoples, p. 93.
60. Ascher Memorandum, p. 4.
61. "Testimony of a Worker," in Permanent Tribunal for the Rights of Peoples, p. 88.
62. Enrico Paglaban, "Philippines: Workers in the Export Industry," *Pacific Research*, Vol. IX, Nos. 3 and 4, March-June 1978, p. 19.

63. Philippine Solidarity Network, "A Call for Solidarity with the Philippine Labor Movement," Oakland, CA., 1981.
64. "Testimony of a Worker," in Permanent Tribunal for the Rights of Peoples, p. 86.
65. Joel Rocamora, "U.S. Imperialism and the Economic Crisis of the Marcos Dictatorship," in Permanent Tribunal for the Rights of Peoples, p. 71.
66. World Bank, *The Philippines: Domestic and External Resources for Development,* Report No. 2674-PH (Washington, D.C.: World Bank, Nov. 12, 1979), p. 112.
67. Paglaban, p. 18.
68. Philippine Solidarity Network, "A Call for Solidarity . . . ." n.d.
69. Rachel Grossman, "Women's Place in the Integrated Circuit," *Southeast Asia Chronicle/Pacific Research* (Joint Issue), Jan.-Feb. 1979, p. 10.
70. Paglaban, p. 21.
71. Grossman, p. 8.
72. Quoted in Paglaban, p. 12.
73. *Ibid.*, pp. 22-24.
74. "Testimony of a Worker," in Permanent Tribunal for the Rights of Peoples, pp. 89-90.
75. Le Anh Tu, "Rough Notes on a Visit to the Philippines (Feb. 20 to March 6, 1976)," Philadelphia, 1976, pp. 6, 7, 8.
76. World Bank, *Industrial Development Strategy* . . . , Vol. II, p. 12.
77. Cited in Paglaban, p. 18.
78. Business International, Asia/Pacific Ltd., "Asia's Labor Market: Tapping the Region's Greatest Resource," Hong Kong, 1979, p. 211.
79. Roberto Ongpin, "Statement," in World Bank, "Consultative Group for the Philippines: Chairman's Report of the Proceedings . . . ," Annex VI, p. 6.
80. "In Search of the Cheapest Calculator," *Multinational Monitor,* Vol. 2, No. 6, June 1981, p. 10.
81. *Ibid.* For the expansion of electronics companies in the Philippines, see also "Manila Export Zones Line Businesses for Overseas" and "Electronics Hums with Home-Grown Firms, U.S. 'Big Boys,' " *Christian Science Monitor,* Sept. 18, 1980, pp. B27, B31.
82. Paglaban, pp. 5-6.
83. Roberto Ongpin, "Statement," in World Bank, "Consultative Group for the Philippines: Chairman's Report of the Proceedings . . . ," Annex VI, p. 1.
84. World Bank, "Philippines—Review of the Philippines and Bank Activities," Memo from David Steel, July 8, 1977, p. 1.
85. World Bank, *Industrial Development Strategy* . . . , Vol. I, p. 5.
86. World Bank, *Transition Toward More Rapid and Labor-Intensive Industrial Development* . . . , p. 13.
87. Ascher Memorandum, p. 8.
88. Gould Memorandum, p. 10.
89. World Bank, "Random Thoughts on Rural Development," Memo from David Steel to Michael Gould, Washington, D.C., Sept. 1, 1977.
90. World Bank, "Meeting of the Consultative Group for the Philippines, Nov. 30 and Dec. 1, 1978, Report of Proceedings by the Chairman," Washington, D.C., 1979, p. 66.
91. World Bank, "Meeting of the Consultative Group for the Philippines, . . . Dec. 13 and 14, 1979," Annex II, p. 3.
92. *Ibid.*, Annex XIV, p. 1.
93. Roberto Ongpin, "Statement," in World Bank, "Meeting of the Consultative Group for the Philippines . . . Dec. 13 and 14, 1979," Annex VI, p. 5.

94. Roberto Ongpin, "Statement," in *ibid.*, Annex VI, p. 5; also see Gregorio Licaros, Letter to Mr. J. de Larosiere, Dec. 14, 1979, Attached to International Monetary Fund, "Philippines—Request for Stand-by Arrangement with Supplementary Financing," Washington, D.C., Feb. 6, 1980, p. 31.

95. Andreas Abadjis, "Statement," in *ibid.*, Annex V, p. 2.

96. Ongpin, p. 3.

97. *Ibid.*, p. 2.

98. World Bank, "Working Level Draft CPP," p. 7.

99. Ascher Memorandum, p. 5.

100. World Bank, "Working Level Draft CPP," p. 7.

101. *Ang Katipunan* (Oakland), Dec. 15-31, 1981; see also "Setbacks for Ambition," *Far Eastern Economic Review, Dec. 12, 1980.*

102. International Monetary Fund, "Philippines—Recent Economic Developments," Washington, D.C., July 29, 1980, Table X.

103. World Bank, *Industrial Development Strategy* . . . , Vol. I, p. 32.

104. See World Bank, *Industrial Development Strategy* . . . , Vol. KI,p. 11 for discussion of export earnings in "nontraditional" manufactured exports.

105. World Bank, *Report and Recommendation on a Proposed Structural Adjustment Loan to the Philippines* (Report No. P-2872-PH) (Washington, D.C.: Aug. 21, 1980), p. 15.

106. See also discussion of this in Joel Rocamora, "U.S. Imperialism and the Economic Crisis of the Dictatorship," in Permanent Tribunal on the Rights of Peoples, pp. 72-77.

107. World Bank, *Transition Toward More Rapid and Labor-Intensive Industrial Development* . . . , p. 15.

108. World Bank, "Consultative Group for the Philippines . . . Nov. 30 and Dec. 1, 1978," p. 66.

109. World Bank, *Industrial Development Strategy* . . . , Vol. II, p. 10.

110. Ongpin, *ibid.*, p. 6.

111. World Bank, *Industrial Development Strategy* . . . , Vol. II, p. 15.

112. World Bank, "Poverty, Basic Needs, and Employment . . . . A Review and Assessment," Confidential first draft, Washington, D.C., Jan. 1980, p. 378. Hereafter to be referred to as *Poverty Report.*

113. Figure given by Sen. Benigno Aquino at hearings of Subcommittee on Asia-Pacific Affairs, House of Representatives Committee on Foreign Affairs, Washington, D.C., Nov. 18, 1981. Unemployment figures are, of course, a matter of great controversy. As of Nov. 1981, the official Philippine Government estimate was 68,000 job losses. Foreign Broadcast Information Services, *Daily Report: Asia and Pacific*, p. P2.

114. For example, in early 1982, over 100 workers were laid off by Stanford Microsystems alone, the major semiconductor assembly subcontractor in the Philippines. On recent layoffs, see Leo Gonzaga, "Jobs, Not Wages," *Far Eastern Economic Review*, Jan. 15, 1982, p. 46.

115. Calculated from figures in World Bank, *The Philippines: Domestic and External Resources for Development*, Statistical appendix, p. 56; and IMF, Appendix, Table XII.

116. IMF, "Recent Economic Developments," Appendix, Table XII.

117. World Bank, *The Philippines: Domestic and External Resources for Development*, Statistical appendix, p. 57.

118. *Ibid.*, pp. 56-57. This does not, of course, take into account investment income of foreign corporations gained through such mechanisms as transfer pricing.

119. Ascher Memorandum, p. 7.

120. Edberto Villegas, "The Philippines and the IMF-World Bank Conglomerate," Quezon City, Third World Studies, University of the Philippines, Appendix II, Mimeo.

121. World Bank, *Transition Toward More Rapid and Labor-Intensive Industrial Development . . .*, p. 15.

122. "Manila Export Zones Lure Business," *Christian Science Monitor*, Sept. 18, 1980, p. B27.

123. World Bank, *Philippines: Domestic and External Resources for Development*, p. 9.

124. *Ibid.*, p. 12.

125. NEDA chief Gerry Sicat's figure, cited in Congress Task Force, "Philippine Energy Program, Touted as Solution to Balance of Payments Problems, Comes Under Fire from World Bank," Press release, Feb. 23, 1981, p. 1.

126. Philippine government estimates. For discussion of impact of infrastructure investments, see *Ibon* (Manila), Feb. 15, 1981.

127. U.S. State Department, Responses to "Questions for the Record Asked by the Committee," submitted to House Foreign Affairs Committee, Subcommittee on Asia-Pacific Affairs, Washington, D.C., Nov. 18, 1981.

128. World Bank, "Working Level Draft CPP,", p. 10.

129. The Bank complained at the 1978 Consultative Group meeting: ". . . [F]urther efforts will . . . be needed to increase the progressivity of the tax system, particularly as it affects the highest income levels. Special attention . . . needs to be given to strengthening the personal income tax by limiting the extensive exemptions and deductions which erode its base, and restructuring tax rates, which are among the lowest in Asia. World Bank, "Consultative Group for the Philippines . . . ," Nov. 30 and Dec. 1, 1978, p. 68.

130. IMF, "Staff Report for the 1982 Article IV Consultation," Washington, D.C., March 24, 1982.

131. "Testimony of a Worker," in Permanent Tribunal for the Rights of Peoples, p. 92.

132. Aurelio Intertas, cited in "Wage-Price Squeeze, Philippine Style—A Marcos Drama," *Philippine Liberation Courier*, March 25, 1979, p. 3.

133. IMF, "Philippines—Staff Report for the 1980 Article IV Consultation and Review of Stand-by Arrangements," July 17, 1980, p. 8.

134. *Ibid.*, p. 16.

135. *Ibid.*

136. IMF, "Recent Economic Developments . . . ," p. 12.

137. Quoted in "Marcos Soft on Labor—Suter," *Ang Katipunan*, Aug. 1-15, 1981, p. 3.

138. Ascher Memorandum, p. 5.

139. "Right to Strike Restored," *Philippines* (New York City, Philippine Consulate), Sept. 1981, p. 2.

140. Bruce Jones, "Statement," in "Consultative Group for the Philippines . . . Dec. 13 and 14, 1979," Annex XI, p. 2.

141. Robert McNamara, *Address to the United Nations Conference on Trade and Development, May 10, 1979* (Washington, D.C.: World Bank, 1979), p. 6.

142. *Ibid.*, p. 9.

143. IMF, "Philippines—Recent Economic Developments," Table VIII, n.d.

144. IMF, "Philippines—Request for Stand-by Arrangement with Supplementary Financing," Table XII, pp. 45-47, n.d.

145. "U.S., Philippines Held Entering New Era of Closer Trade Ties," *Journal of Commerce*, Supplement to New Jersey World Trade Conference, Nov. 18, 1981, pp. 1C, 6C.

146. Ongpin, *ibid.*, Annex VI, p. 3.

147. IMF, "Philippines—Request for Stand-by Arrangement with Supplementary Financing," Feb. 6, 1980, p. 22.

148. World Bank, *The Political Market for Protectionism in Industrial Countries: Empirical Evidence*, Staff Working Paper, No. 492 (Washington, D.C.: 1981), p. 22.

149. World Bank, *Industrial Development Strategy* . . . , Vol. I, p. 32.

150. Balassa, pp. 2-4.

151. World Bank, "Korea: Current Economic Developments and Policy Issues," Preliminary draft, April 20, 1980, p. 24.

152. Quoted in John Kelly and Joel Rocamora, "Indonesia: A Show of Resistance," *Southeast Asia Chronicle*, Dec. 1981, p. 16.

153. World Bank, *China: Socialist Economic Development: Vol. I, The Main Report* (Washington, D.C.: June 1, 1981), p. 169.

154. *Ibid.*, p. XVII.

155. *Ibid.*, p. VI.

CHAPTER SIX

1. World Bank, "Political and Administrative Bases for Economic Policy in the Philippines," Memo from William Ascher, Washington, D.C., Nov. 18, 1980, p. 6. Hereafter to be referred to as the Ascher Memorandum.

2. World Bank, "Philippines—Working Level Draft CPP [Country Program Paper]," Washington, D.C., Aug. 29, 1980, p. 17. Hereafter to be referred to as 1980 CPP.

3. Ascher Memorandum, p. 2.

4. U.S. Treasury Dept., "Assessment of U.S. Participation in the Multilateral Development Banks in the 1980's," Consultation draft, Washington, D.C., Sept. 21, 1981, p. 50.

5. World Bank, "Draft of Structural Adjustment Loan Agreement," (Loan No. 1903-PH), July 14, 1980.

6. 1980 CPP, p. 7.

7. World Bank, "Aide Memoire" (of Aug. 30-31 Meeting on industrial policy), Washington, D.C., n.d.

8. World Bank, "Report and Recommendation of the President of the IBRD to Executive Directors on a Proposed Structural Adjustment Loan to the Republic of the Philippines," Report No. P-2872-PH, Washington, D.C., Aug. 21, 1980, p. 21.

9. World Bank, *Industrial Development Strategy and Policies in the Philippines*, Vol. II, (Report No. 2513-PH) (Washington, D.C.: World Bank, Oct. 29, 1979).

10. Interview with Ministry of Industry official, anonymity requested, 1981.

11. World Bank, "Report and Recommendation . . . ," Annex IV, p. 3.

12. See Ferdinand Marcos, "Message," in *Journal of Commerce*, Supplement for the New Jersey World Trade Conference, Nov. 18, 1981, p. 1C.

13. Interview with Ministry of Industry official, anonymity requested, 1981.

14. U.S. Treasury Dept., Appendix V, p. 45.

15. Interview with Ministry of Industry official, anonymity requested, by Robin Broad, 1981.

16. World Bank, "Report and Recommendation . . . ," p. 31.

17. World Bank, *Industrial Development Strategy* . . . , Vol. II, Chapt. 7; also *Asian Wall Street Journal Weekly*, April 26, 1982.

18. *Business Day* (Manila), March 17, 1981.

19. Interview, anonymity requested, by Robin Broad, 1981.

20. World Bank, "Report and Recommendation . . . ," p. 31.

21. *Ibid.*
22. Interview, anonymity requested, by Robin Broad, 1981.
23. Ascher Memorandum, p. 8.
24. *Ibid.*
25. *Ibid.*, p. 9.
26. Interview, anonymity requested, by Robin Broad, 1981.
27. World Bank, "Report and Recommendation . . . ," p. 28.
28. 1980 CPP, p. 9.
29. World Bank, "Report and Recommendation . . . ," Annex IV, p. 15ff.
30. Rene Ofreneo *et al*, "A Critique of the 1972 and 1980 Financial Reforms," Unpublished manuscript, Quezon City, University of the Philippines, 1981, Appendix A-1.
31. *Euromoney*, April 1979, p. 36.
32. Ofreneo, Appendix A-1.
33. Central Bank, "Subject: Report of the Joint IMF-WB Mission on Aspects of the Financial Sector in the Philippines," Memo from Arnulfo Arellano, Special Asst. to the Central Bank Panel of the Joint IMF-CBP Banking Survey Commission, Manila, Oct. 8, 1979, pp. 6-9.
34. Interview, anonymity requested, by Robin Broad, Manila, 1981.
35. Interview, anonymity requested, by Robin Broad, Manila, 1981.
36. Interview with Armand Fabella by Robin Broad, Manila, Dec. 8, 1980.
37. World Bank/International Monetary Fund, *The Philippines: Aspects of the Financial Sector* (Washington, D.C.: May 1980), p. 76.
38. Interview with E. M. Villanueva, by Robin Broad, Manila, Feb. 23, 1981.
39. Interview with former senior Central Bank official, anonymity requested, Manila, 1981.
40. Interview with Gregorio Licaros by Robin Broad, Manila, April 1, 1981.
41. World Bank, "Staff Appraisal Report on Industrial Finance Project, Philippines," Report No. 3334-PH, Washington, D.C., April 7, 1981, p. 30. See also *Business Day*, April 20, 1981.
42. 1980 CPP, p. 13.
43. Interview with Gregorio Licaros, by Robin Broad, Manila, April 1, 1981.
44. International Monetary Fund, "Philippines—Staff Report for the 1980 Article IV Consultation and Review of Stand-by Arrangement," Washington, D.C., July 17, 1980, p. 14.
45. *Ibid.*
46. 1980 CPP, p. 14.
47. International Monetary Fund, "Philippines—Staff Report for the 1982 Article IV Consultation," SM/82/55, Washington, D.C., March 24, 1982, p. 20.
48. *Ibid.*, p. 18.

CHAPTER SEVEN

1. World Bank, "Political and Administrative Bases for Economic Policy in the Philippines," Memo from William Ascher, Washington, D.C., Nov. 18, 1980, p. 9. Hereafter to be referred to as the Ascher Memorandum.
2. "Lenders Won't Give Higher Loans to Marcos," *Ang Katipunan* (Oakland), Feb. 15-28, p. 3.
3. World Bank, "Energy Sector Survey," Washington, D.C., Nov. 1980; see also World Bank, "Working Level Draft CPP," Washington, D.C., Aug. 29, 1980, Attachment 1a (hereafter to be referred to as 1980 CPP).

4. 1980 CPP, p. 19.
5. *Ibid.*, p. 19.
6. Ascher Memorandum, p. 8.
7. *Ibid.*, p. 8.
8. Joel Rocamora, "Bureaucrat Capitalism—A Classic Case," *Philippine Liberation Courier*, Nov. 30, 1979, pp. 6-7.
9. *Ibid.*
10. Guy Sacerdoti, "Cracks in the Coconut Shell," *Far Eastern Economic Review*, Jan. 8-14, 1982, pp. 42-48. See also Rocamora, pp. 5-6; and Rigoberto Tiglao, "The Political Economy of the Philippine Coconut Industry," Quezon City, Third World Studies, University of the Philippines.
11. On CDCP, see "Business Empire that Thrives Under Martial Law," *Philippine Times* (Chicago), Nov. 5, 1979.
12. *Ibid.*; see also *Ibon*, No. 60, Feb. 15, 1981, p. 7.
13. *New York Times*, Jan. 14, 1978, cited in "Some Are Smarter than Others," Manila, p. 8, mimeo (Also known as the "Octopus Study").
14. "Some Are Smarter than Others," p. 23.
15. "Cellophil-Tinggian Controversy," *Tribal Forum* (Manila), Nov.-Dec. 1979, p. 14.
16. Phone interview with IFC Philippine Desk, May. 12, 1982.
17. Rocamora, p. 7.
18. "Petrochemicals: The Philippines Cuts Its Costs," *Far Eastern Economic Review*, Jan. 19, 1979, p. 79.
19. Rocamora, p. 7.
20. Louis Kraar, "The Philippines Veers Toward Crisis," *Fortune*, July 27, 1981, p. 36.
21. "Some Are Smarter Than Others," p. 8.
22. Rocamora, p. 5.
23. Kraar, pp. 36-37.
24. Andy McCue, "Philippine Aid Plan to Help CDCP," *Asian Wall Street Journal*, May 20, 1981.
25. Leo Gonzaga, "The Government Steps In—Again," *Far Eastern Economic Review*, July 31, 1981, pp. 78-80.
26. Leo Gonzaga, "Faith in Adversity," *Far Eastern Economic Review*, Sept. 4, 1981, p. 79; also, "How They Broke the Bank in Manila," *Asia Week*, July 10, 1981, p. 40.
27. *Asian Wall Street Journal*, June 6, 1981.
28. Jaime Ongpin, Letter to Editor, *Fortune*, Aug. 24, 1981, p. 24. Ongpin is president of Benguet Corporation, whose subsidiary Engineering Equipment is the main competitor of Cuenca's CDCP for government contracts. See *Far Eastern Economic Review*, July 31, 1981, p. 79.
29. *Asian Wall Street Journal*, June 6, 1981.
30. See Chapt. 6.
31. James Bartholemew, "A Blue Chip Goes Begging," *Far Eastern Economic Review*, June 12, 1981, p. 80.
32. Central Bank of the Philippines, "Industrial Finance Fund," Memo from E. M. Villanueva, ADFU to Jaime Laya, Governor, Central Bank of the Philippines, Manila, April 14, 1981, Exhibit A, p. 3.
33. Andy McCue, "CDCP Gets Manila's Aid, New Chairman," *Asian Wall Street Journal*, June 6, 1981.
34. Leo Gonzaga, "Official Help Wanted, *Far Eastern Economic Review*, May 1, 1981, pp. 56-57.
35. "On the Takeover Trail," *Far Eastern Economic Review*, Sept. 11, 1981, pp. 60-61.
36. *Asian Wall Street Journal*, Aug. 3, 1981, p. 2.
37. Kraar, p. 36. The Justice Department later dropped the lawsuit after issuing a warning to UNICOM not to try again.

38. IMF, "Philippines—Staff Report for 1982 Article IV Consultation," Washington, D.C., March 24, 1982, p. 9.

39. Ascher Memorandum, p. 12.

40. Daniel O'Donohue, Acting Deputy Ass. Sec. of State for East Asia, State Department, "Statement," at Committee of Foreign Affairs, Subcommittee on Asia Pacific Affairs, *Hearings*, Nov. 18, 1981.

41. U.S. State Dept., Responses to "Questions for the Record Asked by the Committee," submitted to House Foreign Affairs Committee, Subcommittee on Asia-Pacific Affairs, Washington, D.C., Nov. 18, 1981.

42. *Ibid.*

43. Interview with World Bank officer, anonymity requested, by Walden Bello, Dec. 13, 1980.

44. Ascher Memorandum, p. 10.

CONCLUSION

1. Newspaper and periodical articles based on exposés headed up by the Congress Task Force and *CounterSpy* include the following: "A Chiller for Manila: Reduce Borrowing and Cut Growth Targets, IMF Tells the Philippines," *Far Eastern Economic Review,* April 30, 1982; "President Marcos' Authority is Eroding, According to Study for the World Bank," *Wall Street Journal,* Dec. 3, 1980; "Bank Criticizes War on Povety in Philippines," *Asian Wall Street Journal,* Jan. 16, 1981; "Philippines May Need to Find New Creditors as U.S. Banks Near Caps, World Bank Says," *Asian Wall Street Journal,* Jan. 20, 1981; Walden Bello and John Kelly, "Les pays occidentaux protecteurs des Philippines s'inquiètent de la dégradation financière du pays," *Le Monde,* Feb. 3, 1981; "Seoul Encounters Problems Instituting Major Reforms Urged by World Bank," *Asian Wall Street Journal,* Jan 5, 1981; Apolonia Batalla, "World Bank Lending," *Bulletin Today* (Manila), Dec. 8, 1980; Walden Bello and David O'Connor, "McNamara's Second Vietnam," *Asia Record,* June 1981; Walden Bello, "Rural Debacle: The World Bank in the Philippines," *Food Monitor,* July-Aug. 1981; Teodoro Valencia, "WB-IMF Formula Could Sink RP Economy," *Philippines Daily Express,* March 2, 1981; Walden Bello and David Kinley, "McNamara's Second Vietnam," *Pacific News Service,* July 7, 1981; "Study Asserts Philippines Overestimates Energy Potential," *Asian Wall Street Journal,* Feb. 24, 1981; Walden Bello and David Kinley, "La politique de la Banque mondiale a l'heure de l'orthodoxie libérale," *Le Monde Diplomatique,* Sept. 1981; Walden Bello, "The World Bank in the Philippines: A Decade of Failures," *Southeast Asia Chronicle,* Dec. 1981; John Kelly and Joel Rocamora, "Indonesia: A Show of Resistance," *Southeast Asia Chronicle,* Dec. 1981; "The Poverty Puzzle," *Far Eastern Economic Review,* March 27, 1981, pp. 125-131; Walden Bello, "Multinationals Under Marcos," *Multinational Monitor,* Feb. 1981, pp. 8-11; Walden Bello, "Secret World Bank Document on Marcos: An Alliance Coming Apart?" *CounterSpy,* Feb.-April 1981; "Dustere Thesen für Zukunft der Philippinen," *Tager Anzeiger* (Zurich), Dec. 6, 1980; "The World Bank and Marcos," *Journal of Commerce,* Jan. 21, 1981; Walden Bello and John Kelly, "The World Bank Writes Off Marcos and Co.," *The Nation,* Jan. 31, 1981; "Indonesia," *Far Eastern Economic Review,* May 29, 1981; Walden Bello and John Kelly, "China: World Bank Report Sets Stage for Taiwan-Style Development," *Multinational Monitor,* Feb. 1982; "Philippine Mayor Resists Slum-Improvement Project," *Asian Wall Street Journal,* Sept. 4, 1981; Walden Bello, John Kelly, and Robin Broad, "Comment Washington intervient dans la politique economique du Honduras," *Le Monde Diplomatique,* May 1982; "IMF Urges that South Korea Devalue its Currency . . . ," *Wall Street Journal,* May 10, 1982.

For these exposés, the Congress Task Force and *CounterSpy* magazine were denounced by *Human Events,* President Reagan's favorite newspaper, as being made up of "far left extremists, some of whom . . . are dedicated enemies of the United States." *Human Events,* Sept. 5, 1981. See also " 'CounterSpy' Counterattacks," *Human Events,* Oct. 17, 1981.

2. U. S. Treasury Dept., "Assessment of U.S. Participation in the Multilateral Development Banks in the 1980's," Consultation draft, Washington, D.C., Sept. 21, 1981.

3. James O'Connor, *The Fiscal Crisis of the State* (New York: St. Martins Press, 1973), pp. 5-8.

4. World Bank, *Rural Development: Sector Working Paper* (Washington, D.C.: 1975), p. 40.

5. State Department response to "Questions Asked by the Committee" at House of Representatives Committee on Foreign Affairs, Subcommittee on Asia-Pacific Affairs, *Hearings,* Washington, D.C., Nov. 18, 1981.

Selected Bibliography

This book was primarily based on 6,000 pages of highly confidential World Bank and International Monetary Fund documents. All documents used are footnoted. The following is a selection of key secondary sources which proved particularly helpful in the project.

1. Anti-Martial Law Coalition, *The Refugee Crisis in the Philippines* (Chicago: AMLC, 1977).
2. Walden Bello and Elaine Elinson, *Elite Democracy and Authoritarian Rule* (San Francisco, Philippine Solidarity Network, 1981).
3. Walden Bello, Peter Hayes, and Lyuba Zarsky, "500 Mile Island: The Philippine Nuclear Reactor Deal," *Pacific Research*, Vol. 10, No. 1.
4. Walden Bello and Severina Rivera, eds., *The Logistics of Repression and Other Essays* (Washington, D.C.: Friends of the Filipino People, 1977).
5. Renato Constantino, *The Nationalist Alternative* (Quezon City: Foundation for Nationalist Studies, 1979).
6. Noam Chomsky and Edward Herman, *The Washington Connection and Third World Fascism* (Boston: South End Press, 1979).
7. Amado Guerrero, *Philippine Society and Revolution* (Oakland: International Association of Filipino Patriots, 1979).
8. International Labor Office, *Poverty and Landlessness in Rural Asia* (Geneva: International Labor Office, 1977).
9. Michael Klare and Cynthia Arnson, *Supplying Repression* (Washington, D.C.: Institute for Policy Studies, revised, 1981).
10. Louis Kraar, "The Philippines Veers Toward Crisis," *Fortune*, July 1981.
11. Frances Moore Lappé, Joseph Collins, and David Kinley, *Aid as Obstacle* (San Francisco: Institute for Food and Development Policy, 1980).
12. Alejandro Lichauco, *The Lichauco Paper* (New York: Monthly Review Press, 1974).
13. Cheryl Payer, *The Debt Trap* (New York: Monthly Review Press, 1974).
14. Cheryl Payer, *The World Bank* (forthcoming) (New York: Monthly Review Press, 1982).
15. Permanent Peoples' Tribunal, Session on the Philippines, *The Philippines: Repression and Resistance* (London: KSP, 1981).
16. Blondie Po, *Policies and Implementation of Land Reform in the Philippines* (Quezon City: Institute of Philippine Culture, 1981).
17. Jose Maria Sison, *Struggle for National Democracy* (Quezon City: Amado Hernandez Memorial Foundation, 1972).

18. Southeast Asia Chronicle, "The World Bank," Issue No. 81 and "The Philippines in the 1980's," Issue No. 83 (Berkeley, CA: Southeast Asia Resource Center).
19. Guy Standing and Richard Szal, *Poverty and Basic Needs: Evidence From Guyana and the Philippines* (Geneva: International Labor Office, 1979).
20. Robert Stauffer, "The Political Economy of Refeudalization," in D. Rosenberg, ed. *Marcos and Martial Law in the Philippines* (Ithaca, New York: Cornell University Press, 1979).
21. Task Force Detainees, *Pumipiglas: Political Detention and Military Atrocities in the Philippines* (Manila: Task Force Detainees, 1980).
22. Third World Studies Center, University of the Philippines, "TNC Control of the Philippine Banana Industry," *AMPO* Vol. 13, No. 3 (Pacific Asia Resource Center, Tokyo, 1981).
23. U.S. Department of the Treasury, *Assessment of U.S. Participation in the Multilateral Development Banks* (Washington, D.C.: 1982).
24. World Bank, *The Political Market for Protectionism in Industrial Countries*, Staff Working Paper, No. 492 (Washington, D.C.: 1981).

Index

About the Authors

Walden Bello, a Filipino citizen, is director of the Washington-based Congress Task Force of the Philippine Solidarity Network. He obtained his Ph.D. in sociology from Princeton University in 1975 and taught political economy at the State University of New York at Old Westbury in 1975, and rural development and environmental issues at the University of California at Berkeley from 1976 to 1981. He is coauthor of *Logistics of Repression* (Friends of the Filipino People, 1977) and is a regular contributor to *Le Monde Diplomatique* and *The Nation*. His articles have also appeared in *Le Monde*, *Multinational Monitor*, *Newsday*, *New Internationalist*, *We-Forum* (Manila), *El Gallo Ilustrado* (Mexico City), and Pacific News Service.

David Kinley, a freelance writer, is coauthor of *Aid as Obstacle: Twenty Questions about our Foreign Aid and the Hungry* (Institute for Food and Development Policy, 1980). He coordinated the Aid Education Project at the Institute for Food and Development Policy for five years and also served on the staff of the North American Congress on Latin America (NACLA) and the Corporate Data Exchange. His articles on the impact of U.S. aid programs have appeared in the *Los Angeles Times*, *The Nation*, *Le Monde Diplomatique*, *South*, and *Multinational Monitor*.

Elaine Elinson is national coordinator of the Philippine Solidarity Network and public information director of the American Civil Liberties Union (ACLU) of Northern California. She is a former editor at Pacific News Service and coauthor, with Walden Bello, of *Elite Democracy or Authoritarian Rule?* (PSN, 1981). She has reported from the Philippines and her articles have appeared in the *New Internationalist*, the *San Francisco Chronicle*, *Svenska Dagbladet*, the *South China Morning Post*, and other publications.

Robin Broad, preparing a Ph.D. at Princeton, has made three research trips to the Philippines. Her articles have appeared in the *Southeast Asia Chronicle*, *Afrique-Asie*, *Le Monde Diplomatique*, and Pacific News Service.

David O'Connor, pursuing a Ph.D. at the New School for Social Research, has visited the Philippines twice. His articles have appeared in *Asia Record*, *Pacific Research*, *Science for the People*, and other journals.

Vincent Bielski conducted field research on the impact of foreign aid in the Philippines as a project assistant at the Institute for Food and Development Policy. He is a recent graduate of Michigan State University.

About The P.S.N.

The Philippine Solidarity Network (PSN) works to expose and oppose U.S. military, economic, and political domination of the Philippines and to support the Filipino people's struggle for a just and democratic society.

A nationwide organization founded in 1973 just after the declaration of martial law in the Philippines, PSN (formerly Friends of the Filipino People [FFP]) uses public education, speaking tours, and grassroots organizing to reach Americans. PSN produces and distributes literature and slide shows on a broad range of Philippine issues, including the labor movement, women, tribal peoples, U.S. military bases, and the resistance.

The **Congress Task Force** is the Washington-based research and lobbying arm of the Philippine Solidarity Network and the Coalition Against the Marcos Dictatorship. The task force's exposés of World Bank and International Monetary Fund activities in the Philippines, Indonesia, South Korea, the People's Republic of China, Honduras, and El Salvador have appeared in *Le Monde*, *The Nation*, *Multinational Monitor*, the *New Internationalist*, and many other publications around the world.

The Congress Task Force has taken the lead in lobbying against military aid to the Philippines and against the proposed U.S.-Philippine Extradition Treaty.

For more information, contact:

Philippine Solidarity Network
P.O. Box 84
Oakland CA 94668 USA
(415) 839-7066

Congress Task Force
1322 – 18th St. NW
Washington DC 20036 USA
(202) 223-5611

Institute Publications

Diet for a Small Planet: Tenth Anniversary Edition, an updated edition of the bestseller that taught Americans the social and personal significanceof a new way of eating. Frances Moore Lappé, 432 pages with charts, tables, resource guide, recipes, Ballantine Books. *$3.50*

What Difference Could a Revolution Make? Food and Farming in the New Nicaragua, provides a critical yet sympathetic look at the agrarian reform in Nicaragua since the 1979 revolution and analyzes the new government's successes, problems, and prospects. Joseph Collins and Frances Moore Lappé, with Nick Allen, 200 pages. *$4.95* (est.)

Now We Can Speak: A Journey through the New Nicaragua, features interviews with Nicaraguans from every walk of life telling how their lives have changed since the 1979 overthrow of the Somoza dictatorship. Frances Moore Lappé and Joseph Collins, 125 pages. *$4.95* (est.)

Food First Comic, a comic for young people based on the book *Food First: Beyond the Myth of Scarcity*. Leonard Rifas, 24 pages. *$1.00*

Trading the Future: How Booming Farm Exports Threaten Our Food Security traces the worldwide shift from food self-sufficiency to export dependence and shows how U.S. grain exports accelerate this trend. James Wessel, with Frances Moore Lappé and Mort Hantman, 150 pages. *$4.95* (est.)

Seeds of the Earth: A Private or Public Resource? examines the rapid erosion of the earth's gene pool of seed varieties and the control of the seed industry by multinational corporations. Pat Roy Mooney, 126 pages with tables and corporate profiles. *$7.00*

World Hunger: Ten Myths clears the way for each of us to work in appropriate ways to end needless hunger. Frances Moore Lappé and Joseph Collins, revised and updated, 72 pages with photographs. *$2.95)*

El Hambre en el Mundo: Diez Mitos, a Spanish-language version of *World Hunger: Ten Myths* plus additional information about food and agriculture policies in Mexico, 72 pages. *$1.45*

Food First: Beyond the Myth of Scarcity, 50 questions and responses about the causes and proposed remedies for world hunger. Frances Moore Lappé and Joseph Collins, with Cary Fowler, 620 pages, Ballantine Books, revised 1979. *$3.95*

Food First Resource Guide, documentation on the roots of world hunger and rural poverty. Institute staff, 80 pages with photographs. *$3.00*

Aid as Obstacle: Twenty Questions about our Foreign Aid and the Hungry demonstrates that foreign aid may be hurting the very people we want to help and explains why foreign aid programs fail. Frances Moore Lappé, Joseph Collins, David Kinley, 192 pages with photographs. *$4.95*

Needless Hunger: Voices from a Bangladesh Village exposes the often brutal political and economic roots of needless hunger. Betsy Hartmann and James Boyce, 72 pages with photographs. *$3.50*

What Can We Do? An action guide on food, land and hunger issues. Interviews with over one dozen North Americans involved in many aspects of these issues. William Valentine and Frances Moore Lappé, 60 pages with photographs. *$2.95*

Mozambique and Tanzania: Asking the Big Questions looks at the questions which face people working to build economic and political systems based on equity, participation, and cooperation. Frances Moore Lappé and Adele Beccar-Varela, 126 pages with photographs. *$4.75*

Circle of Poison documents a scandal of global proportions, the export of dangerous pesticides to Third World countries. David Weir and Mark Schapiro, 101 pages with photos and tables. *$3.95*

Casting New Molds: First Steps towards Worker Control in a Mozambique Steel Factory, a personal account of the day-to-day struggle of Mozambican workers by Peter Sketchley, with Frances Moore Lappé, 64 pages. *$3.95*

Agrarian Reform and Counter-Reform in Chile, a first-hand look at some ofthe current economic policies in Chile and their effect on the rural majority. Joseph Collins, 24 pages with photographs. *$1.45*

Research Reports. "Land Reform: Is It the Answer? A Venezuelan Peasant Speaks." Frances Moore Lappé and Hannes Lorenzen, 17 pages. *$1.50*

Facts Behind Famine: The Horn of Africa. Nina Friedman, 15 pages. *$2.00*

Export Agriculture: An Energy Drain. Mort Hantman, 50 pages. *$3.00*

Seeds of Revolution is a provocative documentary about hunger, land reform, multinational agribusiness, and the military in Honduras. Produced by Howard Enders for ABC News, with the assistance of Joseph Collins, 30 minutes, 16 mm color. *$450* purchase, *$50* rental

Food First Slideshow/Filmstrip in a visually positive and powerful portrayal demonstrates that the cause of hunger is not scarcity but the increasing concentration of control over food producing resources, 30 minutes. *$89* (slideshow), *$31* (filmstrip)

Write for our free publications catalogue.
All publications orders must be prepaid.

Institute for Food and Development Policy
1885 Mission Street
San Francisco CA 94103 USA
(415) 864-8555